"A raw and honest journey o.
redemption—grounded in a deep love of place and all things
mustang. The best memoirs reveal the deeply personal in order
to see the larger world with renewed clarity and insight—this is
one such book. As Wilder moves from heroin to horses, we see
a substantive journey of recovery and strength—and ultimately,
of resilience."

—LAURA PRITCHETT, author of *Stars Go Blue*

"For too long, the lone cowboy myth has corralled the American West in the barbed wires of dominion and destruction. Tangled in that telling are women and mustangs—their wildness,
togetherness, and vulnerability. In *Desert Chrome*, Wilder bucks
against a story as desiccated as the deserts she has dwelled in—
kicking hard enough to free what was bound, to redeem what
was broken. Listen now, to the thundering of hearts and hooves.
They're coming for us, at last."

—AMY IRVINE, author of *Air Mail* and *Desert Cabal*

"*Desert Chrome* journeys through parched valleys, on wild rivers,
and into deep rock canyons on a unique quest. In this authentic,
hard-won account of her life, Wilder finds the warm, true hearts
she's been seeking and that deserve our humanity, healing, and a
hell of a lot better future than they've been dealt. There's a quiet
heroine at the center of this story, yes, pointing toward a beautiful world. It can be ours if we'll love better, lean closer, and listen
to the voices, like Wilder's own, well worth heeding from birth."

—REBECCA LAWTON, author of *The Oasis This Time*

"Wilder's love of horses and the land is the theme threaded
through her, and her writing makes a heartsong of it all. I could
feel the land rising up as a subject, not background, not setting,

but subject . . . like the land has a story as important as her own, like the land and Wilder's stories make a helix together, like the land has a piece of her heart in it."

—LIDIA YUKNAVITCH, author of *Verge*

"'Blame it or praise it,' Virginia Woolf writes, 'there is no denying the wild horse in us.' *Desert Chrome* is the story of a landscape and the many ways the land sings us into being. It is the story of one of our most iconic North American species, *Equus caballus*, the wild horse. And, most of all, it is the story of a woman coming to know her own wildness—a wildness that is free, and sustaining, and on her own terms."

—JOE WILKINS, author of *Fall Back Down When I Die* and *The Mountain and the Fathers*

"A powerful coming-of-age story, into the age of a woman's strongest power, when, with complete awareness of her past, she can, with might and strength, will the future before her. Wilder writes with all the love, wisdom, and courage it takes to make positive changes for the western landscape, horses, and readers."

—CMARIE FUHRMAN, author of *Camped Beneath the Dam*

"I learned so much reading Kathryn Wilder's book, *Desert Chrome*—about wild horses. About desert and water. About Kat. We were neighbors years ago, but the new paths along which, with smooth and stunning prose, she leads readers into the depths of her life suggest how little we know those close to us. And how huge life can be once we commit with our whole hearts to wildness."

—BROOKE WILLIAMS, author of *Open Midnight*

DESERT CHROME

DESERT CHROME

WATER, A WOMAN,
AND WILD HORSES
IN THE WEST

KATHRYN WILDER

TORREY HOUSE PRESS

Salt Lake City • Torrey

First Torrey House Press Edition, May 2021
Copyright © 2021 by Kathryn Wilder

Published by Torrey House Press
Salt Lake City, Utah
www.torreyhouse.org

International Standard Book Number: 978-1-948814-36-2
E-book ISBN: 978-1-948814-37-9
Library of Congress Control Number: 2020931567

Lines from "The Creation Story," from *The Woman Who Fell from the Sky: Poems* by Joy Harjo (W. W. Norton & Company; revised ed. 1996). Reprinted with permission of the author.

Lyrics from "The Circle" from the album *Tonopah* by Dave Stamey, copyright 1999. Reprinted with permission of the author.

Cover photo by TJ Holmes
Cover design by Kathleen Metcalf
Interior design by Rachel Buck-Cockayne
Distributed to the trade by Consortium Book Sales and Distribution

MIX
Paper from
responsible sources
FSC
www.fsc.org   FSC® C011935

Torrey House Press offices in Salt Lake City sit on the homelands of Ute, Goshute, Shoshone, and Paiute nations. Offices in Torrey are in homelands of Paiute, Ute, and Navajo nations.

For Nancy Park,
who was there
for so much of this

And for wildness,
that it may remain so

TABLE OF CONTENTS

We are all on the run, human and wild. Endangered. Exiled. Refugees.

—Terry Tempest Williams, *Thirty-Year Plan*

Maps and plans lose integrity within the grind of a rapid.

—Craig Childs, *The Animal Dialogues*

Prologue

Last Drink

I lead my grulla mare, Savanna, to water. She is the gray of a mule deer's winter coat, with a dorsal stripe and zebra markings on her legs that trace back to the original wild horses, though she is quarter horse, not mustang. The mustang follows. It is his first time here, to the piñon pine and juniper woodland that defines my desert home. We walk down the rocky path and around to a flat below the cabin, where in the 1930s post-and-rail sheep pens were built right up against the wall of Dakota Sandstone, which forms the back fence of the old pens and the cliff base upon which a modern log cabin sits.

Savanna follows me on a loose lead despite thirst. The big, dark bay mustang, who wears no halter or rope, sticks close to the mare until he smells water and trots up and around and above the creek, missing the trail the cows have made through the coyote willows. Four hundred years ago that trail would have been carved by bison and wild horses, and Savanna might be a direct descendent of the horses brought to North America in the 1500s by Spanish conquistadors. I would not be a white woman in her sixties watering her horses in Disappointment Creek but a young girl nearing a stream that ran cold and clear from the mountains, the rope in my hands plaited grass.

The mustang comes in close to the mare again and I quicken my steps, the willows tight here with no place to veer off if the horses crowd me. No longer a young and nimble escaper, I trip over tree roots or rocks or my own boots more often than ever before. My sons tease me about this, and because I have strong bones I can laugh, too, each time I pick myself up off the ground.

Last week I stepped in a prairie dog hole as I backed up while closing a wire gate. My right leg dropped in clear to the knee (fortunately my left knee—my troubled knee—was spared), and my boot got stuck. I tried to jerk it out and finally had to yell at Ken, my elder son, to come help. He trotted across the pasture with the natural grace of a wild horse and yanked me up out of the hole. "Jeez Mom," he said. That was all.

The next day I stepped backward and tripped over a sandstone slab, falling not just on my ass but all the way down, elbows to the ground, bruises purpling my arms and legs for days.

"Just don't walk backward," Ken said. "You can't step backwards anymore, Mom." Later I will think about this, about which direction I'm going, but for now, falling is still comedy.

I have lived my life outside, on ranches and rivers and the sea. Grateful for strong bones and stubbornness, I still ride and rope and hike and row. I'm not ready to be turned out to pasture just yet, or confined to a space surrounded by walls. But Ken may be right—stepping back may no longer be appropriate.

The horses and I have pushed through the willows and stand on a bank that high water has scoured down to earth and stone. Savanna slides in the mud and dips her nose into a creek that smells of oil shale and spring as it carries snowmelt and silt downstream. The mustang passes her and splashes in, his feet planted in the current. Both horses drink deeply despite the tang and salt and sand—water humans can't stomach—and then the mustang whirls and lunges up the bank on the trail he now knows is there. Savanna and I follow, watching him trot in smooth ripples away, neck arched and body gleaming in the afternoon light as he passes the sheep pens and trots on, sniffing the air. He breaks into a run, flinging his head and bucking, youth and grace and freedom in his bones.

Savanna could pull away to follow him and I would probably fall on the rocks if she did, but today I am her leader. I want to hug her. If I were that young girl I would entwine my fingers in her mane and swing up onto her back; instead, we ascend slowly through rocks and rabbitbrush as the mustang trots ahead, his big bay muscles constricting my heart. Not pain. The ache of love.

YOU MAY HAVE heard: the West is at war. Armed standoffs in Nevada between cattle ranchers and Bureau of Land Management personnel. Old-time Utah residents mounting ATVs to ride public lands in designated wilderness areas, claiming roadways where there were none before. Wyoming ranchers suing for the removal of wild horses, and winning. Mustang advocates across America fighting helicopter roundups in the West with letters and phone calls, on-site activists drawing media attention, and sometimes the law.

In many of these battles, wild horses are the innocent victims, living on BLM-managed public lands. As with some reservations, these government-designated mustang ranges are often in the worst locales. Long ago, white ranchers and farmers secured the most productive lands in the West. Cattle run on good private ground and Forest Service and BLM allotments. The horses and some people get the wastelands—the driest deserts. It's true mustangs often share the terrain with cattle. It's also true that many cattlemen want the horses off, and ranchers and the government have louder voices than wild horses.

I want mustangs to stay wild on lands they know, where their generations have lived, rather than be removed. Or dropped where they stand. An animal or a person or a tree doesn't have to have economic value to have value. Just being, mustangs have value, to the earth, the spirit, like water, air, a falling leaf, a mule deer doe, a vole.

And yet, our public lands as managed today cannot sustain the wild horse numbers. Cattle still rule the range. Mustang adoptions occur less frequently than a decade ago. Without slowing reproduction rates, too many horses competing for feed with other wildlife and domestic cows potentially face starvation. Ranchers know this—for decades they have seen the land depleted by cattle first, mustangs second. For the health of both wild horse and habitat, "removal" is sometimes necessary. Helicopter roundups happen.

Looking at cost in dollars only, the government reports that helicopter roundups are the least expensive way to gather large numbers of wild horses, though the costs to the horses themselves are great: intolerably high stress; running to safety they can't find; being separated from their families—stallions from their mares, foals from their mothers—as they are trucked to processing and adoption centers and short-term holding facilities like the one at Cañon City Correctional Complex in eastern Colorado.

FOR A DECADE, my friend TJ has documented the mustangs of the Bureau of Land Management's 21,932-acre Spring Creek Basin Herd Management Area in southwestern Colorado. She lives seven miles down the valley from me; between our homes no other dwellings exist, just another set of dilapidated, decades-old sheep pens and a modern set of shipping corrals built to aid the cattle ranchers in the area. In addition to documenting the wild horses of Spring Creek Basin, TJ manages a sanctuary for mustangs removed from BLM land. Hers is the voice of knowledge and wisdom when it comes to anything mustang. She went with me to Cañon City to pick up mine.

The big bay gelding had already been sorted into a pen by himself to wait for me, though he didn't know that's what he was doing. I backed the trailer up until it touched the posts of the loading chute, and prison inmates in orange vests pushed the mustang down the alleyway with flags and hollers, sound and movement pressing him forward. Just as he was about to break into a run, he saw the trailer gate yawning open and the dark interior, and he pivoted like a cutting horse and galloped back up the alley, where a closed gate stopped him. Spinning again, he rushed down the alley and leapt into the trailer. I swung the gate closed behind him.

TJ stepped onto the fender and peered inside, speaking to my new horse in her calm way as I secured the gate latch. He didn't fight the trailer. He stood still, breathing heavily, listening to TJ's voice if not her words. I climbed up beside her and offered my shaky voice, wondering if the mustang in my trailer could hear my heart over the pounding of his own.

DETRITUS: WYOMING, 2012. *The mustang's band is spotted by men flying helicopters over Great Divide Basin in southern Wyoming, and one of the helicopters swoops down low out of the sky. The horses bolt into a stampede, their heads high and swinging sideways so that one eye or the other can see behind them, keeping terror in sight; with eyes set on the sides of their faces, not in front like ours, horses have a blind spot directly behind them, which is why you don't walk up to a horse's hind end without first letting her know you are there, as kicking is also a survival strategy. But kicking won't help these horses and they run, run, merging with other bands racing across the dusty sagebrush flats as the huge noisy birds whip through the air behind them; they run as if running is all they can do, running the way their species has for hundreds of years across the same terrain where horses evolved millions of years ago.*

Their necks now fully extended, pointing toward a future they can't see, with legs stretching in long strides and great leaps they grab the miles beneath them but no matter how fast they go, they cannot outrun this predator; there is no escape and no stopping until, miles later, they pour into a temporary apron of orange plastic webbing that leads into an alleyway of portable panels and pens where they crash to a stop, breath coming hard, gasping, trembling, stallions and mares crowding together with fillies and colts.

And there is this dark bay colt without his mother. He is almost a year old but in the wild his dam wouldn't wean him until her next foal was a month or two from being born, and still he would stay with his dam and family band until he was two or three. But now he can't find her in the moving mass of whinnying screaming fighting and crashing into metal as horses try to climb fences and jump fences, this other species loud yelling poking and hitting them with flags and sticks and horses by nature move away from pressure and these are wild *horses and there is only one way away from pressure and they jump into the dark metal box so loud with hooves and banging and still horses scream and he cannot even try to find his mother or sister as mustangs crowd together in terror inside and more come in behind them and he stands trembling within this foreign thing, his ribs heaving as he sucks in air next to horses all shaking so badly they can barely stand up, the bodies of each other holding them in place.*

The possibility of escape closes behind them with a loud bang and then this thing like a narrow box canyon with a very low sky starts moving beneath their hooves and they scramble for footing and tremble more and the sweat from the run and the terror and the closeness of other hot horse bodies drips from their bellies and chests and throats and the big colt stands there and takes it, going calm inside himself like water pooling after a rapid, floating in this moving canyon for long hours as other bright shiny noisy things rush past and he has no room to lie down no water to drink and the smell of sagebrush stays behind as diesel fumes and car exhaust fill the space and he presses his nostrils to horseflesh and closes his eyes and rocks with the movement as there is nothing else he can do—he cannot even stretch his legs out to pee.

When the big rig with its long trailer-load of horses reaches the prison at Cañon City, the truck driver stops at the gate and shows his ID and hands over his cell phone and wallet and any weapons he might have and follows BLM personnel who work inside the prison down the road and around the sweeping curve that leads to the horse facilities.

The driver turns the rig around and backs up to the alley, just as I will do two years later, only my trailer will be empty but for a bale of hay spread loose for the mustang I'm taking home, and the truck driver's load is astir with fear as the mustangs inside smell the horses and burros in captivity, and the male inmates, too, who use their flags to spook the mustangs out, and among the loud voices of men there is a low calming voice, talking to the horses the way TJ does.

The horses don't want to come out, the dark insides of the trailer feeling safe now as nothing new has attacked them inside in the miles and hours they rode, and here are men and daylight and sounds and smells anew, and the horses shudder in the depths of the trailer until the bright flags thrust in their faces scare them into action, into the running they know, and they leap from the trailer as one being and race blindly up an alleyway that leads to a big open pen; no one chasing them anymore they stop at the far fence, still crowding together as they take big gulps of this new air, pungent with huge mounds of horseshit and sweet-smelling alfalfa and water—they can smell water—their thirst the only thing left of home.

They don't want to move away from each other just yet, even for water, and soon another bunch of horses rushes up the alley toward them and they are on the alert again, stallions dazed and confused as their bands are not with them but still they feel the urge to protect and they puff up to greet the newcomers, and there is a familiar smell as the big colt, not yet a stallion, lifts his head and takes in the air.

He whinnies loudly and she stops, rigid, looking into the clustered horses in the pen as he neighs again and this time she nickers back and he trots toward her and right away drops his muzzle to her udder and drinks as she rests her chin on his rump, a big black mare quieting herself to let her milk down for her colt, nearly as tall as she. They don't know the sound of a friendly chuckle as the tall man with the low calming voice watches the big colt nurse, then the laughter subsides as the colt suckles mightily even though the colt doesn't know as the man does that this is his last drink of his mother's milk.

AMONG THE NEGATIVE side effects of annual removals of thousands of mustangs from public lands via helicopter roundups, forced estrangement and permanent separation from family band members are second only to death. Like when I lost my own children in a custody battle—premature, unnatural weaning forced upon my sons and me.

I think the women like TJ who are boots-on-the-ground working toward more enlightened solutions for managing wild horses feel the dissolution of family bands in their guts. Their wombs. I know I do.

Part I

BEFORE / *DETRITUS*

I am ashamed
I never had the words
to carry a friend from her death
to the stars
correctly.

—Joy Harjo
"The Creation Story"

1

Into the Desert Dark

I HAVE LIVED A LIFE OF LEAVINGS. I HAVE LEFT PLACES, PEO-
ple, jobs, lifestyles. Sometimes the act of leaving is enough, the
motion itself the adventure sought. Sometimes leaving doesn't
take me away.

A few decades back, when I lived in Flagstaff, Arizona, I
heard William Kittredge say at a bookfair in Denver that people
in the West moved a lot, searching for the next best place. That
eventually they would find there's nowhere else to go and they'd
have to stay put and fix where they were instead of leaving it in
hopes of something better.

I heard him and left anyway, supporting my lifetime average of moving every year and a half. Perhaps turning my back
on hurt and facing *different* instead of fixing what was wrong
became habit. Habits are not necessarily bad for you—think
yoga or meditation—though I tend toward the other kind. Like
sugar. Or heroin.

Whether leaving is a skill or a malady, I know how to do it.
It's staying that's a mystery.

I'M LIVING ON Maui, in Haʻikū, upcountry. There are two houses
on the property. Mine was built as a shop with a wall of windows by
a windsurf-sail maker—he could see the sea while he worked and

could hasten down the mountain to the beach when the wind and surf were up. My father's house—the bigger house—had a west side of windows, too, facing a gulch so deep and thick with foliage we never saw its bottom, and a view that didn't end. The jagged West Maui Mountains would hover in clouds that embraced the old crater or show clearly if Kona winds blew, the ocean undulating toward Moloka'i, not another house in sight. In my house with its wall of windows I saw that view every day. My father lived part time in the bigger house, my mother and her husband, Ed a mile down the road. Eventually Maka, my fierce Hawaiian-warrior boyfriend, lived with me sometimes in my house of windows.

It's 2010 when an urge to move consumes me. Not to move house, as they say in Hawai'i, or to move *from* Hawai'i or *to* anywhere else, but to move in bigger arcs, across bigger country. I don't yet know I'm *leaving*—I just want to escape expectations and family and reminders of all things sad, and driving in a relatively straight line after years of driving in tight island circles seems a great way to do it.

There's a pull in my na'au, my gut—that place of listening, of reckoning, of guidance if you listen well and reckon right. Na'au also means "of the heart." Tugging at my na'au is a land of long roads and rivers, redrock and hoodoos, piñon jays and golden eagles flying over—the Colorado Plateau. I have lived there before. I know it as country big enough to hold sorrow.

On Maui, I look for my one pair of shoes that aren't slippahs (rubber thongs), but my hiking boots have gone missing. Even the memory of shoes has gone—how they feel on my feet, how cramped my toes get, touching, pushing against each other like the houses in the cities I avoid. I stuff my warmest clothes—a sweatshirt and three pairs of short pants—into a Dakine duffel with glass fishing floats and a photograph of Maka, figuring I'll find the boots next time I'm home.

Home. Home is where my dog is? Cojo, a black, white, and speckled border collie–Australian shepherd cross, will come with me. Run over as a puppy, when I got him at a year and a half his front legs were as bent and twisted as an old juniper. I named him for the California ranch that was in our family for nearly a hundred years, which was named for a Chumash man who walked with a limp.

In the Southwest, some people will know that cojo means "lame." I wonder how Cojo's legs will handle the new terrain. Perhaps the two acres in Haʻikū are a better place to corral his pain, but they are not big enough for mine.

We fly to California, stay two nights with my mother, and I pack my few possessions—the duffel, my grandmother's desk, which I acquired after my father died, some bedding, my dog—into a Subaru Impreza Outback Sport, the name longer than the car, and head out the same driveway I did when I left home at sixteen, my big sister at the wheel. My mother stood there waving until I could no longer see her. She's waving now. My arm out the window, I wave back and pull away.

I change cars the way I do houses and this one is new to me. Cracking windows for fresh air, I fumble with the air conditioning, preparing for a forecasted heat wave. Cojo watches me keenly from the passenger seat—he's a border collie; I'm his job. I rest my hand on his soft coat and feel him panting. A Maui dog, he has not traveled long in a car before—literally every second he expects me to *stop*. When his breathing settles, I settle, and the Subaru settles into the miles ahead.

My agenda is simple: to log more than six hundred miles a day, and to sleep on Arizona. Dropping over the Tehachapi Mountains into the Mojave Desert, skirting the edges of Barstow, we reach I-40 and I accelerate onto the interstate, heading toward another desert life.

~~~

YOU HAVE TO have certain characteristics to be a desert, though heat isn't necessarily one of them. In the deserts of the American Southwest, the amount of water lost to evaporation and transpiration (which is like plant perspiration) will exceed the amount of precipitation received, which will be less than ten average inches of rainfall a year. Sparse vegetation dots the land, and plants develop creative survival strategies, thorns among them. Extreme temperatures can be cold as well as hot.

The Mojave, with an average annual precipitation of five inches, is inarguably desert. A summer day of 113 degrees is typical. I've driven across it at 123, so hot you dare not use the air conditioner for fear your car will overheat, and stuck out there in 123 degrees and no shade is not where you want to be. But after years in Hawai'i, I have forgotten that desert in October is different from desert in July. On both ends—day and night. I have forgotten how five inches of rain spread over 365 days feels in the air. So unlike the rainforest microclimate of Ha'ikū, where the average annual rainfall of seventy-four inches makes toweling off after a shower futile, moisture returning to your surface in moments, lotion unnecessary. Driving, I feel the Mojave Desert sucking the moisture from my skin.

In 1990, after my first divorce, I moved from California's Central Coast to attend graduate school in Flagstaff, and spent a lot of time driving I-40 from Flagstaff to the rest stop west of Needles, or Kelbaker Road, sometimes to Barstow or Victorville, to deliver or pick up my kids for holidays and summer vacation. I drove alone, or sometimes with Smith, my sweet second husband, who would come along just for the ride (six hundred miles round trip, but he's from Montana). Despite the years between then and now, the jagged skylines of the Mojave still feel like arms wrapping around crushing sadness, reflected now in the deaths behind me.

I turn up the air conditioning. The thermometer peaks at only ninety-eight, in Needles, 488 feet above sea level.

Needles. Another part of the story.

I push the Subaru farther, faster, as if east is a direction that can take me away.

I WANT TO stop at the lowest point—the Colorado River, where kids dogs and I would dunk and splash on the hottest drives—but dusk like grief is a cloud around me. Plus I can feel my knee swelling and filling my skin the way I fill my new "skinny jeans" (shopping for jeans in California, I was surprised at how styles had changed since my last purchase more than a decade ago), and my knee and the coming night push me past the private spot by the water. From the bridge that connects California and Arizona I can see the shimmer of river; from there the freeway begins its rise toward seven-thousand-foot Flagstaff on the side of the twelve-thousand-foot San Francisco Peaks.

Full darkness curtains the windows before I reach Kingman. I've made over six hundred miles. Somewhere on the north side of the freeway there's a stack of huge red rocks—I found them once when I let kids dogs me out to pee and found them again, often. The southwestern perimeter of the Colorado Plateau still miles away, the rocks would say to me something like *yes, you're almost home.* That's where I want to sleep but as I scan head-lighted junipers, I can't remember the exit.

Taking a random exit, no lights of civilization anywhere, I drive up a dirt road, turn onto another, and branch off again, confident that in daylight I'll be able to find my way back. In a clearing I circle the little car with the big name around, facing out so I can drive away fast if I need to. Cojo hops down from his seat. We stretch and sniff the dry desert air—a blend of juniper and piñon pine duff and the dust of red earth.

I have my Therm-a-Rest pad from my river-running days, and my sleeping bag. Once slated for zero degrees, in the years of river use, camping on Kahoʻolawe with Maka, and serving as comforter when Hawai'i winters got cold enough to close the windows, it has thinned and flattened and is more a blankie than a real sleeping bag. No tarp, just pad and bag on red dirt I can smell but not see. I climb in fully dressed, the flashlight my mother gave me in one sweatshirt pocket, cell phone and car keys in the other, feet in socks my mother stuffed into my backpack, slippahs beside the bed.

The desert stars poise crisply above me, not muted by moisture like Maui stars. My knee hurts. I don't know what's wrong with it. The Maui doctor wouldn't do an MRI or even take X-rays because I don't have insurance.

Longing creeps in. I don't know what for. Calling Cojo to come share a bit of the bag, I just lie there as the night grows colder. Although I've driven away from it, I hear trucks on the freeway, so I think of rapists, of me without a gun, of sleeping off the road in that previous desert life with two dogs, one part wolf, and my .270. Of how stupid I am to follow this urge to sleep on Arizona instead of in a motel. But I so longed for red dirt—the essence of the Colorado Plateau—that I wanted to touch it if not taste it, as if that is the tonic that will carry me through.

I switch to my side, curling deep into the sleeping bag in search of warmth. That's when Rebecca shows up.

She arrived in fifth grade, her family moving into a yellow house kitty-corner to our white one. Blond and blue-eyed with a chubby belly and so shy, soon every day after school we were climbing an ivy-covered brick wall into each other's lives. It wasn't a girl crush. It was love and devotion. Safety. The one person I could tell everything to, for forty-three years: Rebecca.

We lived together in Berkeley in our early twenties, our lives twisting around each other through boyfriends and college, my marriage and divorce. She never had kids, but she had mine, and she was there for us at each hard turn in the road.

In our mid-forties, I was living in Utah, Rebecca in Oakland, when we met on Kaua'i and backpacked into Kalalau, a deep green valley on Nā Pali Coast accessible only by foot, boat, and emergency helicopter. Nā pali means "the cliffs," and that's what we hiked along, our packs heavy, the ocean hundreds of feet below, the trail eroded in places to pebbles that bounced down the cliffs to the sea. Rebecca went because I wanted her to, even though we both knew she didn't like sleeping on dirt, and no showers. While I stretched her comfort shield, her willingness gave me Kaua'i under my feet, under my body as I slept, that red dirt like skin, like love, that old, old island once my home.

DETRITUS: KAUA'I, 1962. *My big sister and me on the airplane with our father. She's nine, I'm seven, and our mother and little sister are at the house in California, which my mother is packing up and selling. The airplane has two stories and a curly-q staircase. The bar is up there. Our father is up there.*

Out the window white fog covers the ocean and the sky stretches across forever. My big sister and I look for water and islands and hula girls. Or I do, after she starts reading. She always reads. I play with my stuffed animals. And my plastic horses.

Mother said I couldn't take all my stuffed animals to Hawai'i. I had to choose.

I threw them at the yellow wall of my bedroom one at a time— but not the horses. They would break. Then I cried and put all my stuffed animals on my bed and took a nap in the middle.

I hate yellow.

I hate my mother's best friend's husband who won't let me watch the horse races on his TV until after, but I can't tell anyone.

I choose the big stuffed teddy bear to go to Hawai'i with me. I got him for my five-year-old birthday. He had a red ribbon around his neck. Red is okay, but I hate pink. Pink is a girl color. I hate girls. Except my big sister. And my little sister, who isn't a girl yet 'cause she's almost still a baby. I hate me for being a girl. If I wasn't a girl maybe Daddy would like me better and maybe my mother's best friend's husband wouldn't like me as much.

"That bear will fill a whole airplane seat," my mother said. "He will have to come on the boat." He does come on a boat, later, with more clothes, and shoes we won't need. I pick a different animal for the airplane. A soft horse.

The fog stays with California. We get to the first island and climb down metal stairs. The sky is bright, the sun is bright, the sea is bright. There are no hula girls. The wind smells so, so sweet, from flowers on the trees outside the airport building, Daddy says. Plumeria trees. He's happy now, from the airplane landing or the airplane bar I don't know.

We get on another plane and fly to another island. No fog and we can see the ocean and its big waves rolling under us. On Kaua'i there are no hula girls.

We go to the hotel where Daddy will work. Everybody hugs us and kisses us on the cheek. At first I don't like it but I can't tell anybody so I watch my big sister who doesn't like being touched by strangers either, or even people we know, but she lets these ladies whose skin is so soft bend down and kiss her on the cheek.

Daddy says aloha to everyone. We all wear necklaces of flowers. Lei, Daddy says. Mine is yellow. Plumeria. It smells so, so sweet so I decide this yellow is okay, but I am glad my big sister has the pink one. When our mother comes in a month we will have lei for her and our little sister who is not really a girl yet.

When our mother comes in a month she will tell Daddy she doesn't know me. My skin and hair changed color. My feet are wide and brown and tough like shoes, which I don't wear. I still look like a girl, but I look like one local girl, everyone says, and being a local girl is okay.

We have seen the hula girls. At the hotel where Daddy works in the kitchen and bars there is a floorshow every night. The hula girls wear ti leaf skirts, and lei around their necks over their white tops and they smell so, so sweet.

At the hotel where Daddy works there are also hula boys. Only they are not called hula boys. They are called beachboys because at daytime they work at the beach, pushing outrigger canoes filled with pink tourists into the water and taking tourists out on surfboards. At daytime because it's summer we play at the beach, in the water with the girls who dance and the boys who surf but we only swim. And my big sister reads. I never want to read again. Or go to school again. I only want to swim.

After the floorshow when my big sister and I are supposed to be sleeping in the little bungalow we live in with Daddy, we peek through the slats of the windows and watch the beachboys walk by. Sometimes when we watch them walk by in the moonlight and the so-sweet smell of Kaua'i, I feel a part of me that maybe likes being a girl.

When school starts, I still don't wear shoes. It's the best school ever, all our slippahs lined up outside the door. But when summer comes back, we have to leave Hawai'i. Something Daddy said. Drunk. I leave my big teddy bear behind. Inside my big teddy bear I stuff my heart. When we get back to California, my heart is still in Hawai'i.

THE ARIZONA NIGHT grows colder. Stuffed in the Subaru is a patchwork quilt my mother sent along, her foresight much better than mine. I get up, hunched with cold, tug it out, and spread it over my makeshift bed. How is it that my mother still takes care of me when it was both of her husbands who died, and her Rebecca, too, her hānai daughter, adopted by the heart?

My whole family adopted Rebecca. Even my brother-in-law, my older sister reminds me—he fell under her charm when Rebecca went to their farm in Oregon to help with my kids while I attended a writing workshop. Upon seeing the blueberry bushes, she said, "I'm going to crawl in there and take a nap."

I want to sleep, too. I check my phone for the time. Somehow it has crept up to midnight and past. My eyes close and I feel the breath of sleep move up through my chest and that's when Cojo growls deep in his throat. The brush stirs nearby. Cojo's up and barking and I try to see in the dark as a critter crashes through branches, snuffling like a fucking bear, Cojo all raised fur and fury beside me as I fumble with my mother's flashlight, pointing it like a weapon at eyes glowing red in the underbrush, Cojo growling, me all twisted up in the bedding, the beam a moderate pool, but I can count 'em: six. Three pairs of eyes, closer to the ground than a bear's.

One pair separates from the pack, coming closer to where I sit in my knot of sleeping bag and quilt and fear, Cojo crooked-legged in front of me, and I see a raised hump of rounded gray back and the snout face as it snuffs and clicks its tusks and retreats, rejoining the other two javelinas.

Javelina. Peccary. The encyclopedia in my brain is as worn as the old sleeping bag but I ruffle through its pages anyway, searching for facts I once knew. This is what I come up with in the desert dark: a children's book from Northland Publishing where I worked years before, *The Three Little Javelinas* by Susan Lowell, the coyote huffing and puffing and blowing their house down, and why am I remembering *that* when these three are not so little and *they* are doing the huffing and puffing and making little fake charges at *me* all tangled up by my car, which is so loaded I cannot make a bed inside it or put the seat-back down for sleep but will have to backtrack to Kingman or hope Seligman has better motels now or . . .

The three little piggies wander off. I straighten my bed and lie down again and so does Cojo, shivering in the lee of my knees as I pull the quilt over my head, which aches with the cold. That's when the coyotes go off, sounding like fifteen about five feet away, the way coyotes usually sound. Cojo doesn't know this since he has never heard one—or ten—before. He only knows

Hawai'i sounds: dogs barking, Maka snoring, roosters crowing, the pounding of the sea.

I know I slept because I wake up, Cojo still shivering beside me, dawn spreading pale pink around us. I wait for full sun before emerging, remembering another Southwest desert thing: when the sun comes through it's often warm, even in winter. But it isn't winter. It's fall, mid-October, and I have someplace to go.

Changing clothes quickly as it's still nippy out, I see Rebecca snorkeling after we hiked out of Kalalau, the ocean the closest bathtub. Her turquoise thong hidden in water, just her snorkel and the back of her head and her brown bum bobbed above the sea.

I moved back to Hawai'i the year after Kalalau (sometimes leaving was like that—I tasted something and wanted more), farther from Rebecca than ever before. But she would visit, I would see her in California, and we would talk often, a pattern established years before. It didn't matter that we had different lifestyles; we were connected like the patches of my mother's quilt.

I shrug off the missing as Cojo and I search for tracks—how brave we have become in the daylight. In the red dirt around our camp, prints show javelinas circling, one charging from beneath the juniper, but there's no bear sign, coyotes did not come close, and just up the hill sits a house with smoke lifting from its chimney.

THE OCTOBER NIGHT of cold punctuated the meaning of desert for this Hawai'i girl. It's not just those smart desert plants, vanishing wisps of rain on the horizon, and 123-degree days that define a desert ecosystem, but those frigid nights, as well, and the spreads between them. And there's more to it, so much more. I'm returning to the desert to hide but the desert is about exposure. That hot desert air will take you down to skin and bone.

Then it might fill you up with love, or it might kill you. Water can make the difference.

My Hawai'i clothes—shorts and shifts and sarongs—will not fit me in New Mexico at this time of year, that much is clear, but I can't guess how hard it will be to find shoes wide enough for my wide Hawai'i feet. Nor do I guess the depth of the cold toward which I'm headed, or that no matter what I wear, I will not be able to keep the cold out. That my core will freeze.

And where will I find my water? Let alone my heart.

2

PUNCTURED

COJO AND I SURVIVE JAVELINAS AND COLD AND ARRIVE IN New Mexico intact. Next to a Rio Grande tributary and cottonwoods turning to gold sits an adobe casita with a flat roof and flagstone lānai. The casita is empty but for a single-bed mattress on a window seat of the same size. A daybed. Cojo's toenails click across polished floorboards as I open blinds.

The chilly interior chases us back outside. We sit on stone steps in dappling sunlight. My cell phone doesn't work and there is no landline or internet, just Cojo and me in the truest sense. He rests his chin on my knee, his one-up, one-down ears settling against his head as I absently trace the salt-and-pepper markings of his face and watch the world around us—cars on the road disturbing the song of the rio, the canopy of cottonwoods shrinking what sky hangs between the close canyon walls.

Although it's still afternoon, when the sun touches the southern rim the daybed beckons. Sleeping bag and patchwork quilt slowing the chill, I watch heart-shaped Rio Grande cottonwood leaves twirling and falling through the light, and curl into myself like a dying leaf, brittle at the edges.

DETRITUS: OAKLAND, 2008. *In the middle of a December afternoon, a gardener let himself into Rebecca's kitchen using the spare* key he'd been instructed to find under a potted plant on the back porch. He shut his nostrils against the smells—food rotting and cat feces, primarily. The cat, skittering off down a short hallway, whined as it fled, hungry and in want of water and the outdoor litter box it normally used. The man puckered his nose, choosing not to see the cluttered kitchen in the dim light sneaking through closed blinds. His foot kicked an empty cat-food can and it rattled across the floor.

He called out for Rebecca, his voice an echo in the still, dead air of the tiny Oakland home. He took another step, wondering why he was doing this, why Rebecca's sister had asked and he hadn't refused, why they didn't just call the police. He heard the cat in the far bedroom. He'd cleared Rebecca's yard of chest-high weeds, the act ordered by the city for fire prevention, and had called the sister in Virginia when Rebecca didn't answer the door any of the times he'd come over to collect the check. And here he was.

Every window was covered with blinds or blankets. He almost forgot, in his slow walk across the kitchen to the near bedroom, that outside the day held the bloom of winter sun in a clear blue sky. A sky the color of Rebecca's eyes. Standing at the threshold of her room, he heard the cat scamper around behind him, aiming for the kitchen door, which he'd left open for the smell. He glanced at the empty, rumpled bed and the clutter everywhere, hoping he wouldn't find what his nose already told him was there.

Why he didn't turn away and follow the cat outside, he didn't know. Something compelled him forward, maybe the same morbid curiosity that causes traffic to creep past an accident. When he turned on the light he saw a small, pudgy foot in a dirty white sock. He couldn't see the other leg until he entered the room fully and there she lay, my Rebecca, in jeans and a white tank top pulled tight with the bloat, one arm bent at the elbow, her other leg bent at the knee. She looked thick and sort of green and her open eyes no longer held the sky.

No blood or bile anywhere. Just the smell and a quiet Rebecca and the half-empty pill bottles on the nightstand.

WHAT HAND OF grace touches one addict clean and misses another? Rebecca was fifty-three. So many pills, for back pain, insomnia. Mail-ordered meds. She called me the day before she died. She called everybody. Talked to no one. We were all busy. I called her back and left a message: "I love you. Come visit. But you know you can't use when you're here."

She couldn't have come to Maui anyway. She was already death walking. No way she could have navigated an airport.

I could have carried her. But I didn't.

THIRTY DAYS AFTER Rebecca overdosed, Ed, my hānai father, was diagnosed with melanoma, his tumors "too numerous to count." It was in the doctor's report, which he read. So did my mother and sisters. I didn't want to. As if not reading would make it not real. But it was real. I watched Ed's body deteriorate as I felt the loss of Rebecca in my bones. I wanted to talk to her, damn it. I wanted to tell her how I understood better what she was going through as her mother died of brain cancer five years earlier.

Ed died a year and a half after Rebecca, four months after my father.

I arrived at my mother and Ed's house in California on Thursday, the day after the hospital bed. The bed day was a bad one for Ed, being moved from the big bed he shared with my mother to a chair to the new bed. On Friday afternoon, the hospice nurse came—another sign for poor dear Ed that his body wasn't going to hold out much longer. He said he had to go to the bathroom. The nurse guided my mother and me as we helped him rise painfully to two-thirds his old height, grasp the walker with thin yellow hands, and shuffle to the toilet. An emergency call from another family pulled the nurse away, which left my mother and me to help Ed rise again and take his pain-filled little steps back toward the bed, my mother in front, encouraging, me behind him gripping his hips firmly as he sank lower with each inch he gained. I was strong from years of outrigger canoe paddling and no injured knee but I could feel panic rising.

"You have to turn now, like this." I twisted my hips, showing him that I needed him to pivot and back up so he could sit on the bed.

"I can't."

My mother's face over his shoulder, horror-stricken.

"Just a small step. And one more." My hands clenching his hips, so narrow between my palms. "One more step."

He couldn't do it—it wasn't that he *felt* as if he had no more strength but that his body *truly had nothing left.* All I could do was aim his hips toward the edge of the bed at its closest point—the foot—not at all where we wanted him because that meant we would have to pull his poor old tired hurting dying body up the bed in order to stretch it out for him, placing his feet at the foot and his head at the head. Which is exactly what we did, my mother holding a brittle arm, her other hand under his back, me opposite her doing the same, thanking the gods for the small favor of the narrow hospital bed that Ed hated but what we were doing would have been impossible if it were a normal bed.

"You're hurting me," Ed said. My mother and I looked at each other and bucked up and lifted and scooted him with the sheet the way the hospice nurses did until he was in the proper resting, sleeping, dying position, and then the three of us paused, our breathing belabored. It had taken an hour to get Ed to the bathroom and back into bed.

When he got his breath, Ed said, "I think you broke my rib."

We wouldn't see for another day the tumor popping out on his ribcage. When he died five days after the bathroom day, that tumor stuck out a full inch from the bone.

~~~

THE DAY AFTER Ed died, I injured my knee riding my mother's stationary bicycle, desperate for exercise. There was no sudden pain, just thickening and stiffness and an inability to rise gracefully from the living-room floor. I could barely walk down to the canoes on the Maui beach when we paddled Ed and some of Rebecca, given to me by her sister, out to sea.

Weeks later I'm in New Mexico with a thick knee. I don't want to get up from the daybed, but hunger propels me to the tiny store in the closest tiny town. People look at me, a stranger, but no one speaks. I am glad for it. I don't want to speak. I go nearly two years without speaking to anyone in that town.

Fleeing back to the dark canyon, I park the Subaru and wonder how I'll manage to maneuver my grandmother's desk from car to house without hurting my knee too badly—the desk at which my father's mother and my own mother both wrote. I will also write. But not this night. This first night of Cojo and me trying to sleep in the empty house in the cold canyon, I lie shivering in my sleeping bag as if javelinas with their bristles and tusks are stepping through the walls.

I'VE BEEN IN New Mexico a month when my son Ken comes to visit. He is tall and lean with stunning green eyes like Keith, his father, and a college degree (like me). By now I have a real bed and a couch. Ken helps me pick out other basic furniture (a man-chair for him) and shop for tools, a generator. He leaves when his dad calls—Keith is getting steers in and needs help in California.

A month later, Ken takes a job on a ninety-six-thousand-deeded-acre ranch in northeastern New Mexico, just a hundred miles away. Between us rises the swell of the Sangre de Cristo Mountains, not the Pacific Ocean or Mojave Desert or any of the other geographies (or people) that separated us in the past. A new pattern begins: me visiting Ken in his little ranch house on the big New Mexico ranch, this after a twenty-year separation. But I don't feel the joy. I don't feel anything. Each way I turn, the world is dulled by strange orange light. Even Ken.

The next year I'll go on a Grand Canyon river trip. Even there, I won't feel joy. I'll say to another passenger, "I don't understand it. They've been dead a year," and he will say, "It takes two."

During the trip there is an eclipse. The guides give us special glasses to wear. I watch the sun disappear. The whole world turns burnt-orange to match my world. When the sun comes back, the color doesn't change.

Days later, we will round a bend in the paddle raft and see a band of desert bighorn sheep coming to water. Crossing the eddy fence, the drops from our paddles the only sound, we float upstream, watching a full-curl ram dip his muzzle daintily to the river, his eyes with their horizontal irises gazing as if not seeing anything beyond the water at his lips.

WINTER ARRIVES IN New Mexico. The most important activity each day is keeping the fire built up and arthritic Cojo and arthritic me warm. I have lived in cold before, in the Sierra Nevada, in Arizona and Utah, but my body, transitioning from years in Hawai'i, is slow to acclimate. The only time I feel warm enough is inside the sweat lodges to which the chiropractor treating my knee has invited me. Cold fits the new pace I seem to be living.

I wait for my knee to get better.

IN MY MOTHER's California living room, we sat waiting for others to arrive, sharply aware that Ed wouldn't be joining her writing group as he had over the years. I sat on the floor to make room for other women to sit on furniture; I sat on the floor because that's where I'm most comfortable. In a moment of waiting that hung like wet laundry, I felt something different in my left knee. Then someone said should we wait or start writing, and another person spoke and another, and we were no longer waiting but talking, listening, thinking, writing.

We were only women waiting for a short time, but how many years have we, as women, spent waiting? For the right man, for that man to call, for him to arrive at the door; waiting to conceive, for the birth to happen, for the first tooth, the first step. Then, waiting for things to get better. In all those waitings did any of us think we would spend future moments waiting for a man—father lover husband brother—to die?

I did not. That wasn't part of the bargain, the contract going in. At least not on the draft I read. But there we were, women who have waited for that, too—a year and a half of our lives hinging on Ed's health, all the while knowing where we were going, just not knowing when. All of us—my mother sisters cousins aunt kids, our friends, me—waiting.

My younger son, Tyler, stayed in his grandparents' house in Haʻikū when they went to California—when does housesitting turn into living in someone's house? He couldn't decorate or remove clothes from the closet or expired prescriptions from the bathroom drawers because we were waiting to see when Ed would come home. At least for the first year. For the first year we waited while Ed was being treated at Stanford Cancer Center and finally I said to my mother, "We need to know if you think you'll actually be coming back." And we had an answer to something.

When one waits, is one not living? When you were hoping that boy would call, back there in that other life when you were sixteen, was that waiting all-consuming or did you notice the air you breathed, sunlight on pine needles, the smell of rain?

~~~

DETRITUS: SIERRA NEVADA, 1971. *I'm barely sixteen when my big sister drives me north from the Bay Area to a ranch in the Sierra Nevada that is also a camp where I work summers. I'm entering the local high school mid-year. My sister drops me off and drives on to Oregon. The owner and me alone in the ranch house, it takes a long time for summer to arrive.*

But it does, and one hot evening at the county fair a group of us ranch girls walks around the corner of a beer booth and my full cup of Coors splashes up against my chest.

"Goddamnit I'm sorry," a stranger says. Sparkling eyes and a grin like James Dean, he reaches to wipe at the spilled beer. His hand midway to my breast, I step back into the pack of giggling girls.

He stops his hand and says, "Lemme buy you another one," disappearing long enough that I think he's not coming back. But he does, with two full cups of Coors in hand. We wander the fair, watching the rides, the swirling lights, heading to the horse barn so I can show him my mare, Tirade.

It's 1971, clearcutting still popular with the timber companies. Most of the mountain boys who aren't from ranching families work in the woods. Ethics aside, I know that logging makes men of boys. Up in the morning at dark-thirty, they drive into the deep woods with thermoses of coffee and bellies full of breakfasts made by good wives and mothers, dawn showing them the way through old stands of pines and firs to the edge of the forest—an edge they made. They spread out afoot, chainsaws, gas cans, and lunchboxes in hand, and start felling the next growth of trees.

When Craig lifts my chin and kisses me under the soft barn light, I feel a logger's work in his arms and chest. When he pulls me into an empty stall, I follow.

He closes the lower and upper doors. My breath catches as I sink with him into the straw bedding. His callused palm finds its way under my T-shirt. Moving close, closer, he lifts up his shirt, then mine. The skin of our bellies touches.

"Do you feel that?" he says.

Nodding into his shoulder, yes, I feel that: *heat fusing us together. I squirm to get closer. I pull away. I want him to stop, to pull his T-shirt back down. I want him to never stop. That belly-to-belly touch has not ever felt that good again.*

His shirt comes off over his head, muscles rippling. He pulls my hips closer. I push into him. Straw pokes through my top. His Levi's come off.

Callused hands hot on my skin, igniting my skin, he pushes my shirt up above my bra, reaches into my jeans. My body screams yes *but my mind is shouting* no, noooo. *He's almost naked when I say it out loud.*

"No."

Softly, but he hears me.

He hears me say no and he stops and I cry.

SOMETIMES WHEN A child is four or five, she can't say no. Sometimes when a girl is twenty, a woman thirty, she still can't say no. She has been trained not to, threatened or hurt or left for doing what I did in that stall with Craig. Terror and desire swam inside me as I felt his body against mine, my voice stuck in my throat, breath stuck in my chest. When I pushed the word out I risked everything imaginable to a teenaged girl—fists, force. At the very least, he would not want to see me again.

SKIP FORTY YEARS and think, while waiting for Ed to die, did you notice your breath? I know we noticed his. But how did we spend the waiting?

I talked to Tyler, just down the road at Mother and Ed's; to Ken at Colorado State University; to my bio-father, whose wife died of cancer several years earlier; and to my sisters. I hung on to hope that Ed wouldn't go, then hope that he would. So I waited, talked, hung, hoped. I wrote, paddled, and swam. For a while I taught, but I couldn't concentrate well on my students.

In that time of waiting, I got older. My body changed. I swam and paddled and my body still changed and I waited, life on hold waiting for death.

And then my other father died. About to dress for a dinner date in California, he slipped to the floor, looking nearly lifeless when his date found him after the paramedics broke through the back door. He was medevacked to a hospital where he lived for eleven days—long enough for me to fly from Maui to spend several hours over several days with him as he struggled to communicate with one good arm and eyes that kept tearing up, but not long enough to say goodbye. I had just stepped from the shower in the upstairs bathroom of my mother and Ed's house in Palo Alto, hurrying to get dressed and make the drive to see Dad again, when the phone rang. My mother's footsteps heavy on the carpeted stairs told me I was too late.

Earlier that month, my last two-way conversation with my father happened on the phone, him in California, me on Maui. I stood near an upstairs window watching Maka, my boyfriend of five years, load the last of his stuff into his truck. I had broken up with him just days before. Wanting to get downstairs for some sort of closure with Maka—wanting to hold on, to not let him go—I gave my father's voice scant attention. Maka, intent on his business, did not look up, did not see me watching as he walked to the edge of the gulch and looked across at the pineapple fields, the ocean, the island of Moloka'i softened by distance. He did not look for me. Just got in his rusting red Toyota and drove slowly away as my father was saying goodbye. That's how I said goodbye to both of them.

I finished dressing in my mother's guestroom and went downstairs to Ed, who raised himself carefully from his big red chair and hugged me with wavering strength. Stepping back, I looked into his still-clear, still-intelligent blue eyes. "I love you,"

I said. "You know that, right?" Because maybe my other father left without knowing it, like Maka did.

DETRITUS: SIERRA NEVADA, 1971. *Two weeks have passed since meeting Craig. No promises or phone numbers exchanged, I have only the ache of longing. The ranch doesn't have a phone anyway. I tell Rebecca everything in a letter. She writes back. She got in trouble because her boyfriend climbed up the outside plumbing pipes to her bedroom window. Tee hee, she writes in the margin, and I can hear her giggling as I watch the road, letter in hand, hoping to see Craig's Mustang cruise by.*

There's a rodeo and dance in Susanville. As we're getting dressed, the other counselors tell me I look too tomboyish in my T-shirt and cutoffs and dress me up in a lacy, pale blue blouse, tight fitting and scratchy. I feel like somebody I haven't met before and don't much like—a girl.

Entering the grange hall I search the faces and don't see his, so I slip through the crowd to the back wall. The band bangs out songs and the ranch girls dance with boys and men or in fat clumps of each other, knowing how to have fun. The night wears on. It wears me down. I shrug off invitations to dance, try to hide my breasts inside the pale blue blouse, want to bolt as music and laughter and sweating men crowd around me.

And then Craig walks through the open double doors.

I know instantly that it's him, backlit by the porch lights. So do the other ranch girls, and I swear a hush falls over the dancehall as he stands there looking around. And then he spots me. And walks across that crowded room through all those hot sweating bodies right up to me and holds out his hand. It's the best Hollywood moment I've ever seen.

Craig drives me back to the ranch in his '67 Mustang, me so scared of love I think of nothing to say.

With school about to start, the forty-five-year-old ranch

owner informs me that I can't live at the ranch anymore. I told him no that spring when he snuck into my bed one night, and a seventeen-year-old girl who rides like a jockey and has the complexion of a makeup model and perfect pink lips has moved into his bedroom.

Craig about to go back to college down in the flat country, I ask him if I can talk to his parents about staying with them. The kids juggle rooms and Craig sleeps on the couch when he comes home weekends and we move Tirade into their cow pasture. And Craig's family shows me what family life is like when you have a mother and *a father and sisters and brothers who eat dinner together every night.*

Craig shows me more. He shows me that outside is best.

THE FIRST MUSTANG I knew personally was a dark bay mare named Patty that Craig's uncle gave him. Captured somewhere in Nevada before the passing of the Wild Free-Roaming Horses and Burros Act of 1971 (Public Law 92-195), Patty bore no BLM brand. Fat in summer, shaggy in winter, she stood fourteen hands high (a "hand" is four inches—about the width of a hand—measured from the ground to the top of the withers), which made her easy to mount even though she was only partially trained. Dismounting was easier still. It was often her idea. As soon as she felt trapped she would turn her head against the bit and run to a safe corner of the field, or buck or sidestep or head for low branches or into the willow thickets at the end of the pasture where snow became marsh in the spring.

Wild horses must be able to flee—their first and best defense. This is why helicopter roundups "work," according to the BLM: when chased, mustangs run. Helicopters herd them to the traps. That's where the panic sets in. Already terrified, when they realize they are in an enclosure the horses *must* get out. They try with everything they have to escape.

~~~

It's a common saying in the rooms of twelve-step programs: *don't leave before the miracle happens.* I know what that means, there in those rooms. It means don't go back out—don't use again—before the miracle of recovery takes hold. You don't wait for that miracle, you take the steps. You walk you read you talk you pray. Those things are not waiting. *You* are not waiting. You are learning and growing and changing.

The transition from Hawaiʻi to New Mexico remains difficult. I'm cold, regardless of temperature. The change to standard time surprises me—Hawaiʻi doesn't do daylight saving time. Next surprise: the standard-time sun leaves my nameless New Mexico canyon early on winter afternoons (2:53 p.m. on winter solstice). I know there are steps I should be taking, but they hurt too much. I settle into a new me: sedentary, cold, beyond middle-aged, alone with a bum knee and a good dog and a son two hours away, settling easier to do in below-freezing temperatures than in plus seventy-five.

While I have passion only for sleep, some days I force myself into the Subaru to search for places where Cojo and I can walk amid the great basalt boulders and cholla cactus on land the dull color of my heart. I start scheduling my time around sunlight, doing town appointments and errands or walking at the end of the day so I can drive up out of the canyon and catch two additional hours of coveted sunshine.

One afternoon I leave the lonely highway after a few miles, turning onto the first narrow, barely paved two-lane road I see, which parallels a river where common mergansers fish in eddies formed by basalt blocks that have fallen from high up on the canyon rim. The strength in their webbed feet holds the ducks in place in the current as they face upstream and dip heads and shoulders into winter water.

A stretch of wings marks the skyline. Too refined for turkey vultures, too big for ravens, the afternoon light glancing off white tail feathers confirms it: a pair of bald eagles. I stop in the middle of the road to watch their flick and flex of wing as they navigate air currents high above the river corridor. When raptor and rimrock blend together, I drive on.

We come upon a dirt road near the confluence of a small tributary and the bigger river. I take the road to its end, park in a scarred turnaround where others have, and don a jacket, scarf, and gloves but forget my knee brace. Cojo and I start up a path above this side stream, which splashes with clear water. Cojo hops ahead of me, eager to be out despite pain. I feel the same.

The east-west curve of the side canyon offers sun exposure and relative warmth. After a few minutes, I look for a doable descent to the creek so that Cojo can drink and I can watch riffles and eddies and pools in water so different from the sea, but we repeatedly encounter large basalt blocks stacked inaccessibly downward. No problem for the normal me, and Cojo would manage it just to stay close, but my knee keeps me going up the trail, searching for an easy path through red willows and the huge angular rocks—basalt birthed by volcanic activity yet so unlike Hawai'i's smooth flows of pāhoehoe or sharp, jagged ʻaʻā lava.

Suddenly Cojo stops, sniffing over an edge. He takes a hop down. I sniff, too, smelling only the fragrance of freshwater moving. When you're close enough to smell saltwater, you feel it on your skin. My skin just feels cold, even inside my jacket. A cold that turns to chicken skin when I hear the brittle willows rattling near the river. A shadow moves.

"Cojo, stay," I say, as Cojo steps forward to investigate. A mule deer spooked up from a bed in the willows? "*Stay*," I hiss. I want to see it.

Expecting more noise and taller movement, the tops of willows parting as it passes, I watch for the deer's emergence from its protective cover, waiting for it to bound up the far side of the canyon. But the movement remains low, more whooshing than crashing, until against the reddish earth on that opposite wall, which is not all that far away, I see not antlered gray but tawny hide flashing, leaping, lifting, and a long tail following. Cat. Wildcat. Cougar. Catamount. Panther, painter, *Puma concolor.* Mountain lion!

The big cat scampers its vertical way up and more up and out of sight behind a rock outcropping while I stand gawking, hoping to see it again, wishing I'd thought to bring my old loyal Leupold field glasses, given to me by Keith when I used to hunt, or that I had more youth left in my eyes, or still had the trained eye of a hunter, but it's just Cojo and me and my naked eyes and his bent legs and the lion probably over there watching, hearing our hearts. There must be something to *do*, I think, some way to honor. A Hawaiian chant comes to mind but I stand voiceless, and then stumble on up the trail about twenty feet before I turn back to look into the willows to see what the lion was doing in there.

The rocks and a sense of violation deter me from entering the thicket; from the path I scan the tangle of willows until I see something different. Something red. Trash? It's on every Hawai'i beach. A faded-red, plastic, five-gallon gas can?

No.

It's meat. Raw red meat. A carcass, or part of one. The haunch of some large animal. Just one peek closer and I can see the hide—dark. Long dark fur. Too long for a deer. Can't be a bear. Elk? Not really elk country. A bighorn sheep quarter then? I had heard that desert bighorns were released somewhere in the area.

Slowly I realize: the mountain lion had been quietly eating her supper in the dry winter willows beside the stream when Cojo and I interrupted her.

I shiver in the growing cold. Cojo and I walk on up the canyon, me stopping periodically to scan the rocks into which the big cat disappeared, Cojo sniffing every sage bush and chamisa.

The easy part of the path ends and up we go over the rocky trail. The whole canyon is in shadow now, the sun gone even from here, and a voice whispers in the wind—my mother's voice—so for my knee and my mother I turn around and head back down toward the car.

Keeping Cojo behind me in case the cougar has returned, I walk softly along the trail toward the willows, where I peer again at the meat. No one seems to be home and we move on, the tributary rushing along in its bed, bald eagles far downcanyon by now, mergansers tucking in for the night, and the cougar, which was but fifteen feet away when we initially passed, either long gone or watching, waiting to finish her supper.

At the Subaru I notice that I do not feel fear. Have not felt it, not for a moment. Only awe, hope for a better look, and gratitude for the sighting, quick though it was. Not even my mother's cautionary voice and the accompanying stories of mountain lions attacking people on mountain trails or in the hills of suburbia inspire fear.

I have said this before and I think I mean it: I would feel honored by that kind of death. Not to say that during the mauling I wouldn't be terrified, but there's a great rightness in the relationship of predator to prey. I have been predator before and I loved moving that close to the earth, searching for tracks, feeling scat for warmth, smelling it for freshness. Seeking out the story. Rarely have I felt as fundamentally alive as when I've stepped through sweet, pungent sagebrush and the golden grasses of fall, looking for sign and trying to think like a deer. Except on the river, the mundane world sloughing off; or paddling in the ocean far from shore; or, now, wandering into a mountain lion's realm.

After the sighting I picked up someone's tossed Coke can, and had the thought that I could throw it at the mountain lion, maybe scare the big kitty away. Then I thought she might attack Cojo first, a sacrifice for me that dog would readily make. I also thought of the pistol in the drawer at home. If I had it and was attacked, would I use it? Or would my belief in the rightness of the balance of nature prevail? Not likely, in the moment. Primal fear is more like it. But I didn't think about it until after—that maybe I should have had fear.

At 3:16 a.m. it hits me, as though the cold that holds the night has flooded my blood and entered my heart with a rush. I walked within a few feet of a cougar feasting on an animal it had killed—an animal that likely outweighed me and could surely outrun and outfight me and still the sheep or elk had fallen prey to the lion. On only two legs, one of them ouchy, with a crippled dog, I walked past the four-legged creature that bounded up the near-vertical side of the canyon as effortlessly as a shark moves through the sea. I wouldn't have had a chance in hell and at three in the morning that knowledge—that animal awareness—fills my blood.

WHEN I WAS seventeen, my younger sister, a friend, and I rode downstream from the ranch headquarters in the Sierra Nevada, looking for renegade cows. The river strung the valleys together and as we drew close to the river in a narrow spot we saw that on the bank someone had set up a makeshift camp: a tarp stretched between two ponderosa pines, a fire pit with coals smoldering under a coffee pot. A man, white, brown hair, brown eyes, stubble beard, sat leaning against a tree. We nodded and rode on, commenting before spreading out into the next meadow-valley that we must remember to tell the ranch owner about this man squatting on his land.

A couple of hours later, the cattle still unfound, we met near the head of the meadow and chose a new strategy, deciding that I would go back along the river afoot to look closely for tracks and my friends would take my horse and head over the top of the mountain, meeting me in the next valley. I padded my way back up the trail along the river, watching my boots so I didn't miss any cloven-hoofed tracks or trip on pine-needle-covered roots, thinking occasionally to look up through the pines for the missing cattle.

I was almost upon the tarp shelter when I remembered it. One second later a rush of fear filled me toenail to hair follicle for I saw the man and I was alone and afoot and a scream would not penetrate the forest or out-shout the river so I just kept walking, forcing my feet to maintain the same plodding rhythm and not quicken like my heart despite the desire—the primal animal need—to run past the man who lay on his side, prenatal, his rifle cradled in his arms. Sleeping. Armed. Me not twelve feet away. I couldn't hear the river for the pounding in my ears and my feet stepping rhythmically past and the cold fear rose along my spine that was turned to the man as I walked away and away and away, breathing finally as the forest stepped in to cover my back.

Two days later, standing with Craig in a narrow aisle of the tiny local grocery store, we heard the news on the radio: the convicted rapist, out on parole, who had picked up two girls in Reno, one escaping within the city limits and the second jumping from the moving car in Quincy, a town not thirty miles away, had been found dead in his car. *In the car my sister and friend had seen parked on the dirt road above the man's makeshift camp by the river.*

I cannot reconstruct the logic or comprehend how quickly we forgot about the man and sent me back afoot. We forgot to tell the ranch owner. We did not connect the rifle shot we heard in the middle of the night with the rifle I saw the man hugging to his chest in sleep.

I didn't even tell Craig.

But I knew again the icy fingers traveling up my spine as, standing in the aisle of the store, I described how I'd walked past the sleeping man. That's what wakes me at three in the morning: the visceral knowledge of how the blood goes cold the instant you know you are prey.

~~~

KEN TELLS ME not to go back for at least three days. I promise to take my gun. Donning the knee brace before leaving the house, as I park and hang the binoculars around my neck I tell myself it's unlikely the cat will be anywhere nearby, the absence of bald eagles along the river reaffirming that wildlife travels its own course. Slipping rounds into the .38, I feel the cold weight of steel and finality in my palm and wonder if big cats can smell fear the way bees do, or bears.

Cojo and I start up the trail, the day as clear and crisp as the creek, and I remember walking up another river with a different dog before moving to Hawai'i. I had pushed through old tamarisk and dry coyote willows, the soil beneath my river sandals soft with the detritus of previous seasons but not soft enough for burial. Here and there stood small mounds of earth. Looking closely, I saw that these were little hills of shit. Not bad shit—cat shit. Mountain lion dung. I picked up some turds, black and hard and cougar-sized, to test for freshness, breaking them apart to gather data, like what the lion had been eating. I moved from pile to pile, hoping to find something fresh. More information. The rest of the story.

Now I watch the canyon walls and pivot every few feet to see behind me, mentally rehearsing how to use the pistol, and when: only if in close and dangerous company, after other cougar-discouraging behaviors have failed. Fortunately I don't need to cock this gun. Just point and shoot like the old automatic cameras. And remember to do so in the lion's embrace, even if her teeth and claws have found the meat of me. Like sticking a thumb in a shark's eye socket when his jaws have you in their grip.

Copying Cojo, I sniff the air, searching for the smell of a carcass. We are not even close when we find it. The smell. But it's different—different from death but still I know it, somewhere in my brain, and I search its identity in my memory and in the rabbitbrush and sagebrush along the trail. They say smell and memory are closely linked but I am experiencing a gap, a knowing in my senses without a picture or words in my brain.

We get closer. I see the tracks where the cougar began her climb in the loose dirt on the far side of the creek, and then the place where she leapt straight up, her sinewy muscles able to grip and hoist and push and pull her up that near-vertical slope as gracefully as you please. As if the cat were built for this act, like ducks paddling against the current, eagles soaring with it, or a shark slicing through it.

I find the parting in the willows where Cojo first peered in and step as close as I dare in search of the carcass if not the cat. I want to positively ID the hide. I want to know from whence it was dragged. How much the cougar ate, in how many parcels. I want the rest of the story. Then I think of my knee and the gun and my mother and know I will not enter the thicket this day. Not alone, with only compromised Cojo for protection, or diversion, and a .38 pistol that scares me more than the cougar does.

Walking on up the trail slowly, pivoting, pointing the field glasses at each high abutment, I startle at a swipe of movement on the other side of a near clump of sage. It's Cojo. Down. On his side on his back rolling in the smell. The smell that's even stronger now that he's disturbed it.

Spitting a command to stop Cojo's uncanny canine behavior I step close to look at the culprit—green like cowshit with some bits of stuff in it that look like straw. I touch its edge with my boot and it's fresh and soft and smears easily and I stick a stick in it and bring the smell closer and my nose knows what it is though my mind still can't bridge the gap of the years it's been since I hunted, since I gutted an animal, roadkill even, because in Hawai'i there are only dead mongooses and feral cats on the roads, but I have hunted and I have gutted and . . . that's it: *offal.* What the intestines held. Another pile lies close by, this one drier and looking like brown-orange alfalfa cubes and not as compelling to Cojo, thank goodness, and I smell it, too.

Offal smells awful.

A hunter reading this will have known sentences ago what I am smelling but for those who haven't had the pleasure of smelling the raw, dead insides of stomach and bowel I'll tell you that it's worse than human shit or chicken shit or pig shit or any other kind of animal byproduct I've encountered. It's in a rank by itself. And these two piles, one spread and smeared by Cojo and my boot toe and the other a cubed pile, they represent something: a big piece of the story I cannot read. They were not here the other day. They are fresh. But no pile of intact guts lies nearby. No blood anywhere. No carcass that I can see. No cat. Someone dragged part of the body up here and ate everything but this. Who—cougar, coyote, bobcat, bear? No identifying tracks. No tale-telling scat. I don't know. I can't know. Cojo knows and cannot tell. Fumes rise from his fur. We walk on up the canyon.

Again I forget to feel fear, yet I know it's there with the cold on a path beside a creek at the edge of the wild. When the drop to the stream is free of the large blocks of basalt, we descend to the frigid water and I make Cojo stand in it deep enough for me to splash with aching hands where the awful offal clings to fur that fast becomes stiff and cold as icicles. Like my blood in the middle of the night.

We walk more and warm up and head back down through the twilight, wisps of red clouds flaring along the western canyon rim, a near-full moon rising over the mountains behind us. Disappointment hangs for a moment above the stream, where I hope despite reason to see the mountain lion again.

Moonlight has not yet entered the narrow canyon when Cojo and I arrive back at the casita, but the gloom has lifted. I give Cojo a proper bath in warm water but he doesn't like my hairdryer and shivers into sleep on a rug by the fire. I have fed us both, put the pistol away, and iced my knee, and still I don't have the rest of the story. Just the vision of a desert angel in winter's pale light, and Cojo smelling sweet as shampoo beside me.

I TELL A friend the story. I tell her how I have felt as if I'm waiting for something else to happen. Something bad. How the near kiss with a cougar brought me flashes of joy, and then fear. Either way, I felt myself *alive*. She says, *This is your life. Now. You can just sit here waiting, getting older, or you can* do *something—it's your choice.*

And I think, *I cannot wait anymore.*

I see an orthopedic surgeon, who schedules arthroscopic surgery.

The day before the surgery, the hospital calls to reschedule.

"Okay," I say, "but why?"

"Because of the state of emergency."

The winter has turned record cold: twenty-eight degrees below in Taos, minus thirty-five at Ken's, negative twenty-three in my little canyon. The natural gas supply to rural northern New Mexico was cut off so areas of dense population would have enough heat. The hospital in Taos could handle emergencies but not elective surgeries.

I call Ken. He didn't know, either—his ranch house and my casita both heated by propane and wood.

I INJURED MY knee the day after Ed died and six months later I'm in the hospital readying for arthroscopic surgery. I have a needle in my writing hand, the regular IV veins collapsed from overuse. When Ed said his hospital bed hurt him, I didn't understand. Now I do—the hard bed hurts my back and lungs. I can't find the controls to raise or lower different parts of me. Yet I see how the narrow thing with rails gives nurses easy access, and a patient falling asleep won't fall out. I write this down, the needle jabbing into the back of my hand with each word.

I write about being a drug addict, committed to recovery. For years I have told every doctor I see that I am allergic to *all narcotics.*

"What happens if you take a narcotic?" they ask.

"Addiction," I tell them, insisting they write it in my chart.

I tell the orthopedic surgeon that he must prescribe nonnarcotic painkillers. He's young (forties), thin, a skier. Mouth and forehead pinched, he says, "What about Percocet?"

I think, *What* about *Percocet*? Just one. Or two. Five would get me through. I repeat to the anesthesiologist in the pre-op, *No narcotics.* The doctors scratch their heads.

Before I even know where I am as I come to after surgery, I feel deep, pulsing pain. I whimper aloud. "It *hurts*," I say, when the doctors check on me.

The surgeon pinches his shoulders into a shrug.

The anesthesiologist says, "I usually inject morphine into the mix so that people coming out of this surgery don't feel the pain right away. But you said no narcotics."

Morphine? I could have had morphine? "I thought you would give me something else. Is there really nothing else?"

Apparently there is nothing else. The doctors turn away.

After two nights of throbbing pain and little sleep in my queen-sized bed, Cojo occupying the southwest corner despite my disquiet, I call the surgeon. "There *must* be non-narcotic pain relievers out there. Something that *works*."

"You can pick up a prescription at the pharmacy." His voice is tight, as if he's angry with me for wanting to avoid narcotics.

Needing to go to Taos anyway for my first physical therapy appointment, I crutch to my short Subaru, lower my butt to the seat, and with both hands behind the thickly bandaged knee, lift the leg in. Wincing as I shift gears, I head toward relief. For the next three days I take the pills as prescribed. The pain lessens.

I can sleep. I like that. And I like the hum of a drug I can take without using.

A few weeks later, Cojo at the vet's for his legs, the animal doctor prescribes for my dog the same medication the people doctor prescribed for me. Odd, I think, and look it up online. Tramadol, an opioid analgesic. As close to a narcotic as you can get. One website says, "You should not take this medication if you have ever been addicted to drugs or alcohol."

I made it ten days shy of *nineteen years* without a pill, drink, fix, line, or lungful—I went through carpal tunnel surgery, root canals, teeth pulled, and three deaths without anything stronger than ibuprofen. It's not that twelve-step programs prescribe suffering. They have strategies to deal with pain medications. Even an ex–heroin addict like me can take opiates, if absolutely necessary—there are ways to do this that help you avoid relapse—but my intention was *not to take them*, and I had let the world know.

Fuck. Fuck fuck fucking fuck.

Pills disposed of, I ask the vet for something different for my dog.

DETRITUS: SIERRA NEVADA, 1971. *October light leaks in between slats of graying barn wood. A yellow stripe marks Craig's cheek, his shoulder. I taste salt and smell the sun on his skin and in the hay beneath me that makes our bed in the neighbor's old hay barn, a place we run to in daylight. We have other places for the night when it's colder, another neighbor's bunkhouse already shut up for the winter but not locked. I hear Craig's brothers roaming the afternoon near the house on the hill where I live with Craig's family while I finish high school. I hear the wind in the ponderosas I love as I love this boy, this man, whose skin touches mine. We think we're hidden though the wind that slips between the long sweet needles of those big trees slips between hundred-year-old planks of even older trees and I feel a chill as the boy-man-child slips into me. I watch the yellow light on his cheek on his shoulder move like our hearts like our bodies like the day through October and all I know is this moment, this breath, his skin, my depth; I don't know, can't possibly guess, that two Octobers from now he will fall beneath a falling ponderosa, a tree destined to become wood that instead becomes death. That I will leave behind in a daze of drugs the light through the cracks in the barn on his shoulder on his cheek in October and the mountains and valleys and horses and river and all I have known up till then.*

THE LAST TIME I spoke with Craig was from the stairwell of my mother's house in Palo Alto. I'd gone to the University of Washington, breaking up with him first, but we still wrote and I saw him during school breaks and he knew I didn't go back for a second year, and when he called to tell me his uncle died, I thrilled at his voice despite the bad news. At the way certain words curled around his tongue. The stairwell narrow and dark, I twisted the phone cord around my fingers and said, "I'm driving up to Seattle on Saturday. Maybe I'll come by and see you."

"I'll be here," he said. "Come." I sat in the dark until the rush faded.

All the way up I-80 to I-5, right up to and past the turnoffs at Highway 32 then Highway 36, I debated. If you go, you'll spend the night. *If you spend the night, you'll sleep with him. If you sleep with him, you won't leave.*

It was easier for me to fuck a stranger than to spend the night with someone I loved. I didn't even stop to call. That Monday, Craig went to work in the woods. Sprinting out of the way when a branch crashed toward him, he tripped and fell, a sharp stob puncturing his thigh through his Levi's. He wouldn't go to the doctor, hiding the limp, telling no one but his sister. "If something happens," he said to her on the phone, "I won't be able to run away."

Something did happen. He didn't even have time to run. But I did.

I ran away and then I kept on running.

SLEEPING ON MY friends' couch in Seattle, I heard the phone ringing. My eyes opened to a window framing a wet, cloudy dawn. Voices drifted to me, and then the telephone, my mother's voice in the receiver, broken. I lay with the news inside me. I didn't know what to do.

The night before, I had cried for Craig at a movie—*The Way We Were*, Robert Redford and Barbra Streisand. I didn't know he was dead. He died sometime that afternoon, knocked first to the ground then the whole huge tree falling on him. Just his black, steel-toed logging boots showing when his father found him.

My friends made me a hot bath. I sank underwater, my ears filling with a silence that couldn't drown out the truth.

I cried for him again. For a long time. Years.

Craig told me that if he ever died, he did not want an open casket, he did not want people looking at him like that, but I had no voice in the family anymore and there was the casket at the front of the room, open. I sat outside alone. Just me alone on a bench in the damp fall morning, weeping and longing and guilty.

MAYBE A FIRST love doesn't seem so important thirty-five years later, unless you've married him. Or unless he died before you got to the marrying part. Unless he died days after you said you might go see him. Unless he died after you didn't even stop to call.

MUSTANGS IN CAPTIVITY have simple choices: adapt, or die. This is true of abused children, as well. Yet even as we adapt, something dies inside us. I had to find someone else to be.

I went to work for a horse trainer at the racetrack, cleaning stalls, grooming horses, sleeping in the tack room, riding Tirade as a pony horse, loping around the exercise track with a young racehorse running beside us, snubbed to my saddle horn. Even those great, glistening bodies bursting from the starting gate and putting every ounce of strength into a quarter-mile sprint for human entertainment couldn't bring me to feel anything but a heaviness I didn't know as sad.

The racetrack world is transient: all those horses and trainers, grooms, jockeys, and pony-girls moving with the season, living in barns and motel rooms, washing clothes at the Laundromat. One night as I sat waiting for my Wranglers to dry, a tiny jockey and beefy groom offered me a beer. Two. "Why don't you come back with us? We'll watch some TV."

I followed them to their motel room, where I sat on one bed, the jockey on the other, the groom in the single chair. Suddenly the jockey sprang to my bed, wrestling me into the pillows. I saw the big guy at the door, snapping the bolt closed, latching the chain. The jockey ripped my shirt open, grabbed my belt. He was small but wiry and strong. I'm strong, too. I pushed him off and squirmed away.

The groom loomed. He was big. So was the window. When his hands fumbled at his zipper, I charged past him and flung myself at a target of curtains—a mustang trying to break through a fence.

The thick glass held like metal fencing holding against the weight of a wild filly's fear. The men yelling at me to settle down, I lunged again, hitting the window with a shoulder this time. Hurtling through, I rolled on the ground and up onto my feet, running toward the motel office. Running to safety.

The manager, another man.

"They tried to rape me—call the police!"

He shook his head. I sprinted across the parking lot to my red VW squareback, unaware of pain as I found my keys. "She's on a bad acid trip," I heard one of them tell the motel prick. Fumbling at the car door, I felt as if it were true. But I have always been lucky. Most mustangs don't escape.

As the ER doctor probed for glass shards in the three-inch-deep hole in my inner thigh with a six-inch-long cotton swab, he asked if it was a knife blade that punctured me. He didn't see the holes in my heart.

I couldn't ride Tirade. Pulling the stitches out myself, I called Rebecca in Berkeley.

"Come home," she said.

"Home?" I'd left my mother's house three years earlier. I was barely nineteen.

"To Berkeley. We'll find a place together. You can go back to school, and write my English papers." She was an English major who hated to write. I was a wannabe writer with no place to live. It sounded like a good plan. It was the only plan.

REBECCA AND I moved into a duplex on the west side of San Pablo Avenue, down the street from Patty Hearst's boyfriend, Patty Hearst already abducted. Rebecca had grown up slender and cute in a bad-girl way, sassy and sexy like Meg Ryan married to Goose in *Top Gun*. We were bad girls together, though I wasn't cute, just angry.

One day a man sitting at our dining room table asked for an album cover. I gave him Smokey Robinson and the Miracles and he made a pile of brown powder and drew a line. Rebecca abstained but I sucked that powder up my nose as if it were cocaine. It burned in my nostrils and smelled of earth and I snorted more and waves of warm sunshine washed over me and my mind s l o w e d d o w n, Craig's death and what I did to him before he died and what I didn't do receding into the background like Smokey's picture on the album cover, the brown powder all that I saw, all that I felt, all that I wanted, and I wanted *more*.

DETRITUS: BAY AREA, 1976. *Rebecca has moved in with a boy-friend, and I have moved a bunch of times. We meet at my house and pick up another friend, the three of us in our tight jeans and clinging tops driving through the night to a poorly lit parking lot where I pull alongside a trio of young men loitering in a dark corner. One comes to the window. I can't see his face. "Thirty dollars," I say, and we exchange three ten-dollar bills for three balloons. Reaching deeper into his pocket, he says, "Get out of the car." I jam the gas pedal to the floor.*

Heart rates up, we rush the stairs to my room. On the bedside table we place a glass of water, a spoon, a pinch of cotton to filter the drug, and the needle and syringe stolen from a doctor's office. Our practiced friend dumps the contents of her dime balloon into the bent spoon, adds water, and holds the lighter's flame beneath until the liquid bubbles. She drops the wad of cotton in and sucks the drug through it with the needle, then ties off her arm, pumping her hand until a vein pops up.

I hold my breath as the needle pierces her skin. She draws on the plunger. Blood shoots into the syringe, red marbling with light brown. Rebecca's face pales. Our friend pushes the mixture into her vein. I breathe.

Cleaning the rig in the glass of water, I watch her, knowing from how my own face feels when I've snorted enough what she should look like when the drug hits: face suddenly slack, head rolling back.

Shooting dope is faster than snorting. That's why I want it. But there's nothing in her face. Not the tiniest inkling of a high.

She looks at us. "Motherfuckers ripped us off."

My heartbeat slows. "Are you sure? Maybe it's just not very good?"

"It's baking soda. Bunk dope. No fucking heroin."

Sinking—not even enough drug to snort.

"Look at my arm. If my boyfriend sees this . . ."

"He won't," Rebecca says.

"You're sure there's no dope in there?" I say.

She rubs at her arm. "Fucking right. I gotta go."

I sit on the edge of my bed after she leaves with Rebecca, contemplating the two little round balloons in my palm all rolled up tight on themselves like little outie bellybuttons. I unroll each one. Dump the powder into the spoon. Add water. Flick the BIC. Load the syringe, tie off my arm, pump to find a vein. Stab it. Marveling as my own blood mixes with the liquid in the syringe, I push the plunger in and wait for a change in my body, my heart.

I SAT ALONE in my room, my only high that of the adrenaline my body produced, and worked up a plan for more. Sometimes the will to live looks like that—sometimes you want to kill the pain, stab it to death. For five years after Craig died, wanting *more* gave me reason, direction, someone to be. Yet there is nothing attractive or romantic about being a junky. It reduces good people to rot, like our teeth. It impacts those around us and we don't care. I lied to everyone, hurt friends, stole from family, shot up in my mother's bathroom. My tight jeans grew baggy; I wore long-sleeved shirts even on the hottest days. Only Rebecca knew how bad I was. She watched me and loved me and couldn't save me, and finally even she stopped calling—like a convex mirror of what would happen later, when I couldn't save her.

Craig's death shattered me like I shattered that window—I was but slivers of glass on the ground, fragments so small that tweezers and a magnifying glass and a map of my body couldn't have put me back together. Heroin was glue. But heroin is not a drug to mess around with. For one minute the pain does stop. Then the drug takes you. It takes your life.

~~~

WHEN ED WAS dying, all the prescription drugs I was on when I went to treatment were at my mother and Ed's house. I could easily have OD'd like Rebecca. When administering them, I washed my hands carefully after each dose, afraid I would accidentally lick traces of narcotics from my fingers, which could trigger in my body what my mind resisted.

When Ed was gone, I emptied leftover drugs into soggy coffee grounds and stuffed them deep in the garbage—my mother read that this was the best disposal technique so they wouldn't go into the water supply. Or be discovered by trash junkies, I thought.

I'm not saying it was easy, that I didn't flinch as I tossed out the same opiates that steered me toward treatment. That would have been a good moment in which to relapse—I had cause, and means. But why would I want to revisit a lifestyle where I was comatose half the time, sick the other half, death a daily threat and temptation? Eighteen years clean, did I want to experience another hangover? Or withdrawals? Ever? Again?

What I wanted was *not to use*. And six months after I fed Ed his meds, a Taos doctor prescribes a drug I haven't heard of and I trust him and take it.

I *want* to trust him.

I *want* to find a drug I can take.

I want the pain to ease.

In a cold dark canyon in New Mexico, I want that change.

ED COULD HAVE OD'd—he'd been planning to for months, storing away a certain mix of pills that he could take when the time came. Only, he couldn't. When the time came, he hadn't the strength. And it was better that he didn't go that way. Instead he walked right up to death's door. And then he opened the door and in his brave, gallant, gracious manner, he walked through.

Overdosing would have robbed him of the opportunity to pre-pare himself, of the experience of moving one moment at a time along this journey toward death.

He would have died either way, so what am I saying? I'm saying that Rebecca took one pill too many and fell on the floor and died, no witnesses, no loved ones standing by, no reconcil-iation with whatever she needed to reconcile with. No me. Just . . . dead.

Ed went through the *process* of dying. Like me *preparing* for surgery. They have talked to me, asked me questions, disrobed me, scrubbed me, IV'd me, and left me. They know and I know what will happen next: I'll get rolled down the hall, leave one uncomfortable bed for another, and go to sleep while the sur-geon bores into my knee and scrapes debris away. Then, gods willing, I'll wake up.

We prepped Ed in his hospital bed the best we could, want-ing him comfortable, ready. When on Monday a hospice nurse came to bathe him, he said no, it would hurt too much.

"I can't come back until Wednesday, honey," she said.

Pushing the words out through dry lips, he said, "That's good," and I knew.

I lie here waiting for surgery thinking of Ed lying there wait-ing for death. Neither Ed nor I are good waiters. I'm not actually waiting, I'm writing. Ed wasn't just lying there waiting, either; he was processing, surveying, journeying, reconciling, accepting, and he was dying.

To die is an active not passive verb. Ed taught me this. He let me go with him right up to that door. I journeyed beside him until he was so focused on dying that he did not need to know any longer that I, that anyone, was there. He was in the tunnel, I was sure of it, his breath finally even—not in sleep but in dying. He was lying there dying while I finally slept.

I tried earlier in the living room on my portable bed—the Therm-a-Rest pad and old river sleeping bag—where I'd spent each night so I could hear what was happening in the bedroom down the hall.

That night I heard clocks ticking. Ed had six clocks on the wall above my mother's orchids—her orchids loved the northern light coming through that window—each clock set to a different time. He'd researched and come up with odd times, like 4:27 a.m. somewhere in the world was noon in California, so subtraction or addition to Pacific Daylight Saving Time was nearly impossible. One clock held Hawai'i time. That is what I went by, but that night, time was too loud. I got up from the floor—easy, then—stood on a chair, and took each clock down. Hid them away in a closet. Lay down again, but the kitchen clock roared. I removed it and still something beat too loudly for me to sleep. It was my heart.

I went back to Ed. My mother was asleep or drifting in her newly purchased twin bed in the corner of their room, while Mele the night nurse dozed in a chair near Ed's foot. She was Tongan, slightly plump, an angel. Even her name: Mele. In Tongan as in Hawaiian, mele means "song." Ed played kī hō'alu, slack key guitar, his love of Hawaiian music helping him move to Hawai'i, which helped my mother have her dream of living in the Islands again so many years after living there in the sixties, my mother and Ed moving to Maui after Tyler and me, which gave me my parents and Tyler his grandparents because it also brought my bio-dad back to Hawai'i, and for a breath that was the choreography of our lives: both of my fathers and my mother and Tyler and me, sisters and cousins visiting, Hawai'i doing what Hawai'i does—creating, and in our case recreating, 'ohana. Family.

Pulling a chair up to the hospital bed, listening to death-rattle breaths, Mele awake, offering solidarity, I scooted as close to Ed as I could, holding his hand, feeling his spirit, watching him move toward the tunnel. The death rattle went on for an hour and a half—I did not remove the clock in their room; it was after one a.m., then after three—and I grew sleepy.

Mele nodded as I gestured toward the bed. I squirmed my chair closer and wished that we had not gotten the hospital bed so that I could lie all the way beside him, but I couldn't so I put only my head down right next to Ed's, and the death rattle stopped—right then, me head-to-head with Ed—and a slow, even, peaceful breathing took its place. I slept, or drifted like my mother, aware that Ed didn't consciously know I was there but his spirit could feel me and was, I thought, happy. Sometime before dawn, I sat up and looked at him and could tell that he was well into the tunnel, so focused on the journey that he no longer needed the people on our side of life.

I got up and left him and Mele, dragging my bed to the floor of the room a few feet away, and lay down and slept. For an hour maybe or minutes, I don't know—Mele standing over me telling me to come, quickly, and I rose like a spirit myself and floated back to Ed's side, my mother on the other side, him breathing so slowly, my cousin and older sister who had been asleep upstairs coming into the room, Ed's eyes unfocused but seeing, I felt sure, my mother, his blue eyes on her face, a tear forming and rolling down his cheekbone, a breath, a pause, the waiting, but the next breath didn't come. And that was it, it was over, his work done, all his grand efforts to stay alive leading to this one inevitable moment of death followed by a silence that felt, despite all forewarning, as sudden and absolute as Rebecca's.

I told my mother he would die on Wednesday. And he did, Wednesday morning at seven a.m. on the dot. Four a.m., Hawai'i time.

THERE IS ALWAYS a before. Sometimes there is an after. The year of my fathers' deaths was the dividing line, the ridge separating two watersheds—the before and the after. I learned to walk and for fifty-four years I walked uphill and slid back down and climbed up and plateaued out in the random rhythms of life, but when Rebecca died the world tilted and I fell. The year I turned fifty-five, I waited while two other people I loved died. And then I limped on, stumbling along the top of the ridge. From there I could see the rugged terrain behind me but not the landscape of my future.

My knee healing, I begin the slow walk down the backside of the hill. A careful descent, because even though the slope appears gradual it's sandstone and the grains that surface as individuals beneath my feet could cluster together to become little rolling geologic marbles—at any moment, I might fall on my ass. Again.

In the past, drugs have given me motivation, direction. Now I don't know what direction to take. I peer inside myself, and inside seems empty, as if *I* am missing, too. As if part of me already left, slipping into that tunnel with Ed.

Sometimes I don't mean to leave. Sometimes I don't know I'm gone. Now I don't know how to come back. I can't do what I did when I was eighteen, nineteen, looking for someone else to be. I have to find who I already am.

3

DEVIL DOG ROAD

THE FIRST TIME I SAW MUSTANGS WAS ON THE NEVADA SIDE of Susanville, California. They had been herded by helicopters, captured, and were being held in confinement while their fates were determined. Standing in shadeless pens, they looked scrawny and shaggy compared to the quarter horses I was used to, like Tirade, sixteen hands high at the withers with the sleek lines of a racehorse. Bunched together against the far fence, snarls in their long manes and tails, ribs showing, these mustangs looked sad, not wild.

My summers in Hawai'i and at the Sierra Nevada ranch were followed each fall by shoes, paved streets, the confines of classrooms. I would shelve the wild-girl me and endure, knowing the opportunity for escape would come. These horses did not know that. Wilting in body and spirit, they stood in the hot sun, waiting for nothing, their dejection a barometer of loss.

When Kenney was a toddler, my mother and younger sister babysat while Keith and I hunted ahorseback in Utah. At every waterhole we saw mustang sign—wide, round, unshod tracks, mud from those hooves still wet on the trail—but we did not see the horses.

We met two local Utahns who offered to accompany us through the desert uplands, guiding us toward mule deer bucks. As we rode, they told us about chasing wild horses, how when they came upon a band they would spur their own horses into a race with mustangs, galloping after them until a fence stopped them or their horses gave out. Sometimes they'd get close enough to rope a mustang. They did this for fun. It was 1986, fifteen years after the Wild Free-Roaming Horses and Burros Act established government protection. Mustangers had been chasing wild horses for generations. Habits die hard in the West.

Keith shot a buck. I didn't want to.

I HAD JUST kicked heroin when I met Keith. Living with my older sister in Santa Barbara so that we could go out to the Cojo, the family ranch, as often as possible, I found a job working for a horse trainer. Keith managed a neighboring cattle ranch. Lean and long-legged and Marlboro handsome, he was married to someone else. I asked him to teach me to rope. He stood close behind me in the barn, his hand warm on mine as we swung a loop over my head.

Two years later he was married to me.

He got meaner as the years passed.

DETRITUS: SANTA YNEZ VALLEY, 1990. *Rebecca has come to help us move. I'm driving a big U-Haul truck loaded with all the possessions I think my young sons and I will need for our new life in Arizona, and whatever Keith threw at me as I packed. Rags, wrapping paper. With no horses and no dogs, I drive out the ranch driveway to highways heading south then east toward the desert— the Mojave followed by the Colorado Plateau. I will start Northern Arizona University's creative writing graduate program mid-year, will be there five semesters. That's all the plan I've got.*

Tears on my face I had hugged Keith goodbye, Rebecca watching from the door of the tiny barn apartment where the kids and

I had lived since the day of separation. Keith held Kenney, almost five years old, Kenney's long legs dangling from Keith's hip. Tyler clung to me as Keith cussed and pushed me away, putting Kenney down and stomping to his truck, backing quickly around. Kenney pulled loose of my hand and ran down the driveway after his dad's pickup. Rebecca called to him, trotting down the road and scooping Kenney up in her arms.

Two-year-old Tyler is buckled into his car seat beside me in the U-Haul truck, Rebecca following in my S-10 Blazer, with Kenney and our cat as her traveling companions. I know nothing about the Colorado Plateau, and have only been to Flagstaff twice. It has trees—the biggest contiguous ponderosa pine forest in North America—that's what I know. That and how it feels to drive away from a marriage. From California. Body and breath pulled out of my skin.

The U-Haul loaded, the Blazer loaded, Rebecca and me loaded. Through the years of my marriage I had not used hard drugs. Now, low on grit, high on cocaine, I lead that train through the desert, stopping when the kids sleep to snort more, more, bending to lines on a mirror, ignoring my face, as desert-night air enters through the window we leave open so I can hear Tyler if he awakens to the dark of the U-Haul cab alone.

The fuel of Keith's anger is not enough to get me all the way across the desert. Leaving behind horses and dogs, blood and years and generations, I'm tearing us apart from what made us: California, her oaks, golden hills, gray pines; the ranches we have known. The Cojo, in my family for now five generations. Their dad. I need the rush to keep going.

Too soon I will know Keith's pain magnified a million times—a mother's grief prolapsing my heart when a judge orders that my boys will live with their father, the gavel the judge slams on the desk knocking me to the floor. To the very bottom of my life.

~~~

DURING MY FIRST semester at NAU, Keith threatened me with court, saying he made the better full-time parent. He didn't even know whose clothes were whose, leaving that up to his new wife to figure out.

I had to travel to California to visit with my attorney—a woman with stiff hair who teared up when she first met Keith because he was "just so sweet." In her plush office in Los Olivos, she said to my mother and me, "If we go to court, the judge will likely 'split the baby.'" She cited a biblical story.

I stared at her.

The parents torn apart one way, the boys separated from each other was a risk I couldn't take. The attorney and my mother talked as I stepped outside. I needed to breathe.

The foliage on the trees was lush and dry at the same time. I was a single mother, full-time student, teaching half time, grading papers and writing them. The piles of laundry grew exponentially. Grocery shopping and cooking and bath time and bedtime ran into each other, followed by breakfast.

When I came back in, I said, "What if we split the next two years I'm in graduate school instead of risking splitting up the kids? They're already with me. They can live with Keith the following school year." Maybe I wanted to go to Joe's bar sometimes after an evening workshop, have a beer and shoot pool with the other grad students. Sometimes a single mother thinks like that when days off are months apart.

Her hair crunching against my cheek, the attorney hugged me, offering no forewarning of where this could lead—no hint that when Kenney went to live with his dad at six, he would not ever live with me again. That the boys would ultimately be separated from each other anyway.

THE DAWN HORSE, *Hyracotherium* or *eohippus*, stands in the Eocene Epoch about fifty-five million years ago, at the beginning of horse evolution. A third the size of my border collies, it had four toes on its front feet and three toes on each hind foot, which ended in little hooves. Its back was rounded like a rabbit's, and its teeth—one of the most critical physical traits in horse evolution—were small and included grinding molars, useful for chewing leaves and berries.

I grew up knowing about this foxlike creature, ancestor to my horses. What impresses me most now is that even those many millions of years ago, the dawn horse was a herd animal bound to its band. In 1952, when twenty-six *Hyracotherium* skeletons were recovered from a mass of bones in southern Colorado, there were far more female skeletal remains than male. The males were noticeably larger. As is true today, there appeared to be one dominant stallion to each band of mares, the family unit ever important to survival.

The mustangs in the pens east of Susanville had already been separated from family band members. They were suffering not just from their rip from freedom but from real broken hearts.

MY BOYS WERE still with me when Smith from Montana arrived in the creative writing program a semester after me. Tall and blond and seven years younger, he was my biggest fan, writing sweet comments in the margins of my stories. He would come to the house and sit with Kenney and Tyler on the couch by the picture window as I folded laundry, pointing out airplanes leaving tracks in the sky. He split firewood and shoveled snow and generally made himself useful.

When he returned from Montana after winter break, we kissed.

Then the kids left for half the summer, then for that next school year. Each day without them took me deeper into a dark hole. An ache grew inside me like the laundry pile. Corona with lime at Joe's or a glass or bottle of white zinfandel at home didn't touch it. Soon I was steeped in an addiction I thought was over after kicking heroin twelve years before. I scammed pills from doctors, begged them off friends, stole them from friends, Rebecca sent me cocaine through the mail, Smith usually had pot, and if there was nothing else, I could have another glass of wine. The near-perfect high—the closest I could get to what heroin felt like—was the right mix of all of the above.

And yet, I functioned, swallowing pills discreetly, combining them with alcohol only sometimes, using cocaine only when I had it. I thought this was different from being a heroin addict, using to live and living to use. The reality is that a drug addict is not addicted to *one* drug but to *all* drugs.

Smith offered the remedy he knew: *outside.* He'd throw camping gear in the Blazer and drive us past sunset, turning onto a Forest Service or BLM road and making our bed in the dark. At dawn my eyes would open to layered mesas, a canyon, a river, even the Mojave Desert looking spectacular when viewed at first light after such a night. Smith did it all so well, including what happened as the fire burned low. But it didn't fill the hole.

We traded the old S-10 Blazer for a four-door, for the kids and us though the kids weren't there. The car could crawl up the steepest hillsides, slip through scrub oak that would key a truck, and accommodate Smith's six-foot-two-inch sleeping length. The first fall the boys were gone, Smith went with me to hunt the Arizona Strip—that piece of Arizona that stretches between the north rim of the Grand Canyon and Utah.

Keith taught me to hunt. The season lasted weeks in California, my boots raising puffs of dust as I followed sign, learning the trails and heat and heartbeat of the terrain in a closer way than what I knew ahorseback. Even at the cold end of October in Arizona, hunting tied me to the California hills and my boys.

After waking in the Blazer to our breath frozen on the windows, Smith would drive through dawn to the rimrocks, drop me off, and meander down dirt roads to the valley floor, the Blazer looking like a toy down there. Working my way from the forested edge of the Kaibab Plateau through yellow limestone ledges, my .270 slung over my shoulder, I was aware of danger, aware of beauty, aware of everything greater than me—light angling on stone, that blue Arizona sky. No wind, no sounds but my own breath and boots until the cries of piñon jays burst overhead, denim blues flashing as they swooped and soared and flew away, and then the quiet again, the silence of stone, the only record of my passing the track left inadvertently in a crust of cryptobiotic soil, me so small and walking along, pine pitch in my hair, sagebrush my perfume, moving across the bottom toward Smith leaning against the Blazer, golden in the sunlight. I felt *right* there, right inside myself. If I had known anything about spirituality or God I might have understood that the ingredients of a *place* had answered prayers I didn't know I made.

One October evening, encircled by Smith's tent, the camp kitchen, and the arms of darkness, Smith added a log to the fire and sat in a camp chair beside me. Firelight cavorted into the night. We'd just eaten, empty plates and pans ready for washing. I leaned back, stretching out my thighs and calves, the muscles that kept me from toppling over as I made the steep descents. I had seen no bucks, just beauty—lots of it. Still, sitting near the campfire with Smith and our dogs, there was such an ache in my belly I thought I must still be hungry.

I bent forward, wrapping my arms over my stomach, applying pressure. And then stood and went to the Blazer, rummaging through my gear until I found the bottle of pills.

When Smith popped another beer and handed me one, I popped a pill. We were really so young (me thirty-six, him twenty-nine), getting high in the cold desert night like teenagers. Then, as if we were adults, we talked about life after graduate school. Smith didn't just pop the question with the next beer tab. We talked our way toward it, and then he asked.

I would have my boys back. Maybe with Smith we would feel like a family. Looking into the flames, I said yes. When he reached for my hand, I jerked like a startled mustang.

In the horse world—I should say in the world of horses being bred for horse shows and performance competitions—large ears are not a desirable physical trait if you're looking for perfect conformation. But for the wild horse, they represent a survival strategy that leaps back to the Pleistocene, when *Equus caballus*, or true horse, appeared. By this evolution, the horse's legs were longer than earlier versions, and toed in a hoof; its neck and face were also longer, and the eyes were positioned higher on the head and to the side of the face, giving *Equus* lateral vision of 340 degrees. The tapetum lucidum, a layer of tissue behind horses' retinas (and the retinas of other species) that reflects light and affords the animal good night vision, had already developed, but now *Equus caballus* also developed larger eyes, and larger ears.

A horse's ears will often pick up potential danger before the eyes do—my mare Savanna's large ears will pivot toward snapping twigs in a far thicket that could hold calf or bear. Mustangs notice ear movements of lead mares and stallions and everyone else, as the slightest flick could mean danger, or get the hell away from me.

If it's danger, those long legs come in handy, even on a foal. I watched a mustang filly in her second hour of life keep step with her mother as the mare grazed up a steep hillside, hungry after her birthing work. The foal's legs, still bent at fetlock and knee joints from the cramped quarters she had so recently vacated, managed the gradient, albeit a bit awkwardly. Soon she would run circles around her mother, those legs, from the elbow to the ground, already half of her adult height.

Her ears, too, large and active, like her eyes and nostrils, parts of her that for her lifetime will draw data into the brain for processing.

Horses by nature are both wary and curious. One of friend and neighbor TJ's sanctuary mustangs got bit in the muzzle after puzzling a rattlesnake at close range. TJ could do nothing for the wild girl beyond mixing anti-inflammatory pellets into some grain and pushing the tub in her direction. The mare's face swelled toward nostrils closing before the power of the poison reversed.

As the new filly nursed—her first long drink in the big new world—band aunty and uncle came close to sniff at the tiny, leggy creature and the remains of afterbirth. The mama mare wheeled, teeth bared, ears flattened, breaking suction and bumping her baby out of the way as she charged. This human aunty, watching from a distance, did not impose on the natural process but worried as the little one limped away, her mother as inexperienced as I was with my firstborn. The band stallion and older mares— even the grandma—grazed nearby as twilight descended, seemingly unconcerned. It was the yearling colt and two-year-old filly who crowded. Curious, fascinated, like me.

Mishaps can easily occur under these circumstances—no stall of fresh shavings in a warm barn, no vet looking on. I've helped deliver foals under such safe conditions, tugging on slimy forelegs during the mare's pushes until the foal slipped out. Things can happen under the best of circumstances, but in the world of wild horses, foal mortality is relatively high.

Hence the big ears, large eyes, and longer legs of *Equus caballus*—physical traits that helped keep *Equus* alive on the steppes of North America from about 1.7 million years ago to the era of extinction, which, according to various scientific theories, occurred anywhere from 10,000 to 6,500 years ago. Mitochondrial DNA links *E. caballus* to the horses of Cortés— those traits that evolved so long ago still serve the mustangs of today.

~~~

VALENTINE'S WEEKEND THE second year of graduate school—my second semester without my boys—Smith and I drove to California. We were contemplating midsummer for the wedding. We picked the boys up and took them out to the Cojo, and even there, on the most secluded private beach left in California, I was popping pills. Afraid of running out before our return to Flagstaff, I called a doctor and sent Smith to a pharmacy in town an hour away to pick up the refill. I had to get high, stay high—because the whole time we were there, I knew I had to leave. Would have to drive away from my boys, four and seven years old, and head back to my empty house and the dark hole of my life that Smith, school, and even drugs could not fill.

Drugs had taken over, eroding the hole, making it bigger, carving it deeper. They scoured my insides of anything good I might feel, the need to get high, stay high, so powerful that even though I was with my two little boys for the weekend, I was not *with* them. I was high.

When we dropped them at Keith's and the stepmother took Tyler in her arms as if he were hers, Smith put his hands on my shoulders and steered me to the Blazer, driving us through the maze of freeways and cars and too many people, heading east toward I-40, the desert, the Colorado Plateau, home—he drove as I choked down pills with a Michelob Light; high, I just needed to stay high for the six-hundred-mile drive away. But the ache eked through, I felt it, them, my babies slipping from my grip. The whole way home, slipping.

We had our dogs: Hayduke, Smith's black lab–chow mix who showed up at our door one dark and blustery night, and Oso, my border collie–Aussie pound puppy. We stopped at the Colorado River, though it was too cold to swim, and the redrocks near Kingman, and then Smith pulled off on a dirt road winding through the pines. Devil Dog Road.

He killed the engine. Let the dogs out. We all did our business. The ponderosas smelled of caramel. Flagstaff. My empty house.

And just like that, a back tire went flat.

"Fuck," Smith said. Like most men, he took flat tires personally, and tore into the contents of the car to get at the jack and the spare, cursing under his breath.

As suddenly as the tire went flat, the dogs started fighting. They never fought. Ever. Until that moment on that already very bad day.

"*Oso*," Smith yelled. "*Goddamnit Oso*."

He was yelling at *my* dog. But Hayduke was on top.

"Get your fucking dog off him," I yelled at Smith . . .

. . . who yelled at Oso . . .

So I hit him. Smith. Punched him in the shoulder, hard as I could.

Wincing, he turned slowly toward me. "Don't you ever do that again," he said, his voice quiet, calm, meaningful.

What can I say? I hit him again.

The dogs stopped fighting. Stood there staring at us, at Smith staring at me. I got in the Blazer, sat with my arms locked around my knees, my face hidden, pulling all my feelings back into the space of my body, where they continued to burn.

Without a word, cuss or otherwise, Smith finished changing the tire. With Oso and Hayduke in the wayback, quiet as kids watching their parents fight, Smith drove us home. Out of the car before he came to a complete stop in the driveway, I slipped under the rising garage door, past the silence of the boys' bedrooms, down the stairs.

Closing and locking our bedroom door, I took my .270 from the closet. Held the weight, ran my fingers down the smooth stock, checked to see if it was loaded.

I sat there feeling it as Smith called to me, then pounded on the door.

"Go away."

He went around outside to the window. I closed the blinds.

"Please, Kathryn, let's talk."

So I talked. "Fuck you," I said.

The world was spinning the wrong way. It had been since my kids went away, but drugs weren't working anymore to slow it down, stop it, set it right. I wanted out. That's all I could think. I wanted away from myself and could see only one way to go.

"Call my friend from Group." I knew Smith could hear me. "Tell her to come."

This friend and I went through a sexual-abuse survivor's group, graduated, and picked up men together at Flagstaff's infamous Museum Club, nicknamed The Zoo. Now she had a steady boyfriend, and so did I. She might understand.

As I unlocked the bedroom door to let her in, I saw myself in the mirror—red-rimmed eyes, skin pasty, hair a mess. "Take me to the hospital," I said. The hospital or jail seemed the only safe places.

She led me through the house to her car. I didn't look at Smith, or even Oso. Just got into her car and let her drive me along Flagstaff's pine-lined streets up the hill to the hospital.

"When did you last do cocaine?" the doctor asked.

I squirmed in the vinyl chair. "Christmas."

Rebecca sent it. I had a party for graduate students and friends. The kids were at their dad's. Keith got them for Christmas that year; I had them for Thanksgiving. Rebecca came for that holiday—we did coke and mushrooms, pot and alcohol, while the kids slept.

Smith had never seen me laugh as hard as I did with Rebecca. He was stern-faced, watching. I didn't care. Rebecca was there.

But she wasn't at the hospital. Just this friend who had not known me long and was not a drug addict. She could think clearly. As the doctor asked me more questions about alcohol and other drugs, she called our incest survivors' group leader, who arrived with a suicide pact in hand. I signed it, agreeing not to do it for at least thirty days.

"Let's talk about treatment," the therapist said.

DETRITUS: SONORAN DESERT, 1992. *Smith drives me south through the desert, to Tucson, to treatment. I write as he drives, journal in my lap, pen in my grip. I try to keep my eyes open, to see those giant saguaro cacti, their angular arms rising to snag the sky; sun too bright, my eyes keep closing behind my shades. I've popped so many pills. My head drops to the side. I try to lift it, to watch the desert grate by, but the sun glares and my eyes close again. Smith's talking and I want him to stop, to not care, I want to not care. I can't lift my head. My mouth slack, breath slow, I feel the nod through the slow warm buzz of near death and I sink into it all the way. The pen falls from my hand.*

Smith shakes me awake as he pulls into the circular drive-way of the women's treatment center and when I open my eyes, the first staff person I see is a man. Anger burns through me as I step from the Blazer. Smith tries to hug me but I'm on the fight, swinging a suitcase the man takes from my grip, not to help me but to go through it, confiscating shampoo for its alcohol content because, what, I might drink shampoo? Are you fucking kidding me? *and Smith drives off into the desert night alone. After an hour of questions and signing papers, a female nurse coerces me into a bed, giving me Benadryl (pills, not a shot) and I'm gone.*

DRUGS KEPT ME going as I lived without my children. But drugs like a marriage can eventually stop working and I was sinking to the floor of the deepest body of water I could find and I wanted to stay in that quiet darkness . . .

. . . but my kids, my boys . . .

~~~

Detritus: Santa Ynez Valley, 1985. *I'm on a leggy bay gelding trotting off behind Keith, leaving truck and trailer parked in the shade of a California live oak as we ride out to get some bulls that we have to gather today, my baby but a month old bundled up in blankets on top of blankets on the floor of the pickup—I leave him there and trot off after Keith, breasts full and nipples seizing as I leave my baby to follow a man.*

Not gone long but does it matter? My baby crying when I return, my breasts crying, too, clear through my shirt, and resentment sets in. Not for the baby-love of my life—no!—but how does anger not curdle your milk?

Hastily tying my gelding to the trailer, I pick up my bundled baby from his nest on the pickup floor. Lifting baby and shirt, I feel his tight lips find the nipple and pull. And say to me in the language of animals, Mother. You are a Mother now.

A young mother, even though I'm thirty. A naïve mother, even though I wanted this baby with all the want I've ever had.

My breasts and baby know what to do, but not me.

Baby nursing, husband angry—we found and corralled the bulls but my hurry to get back annoyed him. Would I ever learn to say no to the right person? The wrong person?

Elk and deer and mountain lions and bears fight to raise their own. Wild horses run with their foals to protect them, and if that doesn't work, the stallions fight the enemy. Cows are forced to leave their calves, each season of weaning a heartbreak. How is it that a human mother can leave her baby, even for minutes, and a human man doesn't understand the anguish?

I sit on the pickup seat and see love in liquid blue eyes as my hot mother's milk fills my baby's belly. But my body jerks when I hear the trailer door open and feel the horses stepping in—my job to load my own horse and here I am, nursing my son.

~~~

BENADRYL AND THE high I came in on carried me through the first night in the Sonoran Desert treatment center. The next evening, my legs and stomach cramping, I wanted to throw up, throw punches, scream, curse. I wanted to use. Get out-of-my-mind loaded the way I was the day before. My thighs kept cramping the way they always did kicking—that's why it's called kicking—feet thrashing at the sheets, the walls. The nursing staff refused me more Benadryl. They observed me from their office across the hall. I counted how many times a night their lights flashed in my face. Seven, four, two. Four nights. Finally I slept.

Clinically diagnosed with PTSD, depression, a tendency toward suicidal ideation, and, of course, addiction, I sat rocking in a chair or on the floor, my arms folded tightly over my stomach, holding breath in, pushing it out, as therapists chipped away at the hole I'd been trying to fill with drugs. Then on short, supervised walks around the facilities, I started noticing birdsong. Different voices, like the colors sparkling in the saguaros and palo verde trees. Tucson's seasonal migrations just starting.

The treatment center had an outdoor pool. The brochure advertised a heated pool but when I dipped my toes in I found the water as cold as the February nights. I rallied the women and we marched into the office, demanding that they heat the pool. Our group therapist said I was making this an issue to distract myself from what I was supposed to be doing—like, recovery. I didn't care. The pool got heated. I dove in.

IN 1962, WHEN my big sister and I first arrived on Kaua'i, I knew how to swim. I could swim in the hotel pools where our father worked but the ocean drew me like a riptide. Riding the swells was like riding a horse but inside it not on top of it, feeling it all the way through, body to body until there is only one movement. I am water.

Even in the dry spells, I have never stopped knowing how.

In 1992, I swam through that Sonoran Desert winter underwater until I came up for air and felt sunshine on my skin. I mean, I could *feel* the rays touching my skin. I learned again to swim in air, that air can be freedom, too.

I left my heart behind in a big stuffed teddy bear. I left my heart behind when I left my horses behind. I left my heart behind with my children. In a treatment center's heated swimming pool in the Sonoran Desert, I found my body, clean, but my heart was still missing.

AFTER FOUR WEEKS, my time was up. Hard as I fought against being there, I was afraid to leave and begged to stay longer. They gave me another week, but soon I would have to start living life on life's terms, without the use of drugs. I called Smith, telling him where I'd stashed pills, the bindles that held traces of cocaine. "Please find and flush. I want to hear the toilet plumbing at work." I pulled up courage from some forgotten place. "There are syringes and needles in the refrigerator. I know you can't flush them," I whispered into the phone, "but please do something." He must have nodded because no words came. I was that close. I knew it, and now Smith did, too.

My roommate and I left the treatment center together, driving away in her 1974 Cadillac convertible Coupe DeVille, Thelma and Louise on our way to freedom. We hit Dairy Queen first. High on sundaes dripping with hot fudge and whipped cream, we sped north on I-10 through the desert afternoon, pulling into a gas station parking lot just as Smith did, the timing such that it could have been a drug deal. I stepped into my own car, Smith at the wheel, and watched the big fat Cadillac speed away.

"She's going to meet her ex-boyfriend at the stadium to watch a game." I could almost smell the sour beer.

"The one who gave her the black eye?" Smith had come for

the week of family therapy, along with my mother, older sister, and father. They met my roommate, her eye still dark purple.

Suddenly I felt, with all the feeling I was capable of, how much I wanted freedom. Freedom from drugs. Yet it was to me the therapist had said, "You won't make it a year."

I did. I swam underwater and through water and I couldn't breathe, but I made it a year. Even after going back to court and losing my kids all over again, I stayed clean.

In 1990, when I first moved to the Southwest, the pueblo and cliff dwellers who had "disappeared" from places like Mesa Verde were called Anasazi—a Diné word for enemy ancestors. By 1998, when I studied environmental education at Canyonlands Field Institute in Moab, Utah, a transition to "ancestral Puebloan" was under consideration, and today it is commonly used, with some objection because pueblo is a Spanish word meaning "town," and was applied to the phenomenal cliff dwellings and stone villages by the colonizing Spanish. Returning to the Southwest from Hawai'i more than a decade later, I was happy to learn that some scientists had made a turn in their thinking and were in agreement with what Pueblo people had been saying for centuries: the ancestors came *here*, to northern New Mexico, to Arizona. The Hopi village Old Oraibi is one of the oldest continuously occupied villages in North America, human inhabitants spanning at least two thousand years; the Taos Pueblo, one thousand. Ancestral Puebloans, or Hisatsinom (Hopi, meaning "ancient people"), or the Tewa Se'da, "ancient ones," left the Four Corners area between 1200 and 1300.

Scientists want proof, and proof changes. In this case, DNA from turkey bones supported what Puebloans had said for generations.

If theory and teachings have changed in the past twenty years, if paleontologists and archaeologists continue to identify bones and artifacts that trace human occupation of North America back another few thousand years, it is plausible to me that horses may not have gone entirely extinct. Some believe that pockets of *E. caballus* survived on the North American continent after the great megafauna extinction, to join up with horses left by the Spanish in the 1500s. Moose and bears found glacial refuge in the Yukon and Alaska—some horses could have, as well. "It's possible," agrees reproductive biologist Dr. Jay Kirkpatrick in the documentary *El Caballo: The Wild Horses of North America.* Kirkpatrick founded the Science and Conservation Center behind ZooMontana in Billings in 1998, for fertility control research and training. "But I don't make that argument, simply because you shouldn't ... make arguments like that unless you have something to back them up." That was in 2001. People are still looking for evidence.

There is plenty of evidence that horses are native to North America. After fifty-five million years, they have earned that distinction.

If they did become extinct here, then, as Pulitzer Prize-winning author David Philipps points out in *Wild Horse Country: The History, Myth, and Future of the Mustang*, they were only gone for a second. "If the fifty-five-million-year history of horses in North America were condensed into a day," Philipps writes, "horses would be a native species right up until they became regionally extinct at 11:59:43 p.m. When they returned in the last second of the day, why did they no longer belong?"

THE STIFF-HAIRED ATTORNEY who pitied Keith only wrote the second year of graduate school into the agreement—who got the boys after was an empty draft. I didn't know enough at the time to distrust her, or to be proactive in making sure she'd done a more thorough job. Smith in the audience, an attorney beside me who had practiced family law for more than two decades, the judge hit the gavel on the desk and awarded Keith and his new wife *my boys*, because, the judge implied, possession is nine-tenths of the law and they'd been living with Keith for nine months and didn't I know any better, that moving them back and forth was a bad idea, even though I raised those boys for all their lives minus those nine lousy months and Keith still didn't know whose clothes were whose and none of it mattered, the fact that my first attorney fucked up didn't matter—what was truly best for my boys only mattered to *me*.

The blood drained from my heart. Smith helped me from the courthouse to the car as if I'd just come from knee surgery. With Kenney and Tyler we swam in the motel pool. Smith tossed Kenney into the air and he splashed back down, laughing as if his world had not just changed. I ducked underwater. I screamed into its cloudy blue. I wanted to swallow it into my lungs.

For the first time ever, water didn't help me.

Even now, I don't know how I managed.

Except I do. Smith was there.

He was there for those absolutely most awful pain-filled minutes and hours and days as that bad judge and wrong court decision forced me away from my children again. Away from those two boys who had come to this world through *my* body and blood and heart and were still connected *to me* by a love so impossibly expansive that I don't think anybody other than mother-animals who have lost their young before it's time truly understand—it was *my* body *my* breasts *my* hands that birthed and fed and held them while their father was away, always away, always working *away* from us until finally *I* went away with my boys to Flagstaff, which was better for them than living with a father they rarely saw, like me and my father only Keith was angry not drunk and the fucking judge didn't care. He thought *he* knew better than *this* mind *this* body what was best for *my* kids, and he yanked them away.

We dropped the boys off with Keith's wife (Keith already away somewhere working) and Smith stepped into his rental car (he'd flown to California for the hearing) and followed me to Santa Barbara as I drove too fast around the perilous curves of San Marcos Pass, afraid he was about to watch me die.

I wanted to hit that edge and fly.

At a corner gas station at the bottom of the pass, a phone booth stood sentry as if planted there by God. When Smith pulled up, I was talking to my aftercare therapist.

"Suicide is the worst form of child abuse," she said. "Get to a meeting."

Smith found one, and after listening to other people's problems for an hour and a half I quieted down inside enough to live. Through the night. Without my kids. Without drugs.

The next morning, I managed to get up, take a shower, and get dressed.

I did it the next day, too, and the one after that. Smith loved me through it all even though he knew his love could not fix or help but a little.

Neither drugs nor treatment came up in the courtroom. Addiction wasn't part of the equation. The judge simply believed what he believed and no reasoning would convince him otherwise. My attorney quit practicing family law after that.

4

TANGLED

I WAS EIGHTEEN WHEN CRAIG DIED, NINETEEN WHEN I STARTED using heroin, twenty-four when I stopped. During the years with Keith, my using was minimal: pills as prescribed or when I could scam or steal them, and beer or wine a few times a year, at brandings after the work was done and the dust settled.

Divorcing Keith freed me up to use more. Which I did.

Not everyone who gets divorced gets high.

Not everyone who has someone they love die gets high.

When Craig died something was already broken inside me. Or at least cracked. I know so many women for whom this is true. Abused physically or sexually (which can be the same thing) in childhood, we break, are broken, as if those hands reached inside us and broke our bones. But bones mend. And we were just kids. Small girls, and boys, too, our bones malleable. It was our psyches that snapped. Too young to find the kind of therapeutic glue that might help put us back together, we learned new ways to survive.

Some of us used.

Food. Sex. Drugs.

Just trying to feel right again. Whole. Unbroken. In treatment they called it self-medicating, like taking cough syrup for a cough but it's codeine cough syrup and we drink it straight and the cough does not go away. It waits there in the shadows.

If we ever stop using, there it is. Only it's bigger because using augments misery.

I didn't know I was already cracked before Craig died, or that I was self-medicating by doing bad things—punishing myself for hurt that was given to me. Then Craig died and I believed I was at least partly to blame. Medicating with heroin felt good. Felt *great*. But shooting heroin is going a little beyond self-medicating. Junkies aren't just hurt people who need medicine. We're the dregs. I was a dreg.

When I kicked heroin, I had to climb up from that murky bottom, which I did.

When I lost my kids, I hit bottom again. I hit Smith. I had to get clean. Stay clean. I had to get my boys back.

HERDS OF MUSTANGS populate ten western states, living on high-desert lands within loosely defined, or government-defined, habitats. The forming of bands, like a human family, happens naturally within the herd. Band stallions acquire mares, and mares have foals—fillies and colts. Colts grow up to be stallions, fillies grow into mares, and both are eventually driven or stolen from the band.

Young stallions often form bachelor bands—several stallions hanging together like teenage boys for months or even years until they are mature enough to start acquiring their own mares. The fillies usually want to stay with their mothers, but sooner or later a stallion who is not the sire will slip in and steal a filly, or fight and steal her. It's the way of nature.

What I find most remarkable is that a stallion may have his mares for years. And mares will be friends for years, fighting off the advances of other stallions to stay with their band stallion or their mare friend. In Spring Creek Basin, Houdini and Alegre, two regal mares, Houdini nearly thirty, Alegre fifteen, have been with their stallion, Hollywood, a confident little dun, for the seven years I've known them; before that, they were with another stallion. Total, the mares have been with each other most of Alegre's life. When I see one of them, the other is usually just feet away.

While change is part of the survival mechanism of the species, it can be heartbreaking to watch. It can also be heartbreaking for the horses—when a filly leaves her mother, or a younger stallion whisks the mares away from an older stallion who just cannot keep up the fight anymore (which is what Hollywood did). Or when a stallion is injured and one day he shows up alone. Or a mare dies from injury or foaling. Sometimes a foal dies, for reasons unknown. A horse may just disappear, never to be seen again. TJ, herd documenter, may stumble upon the remains, enough left for her to identify him, or her. Later she will tell me in her quiet mustang voice about what she saw.

AFTER THAT BAD judge awarded Keith my kids, Keith and I continued to fight through attorneys and mediators until finally I had to surrender in order to break the cycle. Keith wasn't going to—our sons were the only ammunition he had. So he won. Or he won Kenney, because I got Tyler back, twice. Although I stopped the custody battles, I was still a mother. I did not stop being a mother, scheming about how to get my boys back.

My mother and Ed were spending some time on Hawai'i Island and invited us for a visit. The first day, Kenney wore a long-sleeved shirt, Wranglers, and cowboy boots like his dad ("I'm not a shorts kind of guy," Keith would say when I suggested shorts on hundred-plus-degree days). In his dad's presence, Kenney was not a "shorts kind of kid." But by the middle of the second day, he had slipped into board shorts. Soon his brown back and bare feet and the gold highlights in his brown hair had him looking like *one local boy.* I had to remind him to put on a shirt and slippahs to go into a store or restaurant.

One day as the five of us meandered down the road in the little town of Hawi after eating pūpū and listening to slack key guitar, Kenney said, "Mom, let's move here."

The ocean shimmering in the distance, Maui across the channel, parts of my childhood there across the years, for one moment I hid the thrill—"Okay," I said, so casually—and then in a rush, "You'd come live with me if I moved here? I will you know, if you'd come. I will tomorrow."

Kenney sprinted away down the road. For two years the topic did not come up again. Tyler about to enter high school, Kenney a junior, both living with their dad and his wife, Tyler was quiet when I visited, hands in his pockets, head down. Glum. Dull. Something was wrong that I couldn't fix from afar. I needed to be close to him. He needed me to be close to him. I lost Tyler when he was three, *still my baby*, and got him back just before he turned six. He lived with his dad again in seventh and eighth grades. This time, instead of drugs, I had turned to *place* for survival—the Colorado Plateau—rowing rivers and working in the local bookstore and even going to community social events, determined to have a life without my boys. But a good life could not make me not a mother.

If Tyler got into a good college-prep school in the Islands, how could Keith say no?

Tyler took the tests; he got in.

I had every hope that Kenney would come with us, that his little comment would bubble forth like a spring in the desert. But he said no.

I moved to Maui to get Tyler back, my heart still split in two. Tyler is a Maui boy. No one can take that away. Even if he leaves the island, the island won't leave him—I have decades of knowing this. I also know that the boys were a part of me all those years we were apart. Which didn't stop the pain.

I never got Kenney back.

~~~

BANDS STARTLE WHEN they hear helicopters coming, some horses standing still to find the danger visually, others breaking into a run to escape it. Some mustangs have been rounded up by helicopters and returned to the wild, branded with PTSD. They may be the first to break, unable to hold their fear in check.

The adult horses inevitably run faster than foals or yearlings, and the young may lag behind, get lost in the dust. The helicopter pilots may swoop in close to a colt, terrifying it along, or leave it to its fate as an orphan; regardless of what the pilot does, the mare will make a break to circle back to her offspring. She may die trying, her instinct to protect her young even stronger than her will to live. In fact they may be the same thing: in that filly or colt lives the future of the band, the herd, the species. The mare must protect it. The stallions protect the mares and their foals, as well. But not against helicopters. Against helicopters they are powerless.

WHEN A CHILD is abused and the world tells her she wasn't (implying that she is somehow clever enough to fabricate such a thing at the age of three or four or five, or even twelve), she starts to doubt her reality. What *is* real, if what she saw and felt didn't actually happen, if the ache in her stomach isn't real, or the pain in her privates? A parent doesn't have to accuse the child of lying; just the fact that the parents don't believe her is enough. The fact that the parents didn't notice is enough. How to trust the people whose job it is to protect a child from danger, after they have failed—that is what abused children face.

When I sense or see a truth and others deny it, it's not the lying, exactly, that guts me—it's that my reality shifts and I am that little girl again.

Such a delicate thing, trust. So easy to break. Like the insides of a child.

~~~

DETRITUS: FLAGSTAFF, 1993. *Smith and I live in a partially off-grid cabin in the ponderosa pine forest outside of Flagstaff. We haul water to fill the 1,500-gallon cistern buried beneath the volcanic cinders of the yard. From there we pump water to the house—we have electricity.*

One evening the pump goes out. Smith climbs down into the pump house with a flashlight as I watch from above, ready to hand him tools. The clear night grows chilly. Shivering, I grab Smith's jacket, thrown over a camp chair, and put it on, the soft, extra-large wrapping warm around me. Stuffing my hands in the pockets, my fingers find a pack of lies.

Pulling the cigarettes out, I read their story. Smith looks up from the pit he's in, his face saying what his words deny. I'd asked before if he was smoking. He swore he wasn't, that he'd quit before we met. Now he says, "They're not mine."

I am good at these kinds of confrontations. "Bullshit," I say.

"Honestly, Kathryn, a guy at work asked me to hold them for him. I didn't smoke any."

"It's opened."

"I smoked one when I was getting water?"

Four are missing. My other hand produces a lighter.

I don't have to say fuck you *but I do, and then, like an angry four-year-old, I dump the remaining cigarettes on Smith's head.*

"But Kathryn," he says, his verbal skills not quite equal to mine.

I rush into the house, locking Smith outside, afraid I'll hurt him if he gets close to me.

WHICH HE HAD—I opened myself up to this man because I felt safe with him. Safer than I'd ever felt with anybody. Except Craig, who died. And Rebecca, who was a girl. But Smith . . . pledging honesty in our wedding vows . . . I couldn't bear it. So I hurt him, hurt this man who brought me back to safety because no matter what he did he couldn't bring me back my kids.

I left.

A LIEUTENANT (OR satellite) stallion is often a young bachelor stallion who attaches himself to a band, living at the perimeter, not yet ready to take on a band stallion but maturing toward that goal. The band stallion will allow his presence as the lieutenant fights off other interested stallions, leaving the dominant stallion to focus on breeding and protecting his mares. At the outskirts, the lieutenant stallion maintains a watchful eye for predators, marauders, and other threats, and the dominant stallion can follow his mares to safety while the lieutenant challenges the threat at the back of the escaping band (which is usually the main stallion's job). Sometimes the lieutenant stallion manages to breed a mare himself while the band leader is not looking, and sometimes the lieutenant fights the band stallion outright and steals the mares.

And sometimes, after he steals the mares, he loses them back to the dominant stallion. Sometimes loyal mares just won't go. They'll fight the intruder. Or sneak away to return to their own band.

The lead mare is not necessarily the oldest mare in the band, but the most respected. She will lead the band to new forage and water, and away from danger, while the band stallion follows. She may drift off on her own to protect her young foal or to follow a stolen companion, but ultimately she is safer within a band.

A wild horse cannot fight instinct. Even brokenhearted, those captured mustangs outside Susanville were *alive.* They would stay alive through the adoption process, and would adapt to new circumstances—if they got a good adopter. Or, at that time (early 1970s), they might get loaded onto trucks going to slaughterhouses and die in a state of terror as they were pushed through chutes toward their final blow.

Today they would go to short- or long-term holding; if unadopted, they would live out their lives in the company of other mustangs, forming small bands within the herd, band geldings and lead mares taking their places once again.

DETRITUS: CALIFORNIA, 2008. *The hot, dry air of the Sierra Nevada foothills burns in my nose. Master women's double hull, a short, fast sprint, no turns, just all-out paddling from the flag dropping to the finish line. I'm Seat 3—supposed to call the changes—hut, ho—paddlers switching their paddles from one side to the other. I have to count, to concentrate.*

Rebecca called yesterday, upset because I asked my cousin for a ride from the Oakland airport. Rebecca thought she would be driving me. But she didn't return my calls.

I don't trust my voice. Last second someone else calls the changes. Just follow Seat 1, paddle, breathe; change sides, paddle, breathe. I give it everything. A millisecond not enough for first. Silver-medal seconds.

I fly to Colorado, to Ken in college. He interns at a ranch, caring for cattle. In winter he checks first-calf heifers day and night, pulling calves if needed from the hot insides of heifers into a world of frozen white. He struggles with school—so much of it indoors, and math—but he will graduate. He takes me to a natural lake in the Front Range—freshwater surrounded by granite and green meadows and forests of pine and fir. I watch him fly fish, ten o'clock two o'clock. Seated on warm granite, I smell the mountains.

Back to Oakland, calling Rebecca to confirm she'll be at the airport, repeating the airline and ETA. She gets mad that I don't trust her to remember. Outside baggage claim, I call again—for forty-five minutes, I call every five. Then I hear her voice, small and sleepy, words stumbling over themselves as she struggles to attach them to a thought.

She manages, "I think I fell asleep."

"Just hurry your ass up," I tell her. Half an hour later her old Beamer bumps onto the curb. She walks slowly around from the driver's side, her hands gripping the car's top and trunk, one over the other, like a baby learning to walk.

She's thin and gray. She smells funny. Like a homeless person. Not in Hawai`i, where the beach parks have public showers, but in other places I've been.

She didn't like to wash her hair. Dark blond or light brown and coarse, like horsehair, it would not conform to styles, though she tried many. Inches short, peroxided white. A long purple lock against bleached blond. Convention didn't suit her. When we lived together in Berkeley, she wore it shoulder-length and straight in its odd natural shade, and I would bug her so much about her dirty hair that she would tell me to wash it. I did not understand this hair thing; her mother a spunky, successful real estate broker, a high-school-cheerleader sister, her brother on his way to becoming a cardiologist, and Rebecca wouldn't wash her hair.

Her mother is dead. Five years ago. Brain tumor and Alzheimer's. Or one or the other. The doctors weren't sure. Rebecca pulls into the line of vehicles exiting the airport. Her foot slips on the clutch. She giggles, restarts the car, tries again, all in slow mo like her words. I ask if she wants me to drive, wondering why I didn't think of it sooner. Because I want her to be the Rebecca I know, that's why— whipping through Bay Area traffic like a white-tipped reef shark flashing across the ocean floor, quick and lithe and fearless. That is my Rebecca. Not this one. This Rebecca I do not know. And yet . . .

While housesitting for my mother and Ed on Maui, she got arrested for a DUI after having a bad reaction to a shot at Kaiser for her chronic back pain. In a strained voice on the jail phone, she pleaded with me to come bail her out. I believed her words, not my gut.

She stops the car, climbs over the gearshift, mumbles, "I don't know why I fell asleep and didn't hear the alarm."

"That's why I called you this morning, so you'd be awake and on time."

We stick to directions after that—to her own house, where she's lived for more than ten years, and she can't tell me how to get there.

Rebecca and freebase cocaine, like heroin and me. This during my marriage to Keith and I didn't know until after the divorce, when I stayed with her in Oakland during spring break after driving the kids to their dad's and freebased with her. It felt as good as the first time, that hard rush at the back of your head when you don't know if you're alive or seeing the light and all too quickly you realize it's life and you smoke more and more and it's not ever that good again. Except for me it was since I had over ten years between hits.

The trouble with cocaine, not long into the high you want more. Same with crystal meth. You get frantic and paranoid and have to *have* more. Heroin is different. You want until you have, and then you coast for a few hours before you need more. Rebecca smoked a lot of cocaine. Until she figured out she'd better stop. She stopped one drug but not the others. The way I did at first. She was taking pills—prescribed meds. She wouldn't tell me what. Something for her back and to help her sleep.

In Hawai`i, you leave your shoes by the door. Quickly I decide to keep my slippahs on inside her house. She shows me the piles and stacks she's sorting through, every surface covered. She seems proud that she managed to clear off the bed in the guestroom, put clean towels in the bathroom, but in the kitchen every plate, bowl, glass, and utensil is dirty in the sink or on the counter or table. I gag over smells as I wash a water glass. The food in the fridge is in Chinese-food take-out boxes, stale pizza on a plate.

The only place to sit is on her bed. We pull blankets over dirty sheets. Rebecca's slender body fills the hollow on her side. I climb into a sitting position, pillows at my back, and look around the *room in its dull dusk, the windows so completely covered I think of the blackouts during WWII—in their Berkeley hills home, my mother and her sister would watch San Francisco and Oakland and Berkeley go dark as blinds were lowered and cracks sealed so that no light escaped and the Bay Area became an invisible target for feared Japanese air raids. But Rebecca is keeping the light out, not in.*

"What do you do?" I ask.

"I watch TV." The remote in her hand. "When I can't sleep I just watch TV."

MY FRIENDSHIPS WITH women often last decades, Rebecca and me like Alegre and Houdini, those two mustang mares. Not so my relationships with men, other than my sons.

Some mustangs can learn to trust after capture. Of TJ's thirty-two mustangs at the sanctuary, she can pet a few. She had Nevada, a dark bay, for months before she could do anything but stand near him, then one day he let her stand close enough to pick cockleburs from his mane. With others she can do nothing at all, like rub a hand along a neck, and doesn't try to.

TJ lets each mustang offer what it wishes. Some are so deeply cracked by what they've been through that they will die in the hills or valleys of the sanctuary without ever having experienced human touch beyond what they went through when being processed by the BLM: pushed from corral to alleyway to squeeze chute, freeze-branded on their necks for identification, aged (mouths held open and teeth assessed), hooves trimmed, wormer and vaccinations applied, the stallions castrated. While TJ's mustangs have learned that she will not harm them, some simply cannot let her within their survival bubbles.

Like mustangs, we're all different. Some of us do find wholeness, and I don't dare guess why. It's not a matter of constitution. We are *all* strong—we're here, after all (and maybe those of us who left early, by our own hand, were strong, too, in our convictions). But some of us were done with humans—or the man part of that word—long ago.

Others may keep hoping to mend, finding safety in partnership or friendship or family, staying still long enough for someone to brush the tangles from their hair.

I didn't wash Rebecca's hair.

WHEN I GOT back to Haʻikū after seeing Rebecca, my mother and Ed and I talked about what I could do—get Rebecca, force her onto a plane, and sit on her for three weeks while the drugs sweated out of her system and some clarity seeped in. Would that have saved her? I don't know. I didn't do it. If I had at least told her what I was thinking—how at only fifty-three she looked seventy, how she looked as if she were dying—perhaps that would have made a difference. But I held the awful truth inside me, the one secret I didn't share with Rebecca.

The rest of me she knew—from the stories we shared in a childhood fort to the years we lived and used together, what we did, what I had done alone. She knew me more and better than anyone else in the world. Except she didn't see my last house on Maui. She didn't meet Cojo or Maka. She couldn't come visit and couldn't admit why not without disclosing a secret she thought she was keeping to herself.

If she said it out loud, she knew what I would say: *You have to stop. There's no other way.* Because *I* knew no other way.

But she found one.

Part II

THE LANDSCAPE
OF MY FUTURE

Some women come to the desert to erase previous lives, to seek a different way to live in the world. Others choose home not by familial ties but by color and light.

—Ellen Meloy, *The Anthropology of Turquoise*

5

SUNDANCE

As New Mexico moves into spring, Sundance is the talk of the Taos sweat lodge community. Different groups head toward different places in New Mexico or Arizona—or Utah, South Dakota, Montana—to participate in this ceremony sacred to the Lakota people who have, perhaps regretfully, shared their ways and rituals with wasichu and people of other tribes, nations, cultures, and countries. In the Taos sweat lodges sit mostly people of mixed blood and wasichu (I am white, haole, bilagáana, Anglo, gringa, and wasichu). Few are, as they would say in Hawai'i, 100 percent Lakota. Still they follow the protocol, sing Lakota songs, and make dresses and gather offerings in preparation for Sundance.

Inside the sweat lodges I watch the darkness, listen, sweat, and pray silently to Spirit and Creator and Hawaiian deities. I pray for healing for all, and for me. I wish not to talk because whenever I start to speak, whatever heartfelt comment I meant to make turns into something from my head. Except when I talk about my kids. About the pain that follows me into their adulthood. Now they *should* be separate from me, and they are—talented, intriguing, creative, smart, tall, handsome young men, each following a dream—yet that old ache persists, magnified, perhaps, by the recent deaths. I pray for release from this pain. I think about going to Sundance, imagining that piercing my skin and dancing without food and water for four days might finally pull the hurt up out of my body and carry it away.

AFTER THE FIRST spring rain finally falls on my place, I go out with Cojo at dawn and stand barefoot on the cool lānai, smelling the fresh morning, the big sagebrush releasing its spicy aroma the way it does in the steam of the sweat lodges. I know something of what death smells like in its varying stages but this early morning I smell *life* as all around me the brush stands taller, the rocks cleaner, the earth cleansed.

Rain has washed the sand in my old-riverbed driveway. In place of notations of dog and me coming and going or just sniffing around, a clean slate; on that slate, a fresh set of tracks: round, four toes, no claws digging into the sand. In the audible hush of things growing after the rain, Cojo did not hear the mountain lion walk by. Nor, of course, did I.

Keeping Cojo behind me so he doesn't mar the story, I track the feline downriver. She slipped past the house, angled toward the river then inland to the shelter of Rocky Mountain junipers and narrowleaf cottonwoods. The tracks disappear where the river meets the ragged cliff but there are no tracks on the last strip of sand. The big cat went right up the scree cliff.

Maybe I shouldn't tell about the cougar so close to my house. The neighbors and men who manage the acequia might not understand the blessing, though those in the sweat lodges would. I find another set of tracks in the rain-packed earth, with longer toes, a wide pad at the ball of the foot and another indentation just behind. Almost like a people foot, these bear tracks—except for the claws. Several days ago a man in the little town reported that a bear had stolen and eaten one of his goats. Bears usually come down in the fall looking for apples. Now, still hungry with spring and thirsty, too, the bears are hunting for water and any kind of food—whatever delicacies they can find, including the garbage the human species leaves out.

In order not to frighten him, you're supposed to make lots of noise when in a bear's territory, and then play dead when he mauls you. When I was fifteen, my mother, our Kerry blue terrier, and I toured the West in a Dodge van, traveling through the Sierra Nevada into Oregon, meandering along the Columbia and Snake Rivers, camping for a week by Yellowstone Lake. In Yellowstone I saw my first bear, this after going to a ranger talk about grizzlies. "If you see a griz," the ranger said, "fall down in a ball, put your arms over your head, and play dead. Do not run or fight back, don't sweat, and you may get away with your life if not all your limbs."

We did not see a griz but a black bear, a sow and her cub plodding along beside the road, a line of cars stopping and starting as people oohed and ahhed and took Kodak shots. When my mother pulled abreast, the she-bear swung her big head around and looked at me framed in the open window with my dog in my lap, at least one of us drooling. That mother bear sniffed the air for one second before charging the van, and in a movement swift as hers I lifted my forty-pound dog by his collar and pulled him behind me, rolling the window up with my other hand, putting my body and glass between that bear and my dog.

My mother, gasping and gassing the van forward, started to laugh. She laughed until she cried. "What did you think you were going to *do*?" she finally said.

That same fierce protective drive kept me in court fighting for my boys all those years, but no matter what tactic I took, I could not get them back. One attorney called Keith "Mr. No," because whatever I proposed, he declined. I wasn't brave enough to bet on it, though, by saying he could keep the boys in hopes he would give them back to me. For years people told me Kenney would stop hating me for the perceived abandonment and come around, but I found that impossible to believe. Now we live within a hundred miles of each other, I see him often, and we talk on the phone almost daily, weather usually on the agenda. This feels right as rain.

ONE MORNING KEN calls to tell me he's just seen his first bear of spring.

We hang up and minutes later the phone rings again. "I just ran over Bow," Ken says.

"What do you mean?"

On a rocky part of the ranch, his truck bouncing slowly along, Bow, his border collie–McNab, fell from the bed, and the loaded feeder Ken was towing rolled over him.

"Shit. Is it bad?"

"He can't walk and he's pissing blood."

Keith didn't believe in taking dogs to vets. I splinted legs that remained forever crooked. Ken's boss is angry that the dog is hurt. I make the nearly two-hour drive to the ranch in an hour twenty and load the yelping year-old pup into the Subaru as red pee shoots everywhere.

The vet pins the fractured pelvis together near the hip and cuts the ball off the femur so it won't apply too much pressure to the healing pinned place, and I take Bow to my house by the rio to heal. Cojo is slow going and I have my knee so Bow fits right into the infirmary of our lives. For a dozen days and nights I carry him outside to pee, lifting him with a soft blanket under his girth like a sling, and relive adjusting Ed with a sheet in the rented hospital bed. Bow can't understand why I hurt him each time just the way Ed couldn't there at the end and for many nights and days Bow cries, and so do I.

Then, like me, he gets better enough to hobble around. Eventually he can hop to the river and drink, when there's water, and he likes going in ankle-deep, drinking in great gulps or bites, hopping upriver, his mouth wide open, taking big bites of water as if it's steak, his injured leg trailing behind him in the current.

Inside the sweat lodges, I pray for Bow, too.

IT'S A DRY summer in New Mexico. When I return from visiting a friend on the Navajo Nation, I cry at the sight of the dried and shrunken carcass of my river. Upstream, thick plastic sheets have been stretched tightly across the riverbed, smooth stones anchoring them in place, most of the water now diverted to the acequia—the irrigation ditch that runs between river and road. Some rivers drown in their own water but this one is getting sucked dry by the wineries and farmers upstream and down, the acequia getting far more water than the natural riverbed. My house, too, empty and sad. I fear I have become a sad old single woman, drying up like my river.

In the Southwest, summer is monsoon season. Seven years in Flagstaff (in four different houses) taught me that in a good year, clouds will visit nearly every afternoon, water spilling over sometimes as virga—rain that doesn't touch down—and sometimes in buckets, when the land can't absorb all the moisture and water crashes a course to wherever it can go. The desert greens up with the thunderstorms, streams flowing again after winter's snow has vanished, the cacti growing their imperceptible partial inch. One rain and the ocotillos in the Sonoran Desert sprout buds that turn a radiant red. Prickly pears plump up and offer blossoms to the bees. Jumping chollas' white and pink flowers brighten sagebrush-and-creosote flats. People smile.

This summer, the weather pattern in this part of New Mexico has turned the days generic—clouds swirling high in voluminous thunderheads, charcoal fists pummeling each other until they lose definition as individuals and become the afternoon sky. In the heat that draws clouds, I think of the women and men I know, stepping circles around a cottonwood pole to the rhythm of ancient songs. I think of Ken on the rain-shadow side of the Sangre de Cristo Mountains, rain absent. As the afternoon sun tracks slowly west in a camouflage of cloud cover, the sky blackens to purple in a promise of rain it keeps to itself.

New Mexico is burning up. Six lightning fires, quickly extinguished, have started on the ranch where Ken works. He and a buddy join the volunteer fire department. The biggest fire Arizona has ever recorded crosses the state line into New Mexico. Another fire closes the Colorado–New Mexico border. My house fills with smoke. I cough longing.

The wild prairie rose had its pink blossoms early, eager to dance with rain that doesn't come. A few red willow shoots sprouted leaves, the rest curling into themselves or standing straight as dead sticks. A serious monsoon will rip them up and scour rocks with their pink roots as it rushes them downstream.

Each trip to the post office, rain is the topic of the conversations I overhear.

Inside the sweat lodges, people continue to speak of Sundance—praying for the strength to dance for the four days, a sacrifice of flesh and abstinence they want to make for their small communities, and our larger community Earth. I listen. I think about dancing. I think, *we don't need the lodge to sweat*, and pray for rain. I pray for my own release.

Nothing but a trickle of water, its voice a choked gurgle, escapes the plastic dams in the withering river. Last year, before Ed died, the river raged forty feet wide, filling the acequia with debris: whole trees, logs, tires, the rubbish people throw from their cars, the plastic remnants of previous diversion dams. As I stood on the wooden bridge, the crashing dance of the flash flood pounded through the boards into me as the rio ran wild and free and crazy-happy, racing itself downstream.

Last year I couldn't imagine this year—I knew Ed would die but could not imagine him dead, or my life thereafter: leaving Hawai'i, Ken and me in the same state, me on a spit of river, its flow controlled not by nature or nature's lack but by the hands of men, the native growth—Fremont, Rio Grande, and narrowleaf cottonwoods, red willows, New Mexican olives—going thirsty so someone can water his grapes. In New Mexico as in Hawai'i I live at the edge of a culture shaped by water, a stranger to its ways. And visit another culture, learning songs and chants, wishing I could dance.

By August most of my friends have gone to their sundances. By August I've had only one rain that penetrated the top inch of soil. I say *I* because what happens at my place does not indicate what might happen a quarter of a mile away—neighbors closer than that haven't had even one rain.

At the post office one afternoon, when the postmaster asks how my day is going, I say, "Good," then, "The sky's getting black over there."

"It could rain, no?" he says, and I drive away thinking that that sentence in Hawai'i would be, "It could rain, yeah?" or "Maybe we going get rain, eh?" I drive only as far as that thought takes to think when water hits my windshield so hard I should pull over. Instead I turn the wiper speed on high and stick my arm out the window, laughing aloud.

That squall never reached my house.

TWO FRIENDS INVITE me to go with them to a sundance in Montana. They will both dance for four days and they tremble with excitement when I meet them for dinner to arrange travel plans. They want us to caravan but another friend is coming, too, and I'll leave with him two days later. When he calls to say that something is happening at home and he can't leave the rez, I decide that driving alone to northeastern Montana is part of the experience.

I have certainly traveled solo before—all those road trips to get my kids, the long trips home alone. After losing my sons I've been solo a lot in my life, living in houses with bedrooms for the boys, doors shut against the silence. Motivated by my desire to rectify that loss inside myself, I make arrangements with Ken to watch the dogs while I'm gone. He tells me there's some cattle work to do—gathering cows, sorting bulls off—and asks if I want to help. I can leave for Montana from there.

I get to the ranch in the early evening. Ken's house is small, cozy, with Russell prints and Navajo saddle blankets on the walls. A bronze sculpture of a young horse under first saddle, humped up, ready to buck, which I gave Keith for Christmas one year, stands on top of the TV cabinet. Photographs of Kenney and Tyler as small boys sit on a curio shelf. A buckle I won teamroping with Keith in 1985, the year Kenney was born, sits on another shelf. I gave it to Ken for his birthday—evidence that things were good back then.

Ken bakes a DiGiorno pizza and I make a salad. We eat in front of the TV, watching *Seinfeld*. This simplest of events—eating dinner with my grown son in his little ranch house—takes me to something I felt years before, when he was fifteen and working at the Cojo, his first paying ranch job. Tyler and I were in Wyoming to camp and fly-fish with Smith and his fiancé; before we left, I called Kenney. That's how I found out he was in the hospital facing surgery, his thumb severed from an accident with a horse.

Tyler and I arrived at the ranch in the middle of the night. A sleepy, drugged Kenney lifted his head from his pillow and said, "What are *you* doing here?" A therapist told me once to think the opposite of what Kenney said—*I hate you, I never want to see you again* meant he loved me—so, tired from the fourteen-hour trip, I tried to believe he was glad we had come.

One of the ranch houses made a temporary shelter for us three while Tyler and I fed Kenney and entertained him and drove him around, his reattached thumb healing inside an impressive cast. As soon as the doctor okayed it, Kenney, still casted, went back to work. I would make him breakfast and watch him leave, make his bed, do the dishes, and think about lunch. When I heard his cowboy boots leaping the porch steps at noon and again at the end of the day, well, that was something. I had dreamed it all those years and there it was: Kenney's boots on stairs that led straight to my heart.

In his house on the New Mexico ranch eleven years later, we eat pizza and get ready to work cattle the next day. This followed by a Montana sundance—more than my belly is full.

A MONTH EARLIER, Ken's boss decided to ship the stocker steers. They get steers in around May fifteenth and turn them out on prairie grass; in a normal year the steers come off in October. In July Ken called to ask if I wanted to help gather and ship— months early because the ranch, like the rest of New Mexico, had still had no rain. "Hell yes," I said.

Ken had three colts, greenbroke or unbroke, so the boss offered me his tall, twelve-year-old gray gelding to ride. This would be my second time in the saddle since knee surgery. And in the twenty years prior, I'd only been ahorseback half a dozen times.

"I might not be able to get on," I told Ken as we saddled up that morning. "You might have to push your old mother up into the saddle."

I caught Ken's look. But he came over to make sure I wasn't cinched up too tightly and the stirrups were the right length.

"You can climb on from the trailer," the boss said.

In the dawn light we trailered out over open, rolling terrain, the Great Plains in shadow to the east, the Sangre de Cristo rising in the west. At a fence separating two pastures, we unloaded the horses. As the boss trotted off in a westerly direction to meet other riders, Ken swung easily onto Cisco, his buckskin colt, and waited, facing away. Ken headed east when I made it into the saddle without any aids.

It was *my* saddle, or had been. Keith had it made for me early in our marriage and I'd gathered a lot of cattle, roped a lot of steers and calves, and even won a few belt buckles in it, including the one I gave Ken. I sent him the saddle for his thirteenth birthday, UPS from Utah.

As I sat in my old saddle on a borrowed horse watching my son urge his buckskin colt into an easy lope and head over a rise toward daylight, I forgot about the steers I was supposed to push across the field. When Ken stopped and looked back at me, I jolted into action, squeezing the horse into a trot after a small bunch of cattle near a stand of junipers.

I'd lost my balance in the passage of time (my healing knee not helping) and almost went off when I loped the gelding up to the fence to turn some cattle that Ken pushed toward me, the gelding stopping faster than I was ready for, me swaying forward and sticking him with my spurs by accident, just like a dude, Ken saying *Mom!* and other words I couldn't distinguish as I fought to stay in the saddle—which I did. For two days. Riding so long and hard my ass was sore in ways I didn't know were possible despite earlier decades ahorseback.

We gathered the 1,500-acre holding field that morning, 498 head loaded onto the cattle trucks before noon. I heard myself hollering at the steers as though twenty years hadn't gone by; I heard Keith hollering at me even though I remembered every move.

After lunch we trailered out again to gather the second pasture and another five hundred steers. I was told to go one way, Ken another. We started slowly. Gathering cattle is like watching water, how it finds the lowest spot and heads there across the terrain, moving in trickles toward a whole, braiding as it goes, flowing faster downhill, finally converging into a pond or lake or herd when there's something to stop its forward movement. Like a fence.

The cowboys and I pushed those steers toward an opening I couldn't see, moving quietly back and forth so the cattle wouldn't dam up in front or see a break behind us and run back over the top of us. The inevitable happened anyway. Not the whole herd—just three steers broke back. And not together—that would be too easy; we'd just gather them up in a little bunch—no, these three scattered in three different directions. One got turned around quickly but the other two hauled ass—one in Ken's jurisdiction, the other in mine.

Another cowboy and I took out after it, hazing it—the steer was between us and kept going faster. I pulled up then loped across the open grassland in a wide half circle to get ahead of it. I had my rope down and was building a loop before I even knew what I was doing, left hand holding reins and coils as my right slid the rope through the honda and shook it into an oval, all this while on the run. Another cowboy jumped in, chasing the steer down the fence. He threw a loop, slapping the steer's front feet with his rope. I slowed again, glancing back at Ken, who had his steer roped and facing him, he and young Cisco in total control. Even from a distance Ken looked like Keith.

I kicked into position, swinging my loop. "Get your arm up," Keith yelled from years behind me, then "*Throw the fucking rope.*" I did, and missed. "Follow through goddamnit," I heard him say. The steer, head high, eyes wild, kept on up the fence-line. I went around him on the run and turned him on the fence, by golly (another Keith expression), sticking tightly to my old saddle this time, and had him trotting toward an open gate, and through it.

As I closed the gate and headed back toward Ken nearly a mile away, rain cut loose—their first rain of the season. I hadn't even seen the clouds forming. Ken sat on Cisco near the other gate, waiting for us, their backs to the downpour, the quiet gelding and me wanting to do the same, those fat drops hard and cold against our skin. I pushed him on through rain that washed away the dust from the shipping corrals, the dry year, and any bad memories. It was just me then on that borrowed gray gelding riding across the rolling prairie toward my son. I turned my face up and held out my arms, embracing the rain.

AFTER PIZZA, KEN and I go to bed early. We awaken in the dark, feed the horses, and head out before first light, just the boss and Ken and me. Ken is on Cisco and again I ride the gray gelding. My balance and seat in the saddle have returned, though I'm too heavy in the hands.

DETRITUS: CALIFORNIA, 1964. *I'm riding Buck at the Cojo after Kaua'i, a big bay gelding us kids have to share—a dude horse, I hear the cowboys say, so I'm a dude except I'm nine so maybe I'm just a greenhorn 'cause I don't know anything 'bout riding or cows. My grandmother who died when I was four put me on one of her horses, Robin, speckled like an egg she said, and led me around her ranch on Mount Diablo but she always had a rope tied to my horse. And now I have the reins in my hands and Buck trots up and down the big barnyard that connects all the buildings—the red barns and adobe houses where family stays and the guesthouse my grandmother made and the cowboys' homes painted white with green trim and at the beginning of the barnyard a long driveway leads out through eucalyptus trees I smell when I dream. Someday I want to ride out that driveway. Someday I want to ride on the beach. But today I trot up and down bouncing on Buck's back like a dude, and even though maybe I am a dude, or a greenhorn, I love this feeling. Like the ocean. Just me and air and space and room and the big bay horse trotting up and down and there's my uncle walking toward us.*

"Your hands are too hard on the horse's mouth," he tells me. "You don't need to jerk on the reins. Just pull gently and he'll turn. He'll stop."

My hands don't understand. They do not want to hurt this horse. They rub his neck, feeling the softness under his black mane. I slide from the saddle and Buck puts his big head next to my whole body and I know he doesn't want to hurt me, too.

I hide my hard hands in my blue jeans pockets and walk away before I hurt Buck anymore. Before I cry and anyone sees me.

I don't like my hard hands.

I don't like my mother's best friend's husband's hard hands.

I don't like that no one told my mother's best friend's husband to stop.

I don't know that's why we moved to Kaua`i, to get away from those hands.

I'M ON A horse on a New Mexico ranch riding alongside my son who rides like his father, like my grandmother, Ken twenty-six, me fifty-six, his green eyes bright and handsome, his chaps worn with age like my skin, his spurs and hackamore and the horsehair mecate held in the style of our forebears in hands not hard like mine but knowledgeable like my grandmother's. As we push cattle over the curve of the Great Plains in the shadow of the Rockies I can see that in cattle ways we were raised the same, by Ken's dad and family tradition.

The gelding picks his way through rocks as I watch morning spread over the land, the mountains turning green with light while the shadowy plains drop off toward Texas. This day we're gathering bulls in another large field and again it strikes me just exactly what I'm doing: cowboying, with Ken. I feel sun on my skin and life in my body though my heart is still cloudy with loss—Ken back in my life but not Rebecca, not my fathers, death a force that fills the insides of me and blocks the room a smile takes to make.

We ride through the cattle, pushing small bunches containing bulls and letting the cows fall back until we have seven fourteen-hundred-pound, three-year-old Black Angus bulls and one Brangus, a little bit of ear on him and a hump over his shoulders. He is the problem child. As long as he's in the middle of the pack, he moves along. If he drifts to the side and anyone gets too close, he charges our horses. I stay well away, leaving Ken on quick Cisco to maneuver the bull down the hill.

We reach the gate to the smaller holding field and the boss and I drive the bigger bunch through to the corrals while Ken stays back with the Brangus, who refused to go any farther without a serious fight. We lope back to them and the boss trots off to get the stock trailer—they'll have to rope this bull and load him in the gooseneck to get him out of here.

Ken's loop sails out and settles right over the stubborn head. With the trailer close, somebody has to heel the bull. My loop built, my heart beating wildly, I stand aside to let the boss throw first. He misses; I miss; Cisco faces up to the Brangus and dances away when the bull charges; I rebuild, feeling the weight of the years over my head as I swing, tilting the loop down toward the heels, and throw. And catch a hind leg. Jerk my slack. Dally quick wraps around the horn. Swear. I haven't had anything on the other end of my rope besides a dummy steer—a hard plastic head stuck in a hay bale—in twenty years, and now I have a fourteen-hundred-pound bull on the fight, me on a horse I barely know, only memory telling me what to do, and Ken. "It's okay, Mom. Calm down. You're all right. You gotta take up some slack."

"Shit, I know." As I unwrap my dallies from the saddle horn the bull jumps forward so I have to, too, hanging on as my rope burns through my hand, dallying again but I'm farther away instead of closer, Ken pulling the bull toward the trailer but a big bull or cow will choke down and just fall over and you have to give it slack or it might die right there, I've seen it happen, so

Ken kicks forward and slackens the rope around the bull's neck and the bull jumps up and away and I'm the one holding him then, feeling all that weight and fury pulling tight on the saddle horn, the saddle slipping forward, the horse about to blow, I can feel it, I know that feeling. "He's gonna explode," I say. "*Let loose of your dallies*," Ken says and I unwrap my rope just in time, but Ken barely has time to dally up and stop the bull on his end before the bull gets free.

It goes on like this for minutes, for too long. Adrenaline rushes me like cocaine used to and I want to stay calm and steady but I'm shaking all over. "You're okay, Mom," Ken keeps saying, and I am, really, because I can just turn the bull loose and ride away. Except I won't leave Ken. No, I hang in there until we get the sonofabitch loaded, which Ken and the boss do with the help of the calm, steady, forgiving gray gelding, and me.

The boss drives off with the angry Brangus in the trailer to drop him in the bull pasture, and Ken and I ride toward the corrals. I stretch in the saddle, pushing against the stirrups, releasing. "I think I'm too old for this," I say.

"You did good, Mom," Ken says.

AT THE END of the bull day the boss says they'll skip a day and then they have a bunch of cows to gather and calves to vaccinate. If I want my old skills back I need time on a horse, so I say I'll stay longer if they can use me. Then I have places to go and prayers to make. But I have worked up a good stomachache about leaving Kenney again.

On the in-between day, Ken heads off to fix a windmill and I drive to a huge slab of redrock I found last summer. Four feet wide at the top and eighteen feet tall, truly a slice of rock from somewhere beneath in geologic depth and time, that hunk of sandstone held pockets hollowed out by water; crevices carved into stone by water; smaller crevices that led to big cracks and chunks of rock peeled off from the main stem, helped by winter's frozen water; the soil at the base carved by rivulets leading to an arroyo that held moisture in its damp soil. I sat atop that rock and drank rainwater from its pores. Water is everywhere, I thought, even where water is not.

In this summer of drought, ponderosa pine needles, untouched by rain or dew even, crunch underfoot, releasing dust as I climb. On top of the rock, the breeze calms my sweat and high branches of ponderosas frame the view of a valley, another ridge and another, waves of country like years receding into the past.

I lost my son when he was six. He's twenty-six now. I had to drive away all those awful times before and it hits me up on that slab of crystallized earth that this time I don't have to go. Instead of heading to Montana to pray for healing, I can stay with my son and see my prayers answered.

I stay. I cowboy. I pray. Thank you, gods, for the blessings of rain, the blessings of mountain lions, tall rocks, and borrowed horses.

Thank you, Creator, for this dance with my son.

The next week I get a horse of my own.

6

FUBAR

IT TURNS OUT I BOUGHT A BAD HORSE. KEN COULDN'T GO with me the day I went to look at the quarter horse gelding, but when I called to tell him about the horse, he said, "Sounds like he might be too much for you."

"I *want* him," I said, unable to explain the pull in my gut, or to confess that I'd already told the horse he would be better off with me. That was just stuff I *felt*, after all, stuff Ken would dismiss because, heck, cowboys don't *feel* about such things.

He felt plenty, though, the second day I rode the horse on the ranch, me in the gate, the boss and Ken pushing cattle at me, my job to let cows go through and stop the calves. The new horse, called Howard by his seller because he was from Howard, Kansas, started rearing up and spinning off to the right as the cattle came fast at him, my hands and legs too busy as I tried to anticipate bovine decisions, the horse absorbing the agitation until he just couldn't anymore. His rears and spins grew bigger. I couldn't get him to turn to the left. I was stumped. Scared. Ken was angry. The boss told me to get out of the gate.

The next day, pushing cows down through the pines, Howard reared Trigger-high. Throwing the reins forward and urging him forward with my knees so he wouldn't go over backward on top of me, I got him headed after the cattle again but my heart stayed up on the hill behind us, hanging on the limb of a tall ponderosa.

"Get rid of him," Ken said.

I called the man who sold him to me. It had only been five days but the Christian teamroper from Pueblo, Colorado, refused to take him back. He'd not had any problems with the horse, he said; "It must be you." He was an asshole but probably right—it was me not the horse. I needed more time in the saddle.

The next day, my horse was perfect and I loved him. The day after, not so much. Ken started calling him Fubar. Then came the morning when Fubar went nuts in a stall. Ken and the boss saddling their horses nearby, Fubar suddenly erupted, rearing and trying to jump the stall fence, busting the overhead light and damned near his leg.

"I'm not just saying it, Mom. That horse could hurt you. He has to go."

The good Christian wouldn't take him. I couldn't sell him, the way he was acting. I spoke to two trainers who didn't want to work with him. I didn't know what to do.

A friend had heard about a horse trainer in Montana: Andrés. "They say he's a magician with horses," she said. "Call him."

"Does he know how to move his feet?" Andrés asked me right off.

Well, sure, I thought, he can walk, trot, and lope just like any horse. "I think so," I said. Andrés told me he was giving a horsemanship clinic in Montana in three weeks.

I'd not been to a clinic before, or even considered it—it wasn't as popular a thing to do in the last century as it is today, and besides, cowboys don't need lessons. Keith would have scoffed, as Ken did. But Ken hooked up the trailer, making sure the lights and brakes worked, and we loaded two horses—a sorrel colt of Ken's and my bad horse—for the nine-hundred-mile drive north, hoping this trainer could provide a solution.

"Whatever you do," Ken said, "don't bring Fubar back here."

"Okay," I said, thinking if this trainer says Fubar is fixable, I'll find somewhere else to keep him and give him a real name.

DESPITE HAVING DRIVEN lots of highways through the West, usually alone, as I head out the long dirt road leaving the ranch, the two-horse trailer behind me, I feel as alone as I ever have. I appreciate Ken's help but want his blessing. And maybe more than that, I want forgiveness. For buying the bad horse against his advice, yes, and for more. For losing custody of him all those years before.

The New Mexico portion of I-25 tops out north of Raton, one of the few curvy stretches on an interstate that draws a fictitious line between the Great Plains and the Rockies. "Go slow on the grade," Ken said, and I do, winding through country still ashen from a summer lightning fire. I was driving then, too, heading back to Ken's from a different adventure, when he called to say the freeway was closed at the state line, go a different way. I heed his advice about driving—why not about a horse?

His father once said to me, *You're too goddamned independent for your own good.* "He means you're too independent for *his* own good," said my mother. All that has happened in the last two years has revised this independence. Fear rides in the passenger seat.

Adrenaline-induced fear I know well—cowboying, rowing rapids, jumping out of outrigger canoes into an ocean of sharks and humpback whales. This is different. Though I have directions to the Montana ranch hosting the clinic, I don't know where this road is headed.

A huge log barn and indoor arena mark the facilities as the place I saw online. No one is around. I unload the horses, who spent the night in buffalo pens at the Colorado-Wyoming state line, and tie them to the trailer, wanting to turn them loose, sure they feel as road-weary as I do.

A silver F-250 charges down the road, a man jumps out, asks who I am, and says Andrés will be back in an hour or two. After he speeds away, I pee behind the trailer and let the horses nose through autumn leaves on the lush lawns near the barns. Finally Andrés pulls up with a trailer-load of dude horses and a truck-load of real dudes. A "guest ranch" is sponsoring the clinic—a new name for an old practice of finding ways to help a cattle ranch pay for itself.

Andrés walks toward me, smiling. He's fortyish and handsome in chinks and Wranglers and spurs, his blue eyes sparkling beneath a gray, vaquero-style cowboy hat. "How long have you been waiting?" he asks.

"About three hours."

He shows me the pen in which my horses will live for the week. We get hay and I fill a trough as he walks off to deal with the dude string, muttering about why the boss hadn't just told me where to put the horses.

Fubar and the sorrel gelding drink long at the water, paw at the dust, and nuzzle the hay. Ken's gelding returns to the soft dirt, drops down, and rolls, massaging his back in the dirt, twice rolling completely over—a two-hundred-dollar horse, old-timers would say. The two stay close together while eating, walk to the water trough together, explore the corners of the corral as a pair. They are friends.

As I head to the horse barn to find Andrés, Fubar drops to his knees and then his side, grunting as dirt works into his coat.

The man in the F-250 returns to inform me that the restaurant up the road closes at 7:30, in case I want to eat. Confused, as I paid a fair price for the clinic and accommodations, I hurry to the restaurant–gas station. When I drive past on the way to my room, the horses are eating contentedly, which is more than I can do. Salad and yogurt in the refrigerator, I shower and hit the hay.

The boss-man calls early the next morning. "I'm sorry. You

were supposed to eat with the other guests. You can join them for breakfast." I've already reared up and spun away.

"HE'S A GOOD horse," Andrés says, as he demonstrates with my horse in the round pen, a circular enclosure sixty feet across made of twelve portable panels six feet high set up in the indoor arena. "He's sensitive and quick—he may be too much horse for you."

Watching from the bleachers with the other participants, I feel a red burn at his words. I used to be quick myself, riding fast, spooky horses after wild cattle in rough country, a lifestyle that, of all the people there, only Andrés knows. But not even Andrés sees that reckless girl, just a middle-aged woman afraid of her own horse.

A Japanese woman, who lives in China, rides dressage, and traveled overseas to the clinic with her friend, a British trainer at a Chinese racetrack, looks over at me and smiles.

"He's doing everything he can to get away," Andrés says, as my pretty bay gelding races around the round pen. "He's been hurt, probably beaten, and has no trust of humans. A horse's instinct is to run from trouble, or rear or buck or fight." As Andrés speaks, Fubar runs toward the gate, pushing his nose up over the top rung, eyes and nostrils wide, looking for the way out.

"What did you say his name is?"

I can't think how not to say it. "My son calls him Fubar."

Andrés, from Mexico, has not heard the US military acronym for "fucked up beyond all repair." Although clearly embarrassed by my explanation, he stands calmly in the center of the pen, urging the horse forward, showing Fubar that he can move. Fubar lopes in a circle, trots, sweats. I fidget, scribbling notes in my journal. When Fubar slows, Andrés moves toward his hip, applying pressure across thirty feet of arena dirt. "I want him to use his feet. If he knows how to use his feet, he will not feel trapped."

Fubar moves away, repeating his circle, stopping at the gate to fling his head toward freedom. Andrés moves in the direction of the hip, pushing Fubar away from the gate, to the center and then the outer edge of the round pen.

My feet are getting cold as I sit in the bleachers, the chilly Montana morning slipping in through the gap under the heavy double doors.

"He's beautiful," whispers the racehorse trainer.

And he is—red coat shining, neck arched, black mane and tail flowing with his movement. Lovely in his honesty, his determination to take care of himself blatant and urgent. Escape is all he wants, and he searches for it so hard I hurt. That he should run away and be free is the only answer I can see.

A huge overhead heater starts rumbling as Fubar trots around the circle, his nose still high, his muscles supple under his skin, and the words Andrés speaks are lost to me. I watch Andrés move only when the horse slows, the human body also liquid, his spirit out there dancing with my horse's. Andrés stops, lowering his head and dropping in height just a bit. Fubar slows, his inside eye and a pivoting ear on Andrés, sweat highlighting the deep red of his heaving chest.

Andrés takes a step toward him. I know he sees the details—the eye and ear, the tilt of the head, taut neck, the brace to the outside—and sees that, true to a horse's nature, Fubar has bolting in mind. Andrés stops, takes one step back. Just one. Then he takes a deep breath, sighing aloud. Fubar does the same, visibly relaxing, and Andrés moves a step closer.

Too much.

My breath catches as Fubar rears and spins away, Andrés following him, pushing the horse to show him that he *can* move, there *is* room, he is *not* trapped.

This time when Andrés stops so does Fubar, both sighing

deeply. I think we all do—a big collective sigh. Fubar's head drops a notch, his lips twitching. When Andrés steps toward him he doesn't move off. I lean forward, wanting the horse to lean toward Andrés. Toward safety.

Though still bracing away, Fubar's eye is softer now, almost curious, as Andrés walks slowly to his shoulder and rubs his neck and back firmly but gently. If he patted Fubar with an open hand and any sound at all, the horse would head back to New Mexico. Andrés steps to the point of Fubar's shoulder, reaches under his head, and pulls the outside cheek toward him, turning the animal. Fubar, unsure, finishes the turn to the inside of the round pen and starts trotting around the circle in the other direction. Andrés positions himself near the inside shoulder, girth, hip, whatever keeps the horse moving forward.

Again Andrés stops. He doesn't step to Fubar this time; he turns his back and walks toward the group of us sitting in the bleachers on the other side of the fence. We all lean toward Andrés—even Fubar takes a step toward him. Then he remembers the gate and his quest and spins on his hocks away.

"It's okay," Andrés says through the fence railing. The heater has gone off. I can hear him. "He's learning to use his feet. He's learning to trust."

Quieted by Andrés's voice, Fubar stands still near the gate. We all listen, horse and human. "He doesn't trust because he's been hurt. Somebody has hit him, hurt him, scared him." Andrés peers at me as if reading my past. "He just wants to get away. When he knows he can move without punishment and starts to trust, I will ask more."

Both of Fubar's ears point toward Andrés.

"You see, he wants to trust. He wants a friend."

I glance at the two women who traveled together from China.

~~~

ALL WEEK I watch Andrés work with other horses, and with my two. The others, including the sorrel quarter horse I brought, are younger, their histories with humans known. Most are mustangs, gathered by helicopters off public lands in the West and held in captivity until selected by people wanting to train them for the Mustang Heritage Foundation's Mustang Makeover competitions. These competitions are designed to show off a mustang's intelligence and versatility and help get wild horses adopted. Competitors have a hundred days or so to train a horse and show it in the Makeover; afterwards, the mustangs are auctioned off to the highest bidder. Andrés's boss bids on the quietest horses for his dude string, Andrés furthering their training until they're ready to carry the average un-horsey Joe through the hills of central Montana. Andrés has trained many mustangs. He understands the lean toward wildness.

The mustangs with whom our group is working are not *broke* in the sense of finished bridle horses but they're gentle, having been around our species—and Andrés—enough that they understand their leaders, lead ropes, flags, and personal space. They don't push or crowd the way many backyard horses do. They respond to light pressure and know how to move their feet. Know they *can* move, which keeps them calm. They can trust Andrés because their previous handlers did not harm them.

"I like a mustang." Andrés looks at us. "Their minds are fresh. They have not been mishandled or misused. They do not know to distrust." The mustangs at the clinic, and Ken's little sorrel, trot around the round pen when Andrés presses them but do not show the fear that Fubar exhibits, the desperation. Andrés walks up to them slowly, eases back, approaches, reaches out a hand, rubs a shoulder. If a horse feels pressured, flighty, Andrés steps back, giving the horse space, relieving the pressure.

When Andrés turns his back and walks away, they inevitably hook on—following him around the pen like puppies. A foal learns quickly to follow his mother and band this way—she is his leader, the band his protection. But Fubar just can't let a human be his leader. Sweating, straining against himself, wanting to please yet needing to run, he moves away when there's too much pressure—even too much love.

DETRITUS: UTAH, 2000. *Smith drove from Montana to my house in southeastern Utah and we carpooled with friends to a rally protesting Glen Canyon Dam. Both still clean and sober (and nicotine-free), we stood beside each other above "lake" Powell, where we camped often with the kids, my need for water driving us past the politics behind a dammed river.*

David Brower spoke, rolling to the platform in a wheelchair and standing, with help, at the microphone, apologizing as he had for decades for the part he and the Sierra Club played in damming the Colorado River and condemning Glen Canyon (he died five months after the rally), and Katie Lee, eighty years old and looking fabulous in leggings and a T-shirt, sang. (She died in 2018, at ninety-three. She never stopped fighting for her river.)

We parked our trucks and set up tents in the campground at Lee's Ferry, the most sedate campsite I had ever stayed in with Smith. But I wasn't with Smith anymore. People built a bonfire down by the boat ramp and drank as Katie Lee sang more. Ken Sleight—known as inspiration for Edward Abbey's Seldom Seen Smith in The Monkey Wrench Gang—*appeared out of the darkness and told us how he first met Abbey right there at Lee's Ferry, Ken rigging for a Grand Canyon trip, Abbey the river ranger. They started talking and drinking beer and continued talking and drinking for the rest of that night. For the rest of Abbey's life.*

The river near, the stars brilliant, Smith was in heaven, and so was I. We didn't share a tent or a truck and dawn still produced a pink so fragile I was afraid breathing might make it disappear.

Smith came down to Moab another time to visit Tyler and me and join us in honoring Abbey ten years after his death. Ken Sleight was hosting the event at his beloved Pack Creek Ranch and invited me to read alongside Ellen Meloy, Sleight, and some other desert writers. Smith sat in the audience with ten-year-old Tyler and our friends as if no time, hurt, or divorce had passed between us. His presence felt as natural to me as swimming.

When I introduced him to Ellen Meloy, she said, "What do you call him?"

"Smith?" I said, unsure what she meant.

"You have to have a way to introduce him, so that people will know how you're related."

"Oh, well," I said, "he's my best ex."

And he still is today.

ON THE FOURTH day, Andrés does groundwork with Fubar as I carry my heavy western saddle from the tack room into the arena through the big doors, the chill of the shifting season following me inside. When Andrés leads Fubar over, I brush his back with my hand, cherishing the warmth even as I feel his muscles tighten at my touch. The turquoise-and-red saddle blanket compliments his blood-bay, and my saddle flies up onto his back as if I've been saddling horses for years. Which I have. So why does angst roil through me this time, even with Andrés standing at Fubar's head to calm us both?

Stepping up, I feel the burn in my left knee. I need to be careful.

"Trot him out," Andrés says, and I post in time with Fubar's rhythm, forgetting my knee in the freedom of movement. "Lope him," Andrés says.

Fubar wants to go faster than I want him to and I check him up, trying to collect us both, losing the blend.

"Just ride him," Andrés says. "He needs to move his feet."

Fuck his feet, I want to say.

He *is* a lot of horse—I can feel his strength gathering beneath me like a big cat. I know he knows I'm afraid. So does Andrés, who keeps talking to me, guiding me, calming me the same way he does my horse. I relax a bit more.

Then it's time to get off. Graceful dismounting still difficult due to surgery, I stumble a tiny bit when I touch down and before I can think one word Fubar has stepped on my foot and kicked me in the thigh and is running loose across the pen, stirrups flapping.

Andrés escorts me outside the round pen, where I sit on a log as he works with my horse. I can't quell the sadness flooding up inside me, can't stop the run of tears down my face. Ken is right—Fubar is too much horse for me.

When the morning session finally ends, the two horse-women from China walk over. They speak quietly. One touches my shoulder. I don't recoil. We know that the tears are not from the toe blackening inside my boot or the hoof-shaped swelling on my thigh; rather, the tears are a form of grief that comes, sometimes, with surrender.

Andrés hands me Fubar's lead rope and my beautiful bay horse follows me quietly. I unsaddle him without issue. When I turn him loose he moves quickly away. I go to the sorrel gelding and put my face to his neck, breathing deeply, then follow the two women to the dining room for lunch, hooking on, apparently in need of a friend.

Over salads and sandwiches we talk about the ethics of selling a horse with problems, the risk of him landing in the hands of someone who might damage him further. Taking him back to the ranch is not an option. The women understand the unspoken, as well: I am not thirty anymore, cowboying with my husband, quick enough to stay out of wrecks most of the time, malleable enough to survive those wrecks that are unavoidable. They understand the understated: Fubar is too much horse for the me of today.

~~~

"HE's A GOOD horse," Andrés repeats, even after the kick, so at supper the last night, which also happens to be Andrés's birthday, I present the gift of Fubar. The horse of course is not present in the rustic dining room—what a wreck that would have been as he vaulted log furnishings to escape through the large glass doors—but I cause a wreck anyway.

Flanked by the women from China, I make the public announcement: *Happy birthday; I am giving you my horse.* Andrés accepts shyly. The boss is pissed. In the week we've been watching Andrés work with horses, we also watched how his employers worked with Andrés. While we see Andrés as a brilliant horseman, and maybe they do, too, they seem to want him to think he's an immigrant from Mexico, period. I upend the status quo by giving a beautiful registered quarter horse to Andrés, who can see the fear and work with it, letting Fubar run off because eventually he will come back to himself. And he will come to Andrés, who will give him a new name.

ANDRÉS's BOSS WANTED to buy Ken's sorrel gelding for the dude string and I called Ken. The boss agreed to Ken's price of $2,000. The next morning, as Andrés and I hook up my trailer, the boss's wife approaches. "We discussed the horse last night," she says. "My husband said he's willing to pay you $1,500."

Andrés and I exchange looks. I walk off and call Ken again. From the wind in the phone I can tell he's ahorseback, and smile. Modern-day cowboy. I return to where Andrés and the woman stand waiting.

"My son says to tell you he'll sell the horse for $1,500." I pause. "But not to you." A lesson in cowboy ethics: you don't agree to a price one day and lower your offer the next.

She looks as if I'd slapped her.

Haltering the sorrel gelding, I wish I could hug Fubar good-bye, but know I can't without a struggle. As I lead the gelding from the corral, Fubar rushes to the fence, whinnying after us. Andrés helps me load the sorrel and I start the nine-hundred-mile drive away, Fubar's voice following us out the long driveway, piercing my heart. The sorrel was his friend.

7

MUSTANG DUST

THE COLORADO PLATEAU IS SHAPED LIKE A HEART. NOT THE childhood hearts that frame the initials of someone you once had a crush on, or I *heart* NY, but the human heart, the muscle that pumps life through a body. The 130,000-square-mile Colorado Plateau, which encompasses parts of New Mexico, Arizona, Utah, and Colorado, is that muscle, its river system pumping life through a major portion of the West.

I had long been gone from the Southwest when, running from the rattling grief that followed the deaths of Rebecca and my fathers, I returned to a place I thought I knew. But I went to the wrong desert.

With Cojo I flew across the ocean and drove east on I-40, the buckling asphalt near the border inspection station past Needles so familiar, like the private place on the Colorado River, the ancient maze hidden in obscurity in the thin Mojave soil, the redrocks east of Kingman, and the faint line of the Grand Wash cliffs that marked the nearness of the Colorado Plateau, and home. I thought that was where I was going.

I knew the geologic western parameter of the Colorado Plateau but forgot, in sadness or spinning or desperate fleeing, about the eastern perimeter. Just simply forgot about it. Until I'd gone past it in miles or months and looked up suddenly, head rising above dull emotion for a moment the way the San

Francisco Peaks rise above the clouds, and saw the difference: the Santa Fe Group with its muted hues and crumbling rocks was not the redrock of my heart.

It wasn't only grief that threw me. I'd been in Hawai'i so long I'd forgotten that the American Southwest is not one desert but several. Many. The Mojave Desert. The Sonoran and Chihuahuan Deserts. The Painted Desert and Great Basin. Had I looked up Santa Fe or Taos, I'd have learned in minutes what it took me months to decipher. The rivers and rocks tell of a geologic phenomenon, as rivers and rocks tend to do. Pressure and movement within the tectonic plate caused the Earth's lithosphere to thin and split, creating the Rio Grande rift, a series of north-trending rift valleys and basins in New Mexico and southern Colorado. The Rio Grande rift borders the Colorado Plateau, but bordering something, edges touching like skin, does not make one the other. The Rio Grande rift, with its attractive Spanish towns and solid old pueblos, huge basalt blocks and delicate pink shale, is no more Colorado Plateau than the North American tectonic plate is the Pacific plate.

Standing on the lānai of the casita, looking up, I can see that the pink shale of the New Mexico canyon is beautiful against the clear blue of that desert sky, but I do not love it. The basalt boulders that make walks difficult—for the dogs and for me—I do not like much at all, or the cholla that jumps out and pokes legs and feet each time we get too close. And the Rio Grande flows the wrong way—toward the wrong ocean.

No matter how hard I have tried to make it so, the rift is not my desert.

I'VE ALREADY BEEN driving around. Staying within a day's drive of Ken, I move out in circles, heading west from my non-Colorado Plateau place to Arizona, the rez, up into Utah and Colorado, back down, the circles big or little, it doesn't matter:

I'm on a quest, spiraling out across the desert looking for the next place to land.

When Andrés calls I'm in a hidden valley three hours west of Santa Fe, and pull to the side of the gravel road to listen. We have stayed in touch in the months following the horsemanship clinic. "The boss is still mad about the horse," he tells me. "He won't let me keep him at the ranch. Now he wants me to pay rent for the house we're living in."

Usually in a ranch job like his, or Ken's, housing and utilities are provided. "What did you tell him?"

"I said no. I quit."

I turn off the engine. Let the dogs out. Smell the ponderosas in the breeze. "What are you going to do?"

"I want to train horses, do clinics. I want to work with mustangs, training them for Mustang Makeovers. We want to come to Santa Fe."

I tell him where I am. "I just looked at some property."

It won't work—a sweet house, perfect for one person, tucked into a small box canyon with a hundred acres on a mesa above it, the climb too steep for a horse, for me. No room for an arena, or a family.

WATCHING ANDRÉS URGING horses around the round pen with small body movements, and trotting after Ken across the plains, something in my own body has stirred—I want to be the confident cowgirl I used to be, following in the stirrups of my grandmother. Or maybe it's bigger—I want to be somebody not haunted by sadness. *Someone else.* But I'm not someone else. I'm me.

I call my realtor friend Trish, who finds Santa Fe property that will suit Andrés and his family: indoor arena with attached stalls and pens enough to accommodate a dozen horses, a modest modular for the family, cheap, an hour and a half from Ken.

Papers signed, the property in escrow, I fly to Montana. Andrés picks me up at the small Billings airport on the bluff above the city. We don't know each other well enough to bridge shyness and language gaps for the whole two-hour drive to the ranch.

A U-Haul truck is parked in the driveway, next to the gooseneck trailer already hooked up to his big diesel dually.

And there is Fubar, in a clean pen under the shade of the barn roof. Andrés calls him Howard. The horse looks good though the name doesn't suit him. Nor does Fubar, not anymore. Andrés has cowboyed on him all over the mountains, moving 1,200 cows up to summer country (with dudes in tow), and 1,200 pairs back down to winter in the lowlands. Fubar/Howard is fit and relaxed, his hip cocked. I slip through the fence. He moves away, but not far. Settling for a rub on his shoulder, I go back through the fence to Andrés and his family, joining the procession stuffing plastic bags of clothing and bedding on top of a couch inside the U-Haul.

We caravan almost a thousand miles, Andrés driving the U-Haul truck and me following in the diesel dually, towing the horses. His wife and kids and a Chihuahua ride with me, Andrés's border collies in the truckbed amid saddles and bicycles. My passengers thrill when the radio picks up Mexican music stations but I want silence. I need to think. Trish just called—there's a problem with the survey on the property. The actual property boundary runs through the horse pens and a corner of the house.

Trish finds us a place to leave the horses. Andrés and his family stay with friends in Santa Fe. I drive the diesel truck and trailer to the casita in its narrow canyon. The next day we go to the property. The seller's realtor shows us the stakes and pink tape that cut off the corners of things. Trish and I trail the procession, whispering about what to do. I back out of escrow, failing to see the red flag of relief as a sign.

Andrés is handsome and charming and he likes my horse, and he's fifteen years younger than me, with a beautiful wife and kids. I am not in love with him, yet I have to take him home. In the shade of narrowleaf cottonwoods we set up the dog panels that rode tightly cinched to the side of the trailer. Andrés and his family and the Chihuahua stay in a casita next door, sharing the queen-sized bed and pullout couch. Or maybe some are on the floor. I don't know. I don't go inside. Not even inside myself to figure out what to do next.

Sometimes when you're lost you know where you are and you know it's not where you meant to be. Sometimes you look at your feet and the trees around you or the redrock all the same contour and color and you don't know your way out. Sometimes the signs are backwards. My fathers have been dead two years. I am so far away from myself I don't even know I'm lost.

I ride the momentum like a wave. Trish finds another horse property. The dirt road passes redrock on the way in. Andrés's wife says she wants the kitchen remodeled.

"Fuck her," says the man I have started seeing.

They have emptied the U-Haul into a storage unit. We find a house for them to rent in Santa Fe while the kids start school. Andrés looks for work but he can't read or write English and no one will hire him—he's a star in his own arena but not in Santa Fe. We ride the pale pink hills together, me on Fubar aka Howard, the horse in need of a name, Andrés on another gelding beside me. Fubar and I stay calm in Andrés's presence. Fear follows me home.

Andrés and I cowboy with Ken, once, Andrés on the sorrel colt, me on Howard. We ride drag, trailing the herd, timing our movements with those of the other cowboys at the back of the pack. Ken, riding point at the shoulder of the herd, stops and watches the cows amble across the shortgrass prairie. He watches us, watches Andrés working the sorrel, the colt tucking his chin and getting his butt under himself as he steps backward.

I know Ken sees a trainer more focused on the horse he rides than on the cattle we drive, while I see Andrés maneuvering cattle by positioning his horse near a cow's hip, girth, or shoulder, knowing she'll move away from pressure. Andrés doesn't need to whoop and holler and run back and forth like the other cowboys (not Ken); with body not voice he moves the cows and the sorrel learns not to crowd them. But instead of seeing low-stress cattle handling, Ken sees Andrés manipulating me with pressure of one sort or another.

I want to talk to Rebecca. Or Ed. I talk to Trish and our friend Wendy Beth, an attorney and smart. They urge me to step out of the mess.

I don't talk to Ken about it.

Finally Andrés decides to take his family back to Montana, where he can get a job cowboying. He asks for money, actually using the words.

"Fuck him," says my man friend.

"Tell him no and send him on his way," says Wendy Beth. "Or give him money and send him away. Either way, let him go."

I write Andrés a check and he drives off, family, dogs, and horses in tow, Howard in the trailer with the rest of the dream.

WITH ANDRÉS IN Montana and Ken busy on the other side of the Sangre de Cristo, the dread of spending another winter in the dark canyon starts choking me. When Andrés calls to tell me he still wants to work with mustangs, and with me, I can't see the signs lined up like incorrect property boundaries, or hear Ken's words of warning—Ken doesn't want me giving possibility away to a stranger. I have that orange film over my eyes again, like watching the eclipse through those funny glasses in Grand Canyon. I resume my search for a place that might accommodate everyone—except I'm not on the list. Grief can do that. It can take you out.

I look at a horse ranch in southwestern Colorado. Ken doesn't want to go. The boyfriend goes, and Trish. They see endless possibilities. I see orange.

I TAKE TO my truck one fall morning and drive away from the problems I'm creating. Three border collies on the folded-down seat behind me, a long empty highway under my tires, I drive. For miles. Hours. A memory drifts in through an open window: sitting on a slab of red sandstone watching boaters run Class IV rapids. Years and deaths have dulled the picture but ponderosa pines and redrock show through. Several times I turn off the highway in search of the place but each turn I take does not get me there.

Then I feel it. A shimmer. I *know* the Dolores River is running along somewhere below the vast mesa, know that even though it's flowing north-northwest it's going in the right direction because it will empty into the Colorado River, and I know just where. I leave the highway again, turning right toward the river.

Turning right is the rightist thing I've done in a long time. A wrong time. Heading across a tabletop of farmland, miles of plowed fields framed in big sagebrush and spreading toward horizons everywhere, distant island mountains jutting up here and there, I can feel the redrock and pine trees clutching my heart the way roots clasp canyon walls and I keep driving, sensing I've been on this road before.

Glimpses through piñon pines and Utah junipers show a red sheen to the earth; beyond that, a big valley and distant mountains. And then, boom, the world falls away, the way it does when you approach the Gorge Bridge outside of Taos and find yourself suspended hundreds of feet above the Rio Grande, or follow 89A toward the Vermilion Cliffs and the Arizona Strip and suddenly you see *it* beneath you—the Colorado River deep in Marble Canyon, prelude to Grand Canyon. Out of the farming fields I go, a slight drop in elevation, redrock visible on the far reaches and then, there, the world drops off, the serpentine road coiling somewhere below, just me alone with the dogs and the gods in a truck on a road that disappears beneath us as we face the edge of a world gone away. My heart fills and soars as the valley grows beyond redrock layers and I do the only thing I can think to do—pull off the road and stop in red dirt, to find and follow my heart.

Cojo can leap into but not out of the truck. I lift him down. Bow, now three-legged, can jump out but I will have to lift him back in. Reed, a new border collie cross, can leap anywhere. As the dogs head into the redrock world on parallel adventures, I bend beneath juniper branches to follow a shallow arroyo toward a lip of red cliff that overhangs the valley below.

Natural etchings in the floor of the wash indicate that heavy summer monsoons have repeatedly scrubbed it clean. The wash itself meanders like water through rock, heading ultimately downward. I want to bathe in its red dust as if it were a river. Instead I rub a wet finger on redrock and grains of fine sand find my tongue. Gritty and salty sun-warmed silt.

Sunshine on my back, the desert on my skin, hair catching in juniper branches, piñon pine needles and basin big sage brushing familiar scents over my shoulders and shorts, I do not think of Andrés. I do not think of my sons. The dogs moving at their different paces, we continue toward the edge until finally I realize that the bursting within is not my lungs filled with warm autumn air but that muscle of heart hammering through me—
the Colorado Plateau.

I call the dogs and we turn back to the truck and the road. A two-thousand-foot descent takes us through layers of geology that tell stories I can't remember or never knew. Slowing for the hairpin turns around great chunks of sandstone, we head toward the valley below—a vast shadow between far mountain peaks, cliff faces lining an interior perimeter. Piñon and juniper punctuate rock, roots chasing moisture through stone for so many years that stones and trees have become inseparable. Indian ricegrass waves delicately in the wind.

At the bottom of the switchbacks stand empty corrals, long stacks of one-ton hay bales, and a low stucco building. Cattle and horse smells come in through the windows. And there is the Dolores River, the water not high, not low, just a slow meander around a bend and away.

Beyond the bridge the five-dollar-a-day parking lot for boaters launching at the Slick Rock put-in is fenced off and locked up, the faded, hand-painted sign still there.

No other vehicles behind us on the potholed two-lane highway—I've seen but two in the last hour—I stop near the river, the dogs weaving through coyote willows to get to water that foretells the changing seasons: summer monsoons past, winter approaching. Bow takes his river bites while Cojo laps at the edges. Reed leaps across but makes it partway, splashing to the other side and back. They all smell like wet dog now and I could put them in the bed of the truck on this isolated stretch of road but I want their company. They usually want mine.

I've missed the sought-for canyon and keep going. In earlier years I didn't see this valley beyond its river and now I follow the road instead of the river and then make another right turn. Another right move.

Unsure if I'm trespassing, I stop to look around. The redrock through which I drove as I made the sharp descent stops at the valley's western end, the giant sandstone blocks and massive rounded boulders evidence of a geologic phenomenon I have yet to remember. Though clues lie around me like potsherds from my past I do not see that the valley mirrors, in geologic history if not the same geologic formations, two Colorado Plateau valleys in which I previously lived. Only the words *Mancos Shale* come to mind.

Fall's yellow grasses, some salt-desert shrubs, and a few junipers speckle the grayish soil. White mineral and salt deposits line old puddles. Rabbitbrush blooms bright yellow along drainages. Green mountains line the valley's southern flank, long and flat like the hay bales and building we just passed. Aspens grow up high, their leaves turning in groves, as do ponderosas, the darker conifers underscored by the burnt-orange hue of fall-touched Gambel oak. Near the valley's eastern end, random cliffs tower over ash-colored slopes of Mancos Shale.

I decide to do something conservative: I look at a map. Follow the route I've taken. Hawai'i and California on the perimeter, Arizona, Utah, and New Mexico part of the spiral, I am in southwestern Colorado. A *Dolores River Guide*, purchased some twenty years before and hastily stashed with the map in my truck, says the Dolores changes from a "fairly clean" river to one of the Southwest's dirtiest after its confluence with Disappointment Creek. When living in Utah before Hawai'i I had watched the Colorado River change color with the inflowing Dolores at the confluence above Dewey Bridge. That that color comes from a tributary draining a valley in which I find myself these many years later—now *that* is magic, the lives flanking Hawai'i suddenly connected, bridged by a river.

Map and memories in my lap, I look at the rise of mountains to the west. If the Colorado River is just over there, 130 river miles away, that spine of mountain peaks is . . . La Sal Mountains! The same island mountains I looked upon each morning as I awoke in a Utah valley in that other life, a big yellow wolf-dog sprawled across my bed. I'm just on the other side.

DRIVING ON UP the gravel road, the current dogs panting behind me from enthusiasm not thirst, I pant, too, wanting to stick my head out the window and wag my tail. I don't know how that feels to a dog but I can feel the wag all through me—a buzz, an energy wanting out. Having a tail would help. My heart thumps instead.

We cross some dry creekbeds and round a bend. An old log house appears near a barn and panel corrals and I think *oh!* and maybe say it aloud after a sharp intake of breath the way I did as a kid when I saw a dog I wanted—which was any dog—and my mother would scold me for scaring her, but now only the dogs I have hear me as I covet the ranch house nesting near giant cottonwoods and drive on, dried grasses and rabbitbrush bright with color along the road, cottonwoods just barely yellowing marking the creek, the backdrop of rimrock and promontories and distant mountains shifting and changing with perspective. The valley grows more rugged, arroyos and ridges crisscrossing as the piñon pine and juniper woodland thickens, maybe indicating a rise in elevation, possibly in precipitation.

A couple of miles farther, a blur moves into the middle of the view.

It's a movement of color not gray and muted green like the valley or the dark green and orange of the autumn mountains or watery blue like the desert sky but dark and sharply contrasting light. It steps slowly into my vision, slower still into my brain. Again I stop the truck. Right there in the middle of the road. Not looking behind me or caring if the third car of the afternoon evolves in my dust. Without taking my eyes from the black-and-white movement on the gray hillside I reach for my field glasses.

The dogs clamor to the window, noses aquiver. I turn off the truck, slowly open the door. Standing with elbows braced against the window frame to steady my vision, I bring the binoculars to my eyes.

Across the road, on the other side of a barbed-wire fence, on the other side of a broad arroyo from me: wild horses.

They tell their wildness in their arched necks, lithe bodies, and the way they look askance—at me, my truck, the dogs at the window?—nostrils wide, testing, not like Fubar, afraid, but like deer, wary. Prey animals alert to danger.

The pinto stallion, black and white and wild, stops and sniffs the air, snorting as he stares across distance at truck dogs me. He shakes his head and moves on at a brisk trot over the chalky gray hill, nose up, his tail a banner of color. A bay mare follows with her pinto colt. A long yearling, dark bay but for white streaks on his withers and flank, and two pinto mares follow the first mare and colt. Truck motor ticking, the breeze holding my breath and theirs, I stand in the middle of an empty road in the middle of a huge no longer empty valley in the middle of my life watching wild horses until even the dust from their hooves on the powdery gray trail disappears.

8

Mi Corazón

The next time I enter the valley I don't see wild horses, though I look. And I'm not alone. A Colorado realtor drives. We meet another realtor at a gate.

Researching wild horses online, I came upon photographs of a cabin, a creek, cottonwoods water rock and sky. The rock was not the deeper red sandstone visible from the crown of Slick Rock Hill; nevertheless, before I got anywhere near the end of forty-six pics, I knew I wanted *that* place above *that* creek in *that* valley placed within *the* Colorado Plateau.

From the gate near the gravel-and-dirt county road—the same road from which I first saw the pinto band—I can barely see the cabin roof. The dirt road in is almost half a mile long. The sellers' realtor wants to show off the cabin but I don't want to go inside. Not yet. My realtor settles into an Adirondack chair on the porch while the other man paces. I hasten to the edge of the cliff to look down at the creek. October puddles and the tiniest trickle sing up to me. I sit down on a rock, and look.

Through years of seasonal flash floods, huge flat slabs of sandstone have broken free from the ledges and slid down banks to the present-day riverbed, which is lined with orange-tinged willows and cottonwoods with leaves turning gold. Across the creek, thick sagebrush grows on a bench once riverbed, rimmed by the same kind of rock on which I sit. Piñon and juniper woodlands stretch away toward that long ponderosa-and-aspen-cloaked ridge called the Glade. Farthest view to the west, La Sal Mountains in Utah. To the east, peaks I don't know. On the near side of the creek, sheep pens on the flat below the ledge bespeak a more recent history.

The seller's realtor clears his throat behind me. I shake my head to clear it, and follow him. The contemporary tale is in the dwelling itself. Two couples purchased the property and built the cabin with obvious care down to each pleasing detail. Two of the four are attorneys out of LA. Someone is ill. That's all their realtor discloses of their story, but what he doesn't say speaks up the loudest: clearly they love this place.

Made like the Lincoln-log cabins my sisters and I built when we were little, it's a thousand square feet, with two small bedrooms and a bathroom (indoor plumbing!), the rest of the space one room. A steep ladder reaches to a loft in which my sons could not stand fully. The golden logs, ponderosa floors, aspen ceilings, and ash cabinets with terracotta-colored cement countertops all give off a welcoming glow. A woodstove centers the room. Inside and out, it's the kind of place you don't want to leave.

I'm a silent passenger in my realtor's truck as he drives us out of the valley the opposite way from which I'd originally come, on a dirt road that passes by crimson-and-russet slopes of gambel oak tapering toward wind-sculpted rimrock, and then curls up through aspens vivid with autumn yellows and golds to meadows where cattle are being gathered for their trek down to winter grazing grounds.

The realtor asks what I think.

"I love it," I say. "But." I need an arena and round pen. Barn with stalls. *Andrés said he would come.*

THE FACILITIES AT the Colorado horse ranch include a large horse barn, small indoor arena, roping arena, and large round pen (seven-foot-high walls and eighty feet across)—plenty of room and choices for Andrés to train as many horses as he wants. A house for him sits near the horse barn. Beyond stands of piñon and juniper, down an aspen-lined lane, a house for me. And one for Ken. Or a renter.

I name the ranch Cachuma for my great-aunt and -uncle, Sister and Ed Janeway, and their ranch in Santa Ynez Valley. For that tie to California. Keith and I lived on that ranch for a time, running cattle in the backcountry. Kenney started there.

For many years I thought cachuma was a Chumash word meaning "bear." Maybe Sister or Ed told me that. I have since learned that the spelling of the Chumash word is aqitsu'm. It's the name of an early Chumash village, Spanishized into cachuma, and means "sign." That it refers to spiritual signs not road signs is my guess, though sometimes those point in the same direction. And sometimes they don't.

I make it through the first winter at Cachuma Ranch, sometimes alone, sometimes with the boyfriend. I have dogs and horses. I buy hay and feed hay and ruin hay when the barn floods when it rains after snowing two feet. I tweak my back and tell no one until the boyfriend shows up and finds me struggling to put on my own socks. He helps me dress and feed and moves the hay to a dry part of the barn. He makes snow piles and frees up drainages, balancing ranch work and me with his life in Albuquerque.

He's a contractor and didn't finish middle school. I stop writing more than journal entries and don't read a single book.

FROM THE HIGHPOINT of Cachuma Ranch, four states are visible, mountain ranges landmarking each: to the east, Colorado's La Plata Mountains, part of the San Juans; the Mesa Verde mountains directly across the valley to the south; the Chuska, Lukachukai, and Carrizo Mountains in New Mexico and Arizona to the southwest; and the Abajos or Blue Mountains of Utah to the west. Even the Bears Ears show. And of course Sleeping Ute, rising between Cachuma and the Four Corners Monument on the Navajo Nation. The town of Dolores rests in a canyon nearby; beyond it, the San Miguels and Telluride. The Dolores River flows through Dolores town and is captured by McPhee Reservoir; when released, the river heads northwest to Utah, curving around the north side of the laccolithic La Sal Mountains. Along the way it picks up the salty, silty flow of Disappointment Creek.

The outdoor-loving crowd in the area keeps a steady demand on local organic and holistic farmers and ranchers. At a Saturday farmers' market, I ask a couple about their grass-fed, grass-finished beef. It's easy to be misguided, as grass *fed* does not always mean grass *finished.*

"I've been raising grass-finished beef for fifty years," the husband says, which means he's stayed traditional, not getting sidetracked by the feedlot industry or the practice of finishing cattle on grain. "We finish the heifers and steers on our ranch up the road."

Even a bunch of irrigated acres is not enough to maintain a cow herd of the size necessary to produce as much beef as their ranch does, but the rancher spares me the embarrassment of asking too many questions. "We also run cattle in Disappointment Valley."

"Disappointment Valley? I *love* Disappointment Valley." I've seen their cows—I've been back several times.

They look at me strangely—apparently not that many people say they love Disappointment.

"We drive them up the valley to the forest in April or May—about thirty miles."

I know it's a dead end but blunder into it anyway. "If you ever want any help. . . ." When Keith and I ran cattle, people often offered to help. We rarely accepted. We could pretty much do it all ourselves, with our dogs, and found inexperienced help usually more problematic than beneficial. During branding season it was different—we'd go anywhere to rope calves in the branding pen, and had big brandings of our own, trading labor with the neighbors. In New Mexico Ken calls it *neighboring*. But who, besides my son, would ever invite *me* to help—an unknown, older-than-middle-aged woman, likely a dude mounted on a dud?

"I looked at a place for sale in Disappointment Valley," I say, hoping to deflect attention from my faux pas.

He doesn't ask which one. He knows. Disappointment is a big valley with only a few people in it. "You ought to buy it," he says.

I tell him about the horse ranch. "The trainer's coming in the spring."

I leave the farmers' market with five pounds of grass-finished beef and a stomachache.

WEEKS LATER, AT a film fundraiser for a river advocacy group, the rancher appears in the doorway of a crowded room in the Dolores Public Library. The only seat left happens to be next to me. He nods but clearly doesn't recognize me from the farmers' market. It turns out his ranch is featured in the documentary. "I bet you didn't know you were sitting next to a movie star," he whispers.

When the movie and Q&A are over, I introduce myself, reminding him of our conversation about Disappointment Valley.

He says, "That cabin's still for sale."

I've learned that the 160-acre property with the cabin borders a Bureau of Land Management herd management area—BLM land on which mustangs roam. Hence the presence of the pinto band I saw. *They could be my neighbors,* I think.

"We could be neighbors," he says. "You never know. It's been for sale for a couple of years." He gives me a name. "His number's in the book. Call him. Just talk to him."

I feel a shimmer. I want to wag my tail. A sign.

Even so, it takes some weeks for me to get up the courage to call, and David Temple is so nice on the phone, but I feel terrible.

"My wife died six weeks ago," he says.

"I'm so sorry. I didn't know."

"Let's talk about the cabin," he says.

I DRIVE DOWN the switchbacks toward the valley, intending to look for mustangs and mosey past the property, maybe see the cabin roof, and there's the rancher on a tractor at the Slick Rock corrals, loading one-ton hay bales onto an old flatbed truck. I stop and wait as he climbs down, still long and lanky and fit in his early seventies.

"Howdy neighbor," he says, when he sees it's me.

"Not yet, but I'm working on it."

"I've got to go feed; hop in." A couple of miles past the river he turns off the empty two-lane highway and maneuvers the big truck up a hill to his cows. "You drive," he says, climbing out and up onto the hay. I slide over and put the truck in low, crawling along as he pushes large flakes to the line of cattle strung out behind us.

How many times have I done this in years past? My kids in car seats, the truck in granny gear, I would jump out and onto the truckbed and back into the cab if the unmanned truck got too close to a ditch or tree.

When he's finished, he drives down to the highway as I look out the window at a life I once had.

"Have you checked your water gaps? My cows will be going past your place soon. We better go check your water gaps."

We exchange the big flatbed for a three-quarter-ton Chevy and he drives up the valley to the place that isn't mine. We walk across BLM land the short distance from the property gate to the east water gap, and then the longer distance to the downstream one. Made of hot-wire mesh tape stretched across the creek (which high-water marks indicate is sometimes a river), streamers hanging, the juice comes from solar-powered batteries attached to fence posts presumably above even the highest high-water flows.

The idea of a water gap is that water will move through a loose restraint, but not cows. "Colorado's a fence-out state," the rancher tells me. "These are your responsibility." Meaning that if the property becomes mine and his cows get through a downed fence or washed-out water gap, the loss of feed or any damage the cattle might cause is *my* problem.

The water gaps are intact, free of reaching coyote willows that could ground them, the batteries charged and working.

On the way back to Slick Rock and my truck, the rancher sees vehicles in the yard of the ranch headquarters I coveted on my first impetuous drive up the valley. And then he sees TJ. "You have to meet her," he says, pulling into the yard and rolling his window down as TJ approaches. She's trim and tall with wild, shoulder-length hair, which she says is red but I couldn't see it until I started paying closer attention to horse color. Sorrel comes in different shades, TJ's mane among them.

The rancher gestures at me. "She's the one buying the cabin."

TJ smiles. "I've heard about you." What she's heard I can't imagine.

Later I will learn that David Temple's wife, Pati, who died so recently, was one of TJ's most treasured friends.

THE NEXT TIME I see TJ, I'm pushing cattle up the valley with the rancher, his crew, and Andrés—who said he was coming and now he's here. He brought Howard who was Fubar with him, and that's who I'm riding. Andrés is on Ken's sorrel colt. It's late April and the second day of a three-day, thirty-mile cattle drive.

Though the cowboys and I ride across the valley in full sunlight, it's miserably cold. I'm still not acclimated after years on Maui, my clothing inadequate. I didn't even think of long underwear, and, I'm embarrassed to say, I hadn't heard of baselayers. I have no hat and am grateful for my thick hair, which I still say is blond though others see gray. Lined elk-hide gloves do not keep my fingers warm. Even Andrés, down from Montana, shivers as the wind whips unobstructed across the valley.

A neighbor's Black Angus bull is in with the rancher's cows, and he asks Andrés to sort the bull off. I'm told to stay up on a hill—the rancher quickly figured out that Andrés is a hand; I, on the other hand, am a woman, slated to stay out of the way.

For a minute I stay where I'm told, but when Andrés glances up I take it as invitation enough and guide Fubar down the hill, where I see TJ hiding behind a truck so as not to spook the cattle, her camera with a long telephoto lens clicking away. Andrés steps in behind the bull while I hold back cows, and when the bull tries to slip past me Fubar pivots back and forth on his hind end and my hips twist with him in hip-hop motion, the supple gyrations of a good cow horse working up through my torso. Between Andrés and the sorrel colt and Fubar and me, the bull moves away from pressure and into the pen. I shiver with success, rightness, cold.

Andrés ties up his horse and goes with the rancher to haul the bull back to its own pasture. I tie Fubar beside the sorrel, loosening the cinch so he can catch his breath, and join TJ in her truck, its motor humming and heater blasting. I ask her if mustangs are introduced, feral.

Her hair springs loose from her visor as she shakes her head and frowns. "No. They are native and they are *wild*." This is the beginning of a conversation that has spanned years.

WHY DID *EQUUS caballus* die out in North America 7,600 to 10,000 years ago, after fifty-five million years of adaptations and survival? In the Pleistocene, within three million years of evolution into *Equus*, twelve species of horses in four groups migrated to several continents. During the earlier Miocene, nineteen species of horses lived in North America. In the multitude of years that followed, huge herds thrived in what are today the Great Plains. And Texas. Even Florida. Horses crossed the Bering land bridge, back and forth. They survived the freeze of the last Ice Age, a global phenomenon with glaciated fronts in Greenland, Canada, and other parts of North America. In the Pleistocene Epoch, dire wolves, saber-toothed cats, and mammoths were wiped out, which brings us to the combination of climate change and Clovis culture and the theory of Pleistocene overkill.

Clovis hunters roamed the coast of North America and eventually turned inland, according to Clovis point findings, the first one in Clovis, New Mexico. Within a few thousand years, of Clovis arrival, give or take, it's said that in only about a thousand years thirty species of megafauna disappeared. Locations of unearthed Clovis points, locations of the stone sources from which they were made, and DNA show that Clovis people moved around a lot, and ate a lot of meat, including horse meat. A jaw of a butchered horse dating back twenty-four-thousand years was found in Bluefish Caves in Yukon Territory in 2017, which tells us that there were pre-Clovis humans here, as well. (Even those dates for the first people in North America are conflicting, or, better said, evolving.)

Did Clovis hunters kill and eat *all* the horses, which equaled about one third of the megafauna population? While bones of most or all of the different horse incarnations have been found up and down the Americas, no large kill sites of *E. caballus* have been discovered, just bones scattered by the people who gnawed on them. Additional environmental factors after the Ice Age are likely part of the equation.

From the fourteen-toed dawn horse, to *Parahippus*—near horse—whose molars would continue to grind for decades and whose hindgut developed to process the tough grasses coevolving on the plains, to *Merychippus*, who started in the Miocene Epoch with three toes on each foot and ended with one toe, or hoof, on each leg, to *Dinohippus*—terrible horse—who died off about twelve million years ago, came *Equus caballus*. For fifty-five million years, horses have adapted to change, enduring geologic upheavals, dramatic weather variations, natural disasters, predators of immense size, human-sized predators, forests turning to grasslands, grass types changing from C3 to C4, and much, much more, all of which contributed to their evolution.

We know because of the many archaeological findings in Wyoming, California, Alaska, British Columbia, practically everywhere, that horses lived in North America for fifty-five million years, plus or minus the last ten thousand. Maybe *Equus caballus* of, say, thirteen thousand years ago and a mustang of today do not look like siblings of the same parents, but they are related. *Equus caballus* stood about 13.2 hands, the size of my grandchildren's mustangs, both of whom are full grown at twenty years old. One came from Sulphur Herd Management Area in Utah, the other from a northern state (she's a red roan and her freeze brand is impossible to read).

Many mustangs are small, in the 14- to 15-hand range, and average around 800 pounds (Savanna, my quarter horse mare, weighs about 1,050). Many have large ears. They are skittish, and fast, and can be fierce if running away is not an option. They are herd animals, mourning the losses of band members like elephants. They are all *horses*. TJ's point—that mustangs are wild—is based on behavior study. Wild-born foals of herds that have been wild for generations maintain certain characteristics, from the way their bodies move to the way the band sleeps. America's wild horses are *wild*.

~~~

TJ HOLMES INITIALLY came to Spring Creek Basin in 2002, on assignment for the newspaper for which she worked. Having lived with quarter horses all her life, she was instantly transfixed by the ways of the wild horses that populated the sparse desert country of the basin. Coming back every weekend—driving two hundred miles round trip and sleeping in her Jeep—she got to know the bands and individual horses, chronicling them with photographs.

Five years later, again on assignment, this time to report on the 2007 BLM helicopter roundup, TJ met Pati Temple. A passionate animal-rights advocate, Pati was known to stop semis so a dog could cross the road, or to find vehicle owners in restaurants who had not opened car windows for their pets. For years Pati and David Temple led the fight for humane treatment of the wild horses in Spring Creek Basin. Mustang allies, Pati and TJ formed a quick friendship. When Pati saw TJ's photographs and notes, she knew their inherent value—she had already been researching fertility control methods and knew documentation was key. Now they had it.

By then TJ was naming the animals, making documentation easier. She took on the quest to learn more about mustangs and fertility control, visiting other ranges in Colorado. She brought the idea of native PZP back, and Pati fully endorsed it. TJ wrote the proposal to use PZP and did talks ahead of the roundup in 2011 to help educate the public, with Pati's support.

The reversible fertility-control vaccine, porcine zona pellucida, or PZP, is derived from pig ovaries and injected into a mare's hindquarters via a dart shot across distance. In the rare instances in which mustangs are caught and released back to the wild, mares are injected by hand as they stumble through a chute. PZP causes a mare's eggs to reject a stallion's sperm—she doesn't become pregnant but she still cycles, and herd dynamics and social structure remain intact. The unnatural aspects of PZP are that humans administer it and humans decide its recipients.

Herd documentation is vital. TJ is what makes the PZP program in Spring Creek Basin work.

When the ranch bordering Spring Creek Basin came up for sale, a buyer appeared who wanted to establish a sanctuary primarily for mustangs removed by the BLM from Spring Creek Basin, giving them a home next door to their birthland. When the new owner needed someone to live on site, Pati Temple knew TJ was made for that job. That life. And the job was made for TJ. In early 2012, she moved into the log home on the sanctuary as a permanent resident of Disappointment Valley: full-time resident number five. Living on 3,700 acres next door to Spring Creek Basin, she's with mustangs every day, either at the sanctuary or in the basin or both.

TJ SENDS ME photos of Andrés on Ken's sorrel and me on Fubar. I can hardly see us for all the layers we wore that day, but I can see the horses, and maybe pieces of my life fitting together. Another email follows: an invitation to observe mustangs in New Mexico with TJ and some other folks. This will be a swapping tour—first to the Forest Service's Jicarilla Wild Horse Territory and later to Spring Creek Basin for a tour led by BLM personnel and TJ, the first of what will become hundreds of trips to see wild horses.

FIRST I FLY to California for my mother's eightieth birthday— sisters cousins nieces aunties and friends gathering in celebration. The last time we were together was at Ed's memorial service three years earlier. In the interim I went to New Mexico but didn't stay. They know about Cachuma Ranch. They don't know about the cabin.

There's my aunt Natalie, tall and strong with no expectations or judgments. And my cousin Nancy, who was in the room with us when Ed died. And my sisters and mother, finding their own ways through sadness, my younger sister also now a widow, her husband dying a year and a half after Ed. In fact, that memorial service must have been the last time we were all together. We've had too many such events to keep track.

And there is Tyler, sunshine on the darkest days. He lost everyone, too—Rebecca and two grandfathers and his favorite uncle—but his radiant smile, big hugs, attention to my mother, and big heart burn through the fog as he picks me up and carries me beyond grief.

FROM THE DURANGO airport I drive directly to Jicarilla Wild Horse Territory in New Mexico. Except, I don't—I drive to a place that on the map does not show a locked gate, a place that, were the gate open, would lead me up over a mountain right into the lap of the Jicarilla. Instead I backtrack for miles and find my way on dirt roads to Dulce with the help of two Apache men who have pulled off the main dirt drag to find me looking at my map. They point me in the right direction and drive off chuckling.

Onward, to pavement and off it, winding up through the thick piñon and juniper woodland toward ponderosa pines and an obscure campsite where I'm supposed to meet TJ, but my misreading of the map cost me daylight and again I'm not sure where I am. When I see lights in a stand of trees, I sneak away. Could be anybody camping or partying up there.

Sleeping in my car, my body stays relatively warm in my old and worn out sleeping bag topped by a younger one, packed in the car before flying to California, but I forgot to pack warmth for my head. At daybreak it's thirty-six degrees inside the car. Brain-numb, I find the people—the same group that flashed lights at me through the trees—looking warm and fresh and eager, not at all how I feel.

We split up into different trucks, TJ and me going with a man who has been darting mares in the Jicarilla Wild Horse

Territory for some years. He and TJ have much to discuss. I feel like a little girl, growing sleepy in the backseat as the grownups talk. When we stop, TJ and I trot up a sagebrushed hillside on the scent of a small band of mustangs. Actually she trots, bearing her camera with its huge lens, while I pant after her, field glasses in hand. We follow tracks that skirt low juniper branches—wide, flat hoofprints in the soft earth. And stud piles—mounds of manure to which passing stallions contribute as a way of saying *I was here*. Topping out, we can see the valley into which the horses have gone.

As we reach the edge of juniper cover, TJ drops to a crouch, me copying as I feel movement coming toward us—a wave of energy pushing into my chest as a dark stallion ripples into view, his head high and his long, wild mane flowing, his muscles steamy with warning as he trots directly at our rigid human bodies. Stopping forty feet away, nostrils flaring, eyes wide and glaring, he takes in the details and turns in a circling trot away and back at us, a blow from those nostrils the only voice in the still air, a sound felt in my blood as his stance tells us, and the mares in the valley behind him, what we need to know.

The mares lower their heads to graze. If danger were greater than two women kneeling in pine duff, their band stallion would either rear into fight or have them running over the next hill. We understand, too, and retreat, backing up in our awkward crouches, not reaching full height until we're well away, not wanting to challenge the stallion.

As he trots down the slope toward his mares, I don't think to lift my binoculars. TJ forgets to photograph. The pictures I have are in my mind, and in the sensation of the hair on my arms lifting in the wind of a wild stallion's breath.

Back at the truck, TJ says to the driver, "Your horses have shade." Piñon pines and one-seed and Rocky Mountain junipers reach upward into ponderosa pines, dryland forest trees but trees nonetheless. "And they are fat. My horses are thinner."

Although monsoons are months away and winter's snow-melt has not yet turned the grass green, the Jicarilla horses have managed to maintain their weight, winter's fare of cool-season grasses keeping them in shape.

"We're overstocked by 300 horses," he tells us. As with grazing allotments on public lands, the government assigns maximum capacities to wild horse areas. Whereas the twenty-two-thousand-acre Spring Creek Basin Herd Management Area has a BLM-determined "appropriate management level" of 35 to 65 adult horses (as well as a winter cattle permit for 326 animal units: 326 cows or cow-calf pairs), the Jicarilla Wild Horse Territory is seventy-six thousand acres with an AML of 50 to 105 horses, this also in addition to cattle.

We count 104 horses: stallions, mares, yearlings, fillies, and colts, the youngest foal a day old. Lots of grays, a band of pintos, a bay band in which all have bright white stars or blazes. Bachelor buddies, a lone bay, two large bands melding as they trot away from us. The dark stallion who came up close and blew.

The differences TJ noted between the Jicarilla mustangs and Spring Creek Basin bands were caused by three simple factors: genetics, geography, and rainfall. Due to genetics, the Jicarilla horses were on average taller, bigger boned. They were fatter because they lived in the desert uplands, and they had a better year. This isn't often the case. With 400 horses living in an area governmentally determined to support 50 to 105, and drought years outnumbering good years, trouble could strike with any deep winter snow—or lack of it. Which is why these tours were taking place: government employees and mustang advocates coming together to discuss methods of perpetuating healthy horses on healthy ranges.

WILD HORSES PERSEVERE despite the odds. Their numbers were brutally reduced in the mid-1900s, like bison in the 1800s and

Indigenous people since the first day of European contact, and when Velma Johnston of Nevada, who would come to be known as Wild Horse Annie, figured out that truckloads of mustangs were getting sold to slaughterhouses, she incited a campaign to pass into law the Wild Free-Roaming Horses and Burros Act. In December of 1971, under pressure from the public—including letter-writing schoolchildren—Congress approved the bill, which declares that "wild free-roaming horses and burros are living symbols of the historic and pioneer spirit of the West; that they contribute to the diversity of life forms within the Nation and enrich the lives of the American people; and that these horses and burros are fast disappearing from the American scene." The law directed the Bureau of Land Management and US Forest Service to manage horses and burros found on lands within their jurisdictions, and to protect them from "capture, branding, harassment, or death." Today mustangs live in a spiral of high-desert lands in Montana, Wyoming, Colorado, New Mexico, Arizona, Nevada, California, Oregon, Idaho, and Utah.

Horses coevolved over millions of years with the soil, grasses, and other plant and animal species of North America. Then they disappeared from the fossil record (as far as we know to date), returning to North America with the arrival of the Spanish conquistadors in the 1500s, when they began repopulating those ecosystems their ancestors helped develop. Over time mesteños, the wild descendants of horses brought and left by the Spaniards, mixed with other horses—Indian ponies, cavalry mounts, animals turned loose by farmers and ranchers in poor feed years, stallions turned loose to breed wild mares to "improve" the herds—and that DNA joined the gene pools of Spanish mustang descent.

Some government agencies and individuals still contend that colonizers introduced the modern horse to North America. However, scientists like Dr. Beth Shapiro, professor of ecology and evolutionary biology at University of California–Santa

Cruz, have spent years testing DNA and paleogenomic evidence that shows that horses are indigenous to this continent.

"Horses evolved in North America," says Dr. Shapiro. "They are a North American species. They were a North American species for millions of years." At the UCSC Paleogenomics Lab, research on how the horses that returned to the continent are related to the horses that left is ongoing. "They are the same lineage of horse," Shapiro says. When Europeans brought horses back, they were "reintroducing a native species to the North American continent."

Dr. Ross MacPhee, curator of the Division of Vertebrate Zoology at the American Museum of Natural History, sums it up by saying, "Reintroduction to North America five hundred years ago is, biologically, a non-event: horses were merely returned to part of their former native range, where they have since prospered because ecologically they never left."

Equus caballus crossed the Bering land bridge into Siberia and back, establishing themselves on other continents; therefore, unlike mammoths and saber-toothed cats, the species did not die out—they may have gone locally extinct, as Shapiro says, but not globally extinct.

Deanne Stillman, in *Mustang: The Saga of the Wild Horse in the American West*, writes of fervent ongoing research to prove that ". . . pockets of Pleistocene horses survived, linking up thousands of years later with the horses of the conquest to form new herds." While working on her dissertation, *The Relationship Between the Indigenous Peoples of the Americas and the Horse: Deconstructing a Eurocentric Myth*, Dr. Yvette Running Horse Collin interviewed tribal members of Native nations throughout North America, comparing oral histories that indicate relationships with the horse predate the arrival of Spanish horses.

We know that colonial Spaniards brought horses with them, as numbers, names, and histories of individual animals were recorded—the Spaniards left a paper trail. But to claim that horses are an *introduced* species undermines the beliefs and oral histories of Native peoples, as well as science. As is the case with the "vanished" Puebloans, who in fact populated pueblos to the south, truth can be passed from generation to generation. Sometimes it takes science a while to catch up.

I think fifty-five million years of evolutionary occupation places horses right at the heart of America. Mustangs are *here*, they are *wild*, they *belong*.

AFTER THE TOURS, Andrés and I head to Norco, California, to get our own mustang for the Mustang Heritage Foundation's Mustang Million, in which Andrés will compete. This is the first year the Mustang Heritage Foundation is going to such extremes. Trainers will select and adopt mustangs from pools of gathered BLM horses rather than the BLM holding public adoptions of trained mustangs after the event, its normal protocol. The trainers have five months to work with their horses before the competition in Fort Worth. Prize money has escalated, totaling one million dollars. Two hundred thousand dollars and a spanking new Dodge Ram will go to the top competitor. Andrés lights up when he talks about it. He wants to win.

Driving down I-15 into a valley of rim-to-rim houses, I tell Andrés that the ocean is "over there," waving toward the west.

"It is?" he says. He's eager to see it—he hasn't been to California before.

A new layer of mountains rising up through the smog surprises us both. "I guess the ocean's on the other side of that," I say.

Smog clouds my brain as well as the sky—I got sick after the night spent in the cold of my car and haven't eaten much for days, barely able to swallow enough water to down ibuprofen, my throat feeling as if the sharp holes of a cheese grater ran up and down the tender inside flesh. So far this seven-hundred-mile road trip is not among my favorites. Impending strep throat. Overdosing on ibuprofen. Dehydration. Exhaustion. Mustangs waiting. A future waiting. I decide that being sick is an inconvenience, not a sign.

Some of the mustangs in the Norco pens standing against the farthest fences, heads hanging, eyes glazed over, mirror how I feel. More than sick. Life as we knew it is over. Family bands disrupted, members disappeared, hearts cracked.

As I lean on the fence, one mustang steps forward. His coppery sides are highlighted by his long, twisted flaxen mane and tail, and he has four white socks (horse for a fool, old-timers would say) and a big white blaze on his pretty face. He steps closer, reaching his muzzle toward my outstretched hand before spinning away. That night the sorrel mustang is pushed with three others into a large pen in the brightly lit arena, where they race around, hunting the way out like Fubar in Montana. The sorrel is flashy, which Andrés has determined the judges like. I hold up my bidding number. We get him for $430—cheap. Or expensive? I'm too sick to care.

Andrés takes me to a clinic where a doctor confirms strep throat and prescribes antibiotics. I want to ask for painkillers; don't. We fill the prescription, load the mustang, and begin the drive home. Andrés drives the whole ten-hour leg. At five a.m. we unload the mustang into the pen set up as prescribed by the BLM, and I go to bed and sleep until dark.

THE FIRST MUSTANG stallion I saw in Disappointment Valley, who is not bay and white like some pintos but distinctly black and white, is named Corazón. A large black patch on his left side, which encompasses some of his flank and much of his girth, is shaped like a heart. A bit lopsided and abstract, it is still a heart, of the I-*heart*-NY kind. TJ named the pinto stallion for his heart.

At the cusp of the last two decades, I lost my heart and my hold on reality as I had known them, and drove around hoping to find a grounding and my heart. On a whim I turned right to the rim, and right again inside a valley, and drove with that rightness pulsing through me until a mustang stallion stopped me in the middle of the road. Corazón. Not only did he stop me that day, he stops me every time I see him. Each mustang stallion and mare and yearling and foal brings me to a halt. Never ever, not once have I driven on by without stopping to look at mustangs. And each time, I feel my heart beating.

9

DESERT CHROME

WHEN TJ INVITES ME BACK INTO SPRING CREEK BASIN, I say yes immediately.

She drives her Jeep along the frozen dirt road of early morning, and stops a quarter of a mile from a band of mustangs. The horses pause in their grazing, heads turning as we start walking toward them. Shadowing TJ, my breath shallow, I will my steps quieter in the crunchy spring snow. I have stalked bucks in country miles from many roads, but TJ cautions me: Stalking gives the wrong impression. Mustangs run if they sense you hunting them.

"They used to run as soon as they saw a vehicle," she tells me. "Now when they recognize the Jeep, they usually don't go far," unlike the Jicarilla stallion, to whom we were strangers.

We stop a respectful distance from the band of seven horses. The desert curves around us, the basin surrounded by rocky ridges, an angled peak rising to the southeast and breaking into sculpted ashen hills. TJ sticks her monopod in the snow and snaps the long telephoto lens in place. The band stallion stands still in the tentative sunlight as his mares lower their muzzles to graze. I lift my field glasses. And gasp, the stallion's face brought suddenly into sharp focus, his pointed ears aimed at me, his eyes dark beneath his thick forelock, his gaze steady.

TJ smiles. "That's Chrome."

I know what love at first sight feels like, though it's been a while. My heart swelling enough to fill some cracks. Tail-wagging energy.

Chrome breaks my heart wide open. His neck thick and ropey, his chest solid, his girth lean but not thin, his haunches hard with muscles used to run, and thrust. His light coat is speckled with spots like freckles—flea-bitten gray, it's called—and he has the longest mane I have ever seen, other than in photographs. It sweeps across his powerful shoulder and down his foreleg, a "dirty gray" against his scarred body. He continues to look at me as I study him.

When the band moves off, not in alarm but simply to nose through the snow in search of feed, Chrome stands stationary on the poll of a slight hill. His mares walk down and up onto the next low rise, staying within the stallion's peripheral vision. Chrome watches them.

He watches us.

I watch him.

While this stallion is of a species with which I have been familiar all my life, he is different. The descendent of horses that have been wild in this wild valley for generations—dating back at least to the 1880s—he manages his own life and his mares with little human interference. He is motivated by instinct. Mate and procreate. Protect band and babies. Find forage and water. He is as wild as the ungulates and other four-legged, winged, and slithering critters that share this valley. As the golden eagle that passes overhead and vanishes into the blue. Born wild. Living wild. *Wild.*

I suck the cold air in through my nose. It powers through me. Sharing air with mustangs.

TJ pauses her camera to identify the horses in Chrome's band: his mares, the one yearling (stunning with blue eyes), the young colt and filly. All but one, a buckskin mare, are varying shades of gray, from almost bay to Chrome's light, flea-bitten gray. Gray horses are born any color and eventually reach the near-white stage. The oldest stallion in the basin is snow white.

TJ repeats the names of the seven horses—*Chrome, Winona, Terra, Mariah, Kwana, Jadi, Remy*—and orients me to the landscape by identifying distant ridgelines, hills, swales, and promontories, the high and low landforms marking the basin east to west: a distinctive promontory we name Temple Butte in honor of Pati Temple, followed by McKenna Peak, Brumley Point, Round Top, Flat Top, Filly Peak, the finger hills. Awed by the breadth of the land, I doubt I will remember anything TJ says, but when I look at a topo map later I am able to locate most of the landmarks, and to see that "the basin" is in fact a circular basin within the greater valley of Disappointment. I recite the names of seven horses until I can match them with the images in my mind and the photographs TJ sends: *Chrome, Winona, Terra, Mariah, Kwana, Jadi, Remy.*

To READ THIS valley is not always to be reading water. Regardless of its source, water flows to the lowest spot. Waves pushed onto a beach by some invisible tidal muscle wash up and seep back down to the sea. Rain falls, collecting in the nearest dent of a puddle; overflowing that, the water cuts a rut to the next depression. Flash floods push up a river's banks, carve new ones, carry whole trees downriver, and as the upper valley drains of rain, all that's left are the puddles. But neither Disappointment Creek nor Spring Creek made Disappointment Valley.

Most of the valley is public land overseen by the Bureau of Land Management—the BLM manages mining, oil and gas, recreation (including hunting), grazing allotments, and wild horses and burros. The state monitors water rights and irrigation. Fortunately there is little remaining mining and oil and gas activity within Disappointment Valley. Fortunately there are mustangs.

The northwest-southeast trending Disappointment Valley parallels the Glade, the forested country that tops the Dolores anticline, which defines the southern perimeter. Disappointment Creek, with headwaters high up on 12,613-foot Lone Cone, a pyramid of a mountain and the westernmost summit of the San Juans, drains to the Dolores River. The creek has cut resistant geologic layers, forming canyons through which it now runs before meandering down valley, carrying a combination of silt and salt and depositing it in the Dolores. The names of drainages suggest why Disappointment Creek is the major salinity contributor to both the Dolores and Colorado Rivers: Salt Arroyo, Alkali Wash. And then there's "Disappointment." It's said that thirsty surveyors in the late 1800s saw a ribbon of cottonwoods along the valley floor and hastened there, expecting good water, only to find this source of bitter disappointment when their promise of the wet proved instead dry.

How is a valley formed, if not by water? Even glacial valleys have water in their histories. Volcanic activity can have a hand in making valleys, as well (as in the Rio Grande rift), but that's not what happened here. This valley was not pushed out of the mountains by a giant moving ice pond, carved by a river, or left in the wake of a volcanic spill. It is a *collapsed* valley. Like Paradox, Spanish, and Castle Valleys to the northwest, this valley owes its shape in part to flowing salt.

During the Upper Cretaceous era about one hundred million years ago, shallow seas covered the area, laying down the sediments lithified into the gray Mancos Shale of the valley's floor and badlands. The seas also deposited Dakota Sandstone, now capping much of the land to the east and west of the Rockies. Beneath the Dakota is the Morrison Formation, from which uranium is gleaned—hence the uranium mining craze in the Four Corners area in the last century (some mines are still active). Millions of years before the ancient Morrison Formation ecosystems thrived, sediments that would become the Paradox

Formation were deposited, including a thick salt section—as much as 85 percent halite—as well as large deposits of sodium chloride. Testimony to when the last seas vanished, the numerous fossils I find as I walk the fine gray soil and broken shale were once living creatures in ancient oceans.

With the erosion and collapse of the salt-cored anticlines and domes, the aforementioned valleys and half a dozen more in what is known as the Colorado Plateau's Paradox Basin were formed. As with Disappointment, these valleys often have young streams running the length of them to older rivers at their mouths—the Dolores in Disappointment Valley, and the Colorado River herself in the case of Spanish and Castle Valleys.

In some places, the highest escarpments and rimrocks are Dakota Sandstone, as are the great stone slabs below the cabin that slide toward Disappointment Creek. Folds and faults displace layers at higher or lower elevations, depending on where you're looking. In a cross-section diagram of local geology, Mancos Shale shows on top of, not under, the Dakota Sandstone layer—to me it looks as if the top of the valley fell in.

TJ HAS BEEN all over this nearly twenty-two-thousand-acre herd management area and knows each dirt road and its ruts and holes like the map of her own palm. What is inaccessible by vehicle, which is much of the basin, including the overlapping McKenna Peak Wilderness Study Area, she knows by foot, having walked most every arroyo, swale, rise, flat, hill, and valley to see mustangs. The arroyos that crisscross Spring Creek Basin map the flow of water during summer monsoons, and, in the years of enough snow, spring runoff.

"They're deep," TJ tells me. "You look across and think it's nearly flat, but start walking and it can take you all day if you don't know your way into and out of the arroyos."

Chrome's band continues pushing aside snow for the bunch-grasses hidden beneath. TJ points to a wall of medium-red sandstone. "Spring Creek canyon."

"What's the source of Spring Creek Basin's creek?"

"See those hills?" It takes me a while, even with field glasses, to focus on the ribbed hills—one hill, really, with deep cuts in its three visible sides. "Spring Creek is usually dry, but when we get rain *right there*, it runs."

She zooms in on a foal. "When I find horses, I usually just sit down about a hundred yards away."

"Do they ever come up to you?"

She shakes her head. She doesn't take the mustangs' indifference personally, as others might (by *others* I mean me. My fingers itch to scratch behind ears as I've done with all the foals I've previously known). "It's important they stay wild."

A filly at the sanctuary, born of a mustang mare who escaped back into the basin when frightened by cows the previous spring, lets TJ scratch and rub and pet her all over. The difference is not due to the filly's three-thousand-acre birth pasture versus the twenty-two-thousand-acre herd management area, but what happened after her birth. Mare and foal grew used to TJ's presence, the mare accepting the supplemental feed TJ offered during the harsh winter. From her dam, and from other horses within the sanctuary, including TJ's two quarter horse mares, the filly learned that this human will not harm her. If dam and filly were returned to the wild, the filly would quickly revert to her first language—that of her wild ancestors.

The two foals in Chrome's band come as close as their dams and sire allow, and that is all. Were I not with TJ, the prescribed margin of safety would be bigger, a hill or arroyo between us. But they know TJ by sight, off in the distance with her camera, and by smell, sitting calmly in the green bunchgrasses of summer, the yellowing grasses of fall. I have no doubt she sits in the snow, as well.

If TJ were a mountain lion poised in the grass, or if she lifted a rope in the air instead of a camera and started swinging a loop over her head, the horses would be gone that fast. They know a predator when they see, smell, or sense one. While humans can confuse them, as we are both predator and prey and act like it, TJ's intentions are pure: she is here to protect these horses from our predator side.

Presumably because Chrome knows TJ, and maybe because he can guess I bear no threat, he is able to nap on his little hill. He sleeps like a cat: one eye open. He sleeps like the mustang Andrés is training: dozing, his head is still higher than his withers—aware, wary.

My feet feeling the freeze of six inches of snow, I keep watching Chrome. Both foals lie down—standing, now prone, muzzles resting in snow.

"Why do you never see cattle lying down?" Keith asked me when we first lived together.

"What do you mean? I see them lying down all the time." At that moment there were at least twenty roping steers lying down in the shade of the eucalyptus grove below the house.

Verbal, and verb, confusion: "I mean *lying down*," and I understood that he meant the *act* of a cow dropping first to her knees then lowering her hind end as she folds herself to the ground (apparently I had seen this done). But I started paying attention after that, and realized how infrequently I actually saw a cow or steer *lie down*.

"Why?" I asked, once I got that I didn't get it.

"Because they don't trust us."

The act of lying down puts a cow or a horse at risk. Up on all fours, fleeing is easy. Once on the ground, hopping back up onto all fours is easy-ish. But that act of buckling is hard to undo if running becomes instantly necessary. The adult mustangs do not lie down in our presence. Howard won't lie down if I'm nearby. Tirade would lie down whenever she felt like it and let me climb all over her.

Foals lie flat on their sides, sleeping in the sunshine. For only about ten seconds of slumber does Chrome's head drop so low that ears and withers and butt are in alignment—true relaxation. The mares nap, too. The yearling colt with blue eyes lies down—again I miss it—but not for long. Soon he's up and eating snow, his neck and jaw stretched forward as he rolls the snowball around in his mouth, turning it to liquid—winter water. This is what they get, the ponds still frozen along with the few remaining seasonal seeps. The valley needs snow in winter the way it needs rain in summer: water is what feeds the creatures of the desert. Without it we're all toast, dried up and brittle and hard.

Chrome's far ear twists. He does not shift his weight or otherwise move, just that one ear pivoting slightly, and then I hear it: the sound of a distant engine. I turn my whole head to look, as does TJ, but we cannot spot it until Chrome's muzzle and both ears point out the red dot of a truck traversing a dirt road on the far side of the basin. All the horses, including the foals now back on their feet, turn their heads to watch the slow movement. And they watch Chrome. From him they know if they need to go. If he says *run*, the lead mare will lead the way. But they stay.

Instead, we have to go. "I don't want to get stuck out here," TJ says, hoisting her camera and monopod over her shoulder for the trek back to the Jeep. Although I'm still cold, the day has warmed and the dirt road on which we drove in is thawing. As the raven flies, it's five miles to TJ's house. There's no one out here TJ can call for help, if she gets cell service. She'd have to walk home and drive the tractor in on the next frozen morning, drive the Jeep out, and repeat the hike back in for the tractor. Living in this valley with no near neighbors can be complicated. Yet it's the simplicity that appeals.

From the basin to TJ's log house, built in the 1890s as stage stop and store, to the gravel road, to the paved road heading west to cross the Dolores River and climb the switchbacks, my only disappointment in the valley of the strange name is that I have to leave.

TWO WEEKS LATER, I meet my realtor at the title company to close escrow on the cabin. Standing outside, I feel panic rising. I still have told no one, holding within the doubts about payments and years and practicality. "I don't know if I should do this," I say.

"Take a moment. You don't have to go through with it, you know."

I look around at the main street of town, the asphalt parking lot, the cement steps on which we stand, no soil or earth visible anywhere. I can't feel myself, just the obligation to follow through on behalf of those involved—the sellers awaiting their money, the realtors expecting their cut. "Let's go in," I say.

In a room with a big table and no windows, the escrow officer sets a stack of papers before me. My realtor tells her I'm having second thoughts.

The woman looks at me, her brown eyes kind behind her glasses. "How do you feel when you're out there?" she asks, her voice soft, gentle.

I feel it all through my body—that shimmer. "I love it," I say.

She smiles.

"I love it for me."

Hence the remote cabin—with its solar power and catchment water and intermittent stream on one hundred sixty acres of piñon and juniper woodland next to twenty-two thousand acres of mustang desert and hundreds of thousands of acres of public lands, habitat for pronghorn, mule deer, and elk, black bear, bobcat, and mountain lion, one set of human neighbors five miles east, TJ seven miles down the road in the other direction, mail delivered Tuesdays and Fridays, the closest gas station forty-seven miles away—that cabin now officially belongs to the bank, and to me.

To celebrate, I drive into Disappointment with the dogs for a quick visit. From the dusty road I spot a band of seven horses near the corrals built some years back by cowboy and BLM crews. Leaving the truck at the corrals and the dogs in the truck, I slip through a wire gate. Two hundred yards away stands band stallion Chrome. I walk quietly to the perimeter of his comfort range as he lingers, hip cocked, ears forward—one saying relaxed, the other indicating mild interest. His mares cluster in the trees behind him, a gray face or buckskin or the bald-faced filly framed in the muted greens of piñon and juniper.

Beneath the dreadlocked mane hanging toward his knee, the curve of Chrome's neck is shaped of a stallion's muscle, his shoulders and haunches, chest and jaw thick and solid with purpose. He watches me from the sloping crest of an alluvial fan, mares and foals and yearlings now nosing for grass in the cover of trees in the nearby swale.

That's all Chrome does: watches. Unafraid. Mildly curious. I could be a browsing doe—I'm barely that interesting. Still, I can tell he can tell I'm not TJ—he doesn't graze or doze, just . . . watches.

Until I leave. Not just turn and walk away—he waits until I'm in the truck, backing up. Then he wheels and lopes smooth as liquid silver toward his mares, trotting the last few paces, mane and muscle moving like stillwater touched by wind, undulating. Sunlight at his edges, highlighting Chrome.

IT'S COMPLICATED I know, even for me and it's my story. I saw redrock and a pinto mustang stallion and found a cabin online and loved it, and dropped it for the horse ranch and Andrés. I met a rancher at a farmers' market and saw him again at a movie, and when he suggested I call David Temple, I did. Then Andrés arrived, and we drove to California to adopt a mustang for the Mustang Million, arriving back at Cachuma Ranch at five in the morning.

Starting that day, Andrés worked every day with the pretty sorrel three-year-old from Nevada. The boyfriend stayed more often at the ranch, and though he had no interest in horses before, in the quiet of early morning he liked to sit in a green plastic chair outside the round pen, drinking coffee and watching Andrés and the mustang.

By summer Andrés's wife and children have arrived from Montana. The ranch is full of people and projects. We have meetings Monday mornings and potluck dinners Thursday evenings. Sometimes I feel like a grownup. More often I feel anxious: finances, irrigation water, maintenance costs, payments, hay. I ride Fubar-Howard everywhere, thinking on a new name.

We hold our first horsemanship clinic—fifteen horses and riders circling the arena around Andrés, who rides the BLM mustang. Andrés talks to us all, or rides up to help us individually. I'm on Fubar. Trotting around the arena, through the haze of dust I can see the lines of Mesa Verde, blue sky, dreams coming true.

After the clinic, I watch Andrés change. Elevated from horse wrangler at a dude ranch to horse trainer, he stands taller. He stands up to me. Near a section of gated pipe, we argue over how best to irrigate a field—top to bottom or bottom to top. Beneath the words is the new attitude: trainers don't irrigate.

The boyfriend listens, and then walks away. Later I ask him why.

"Fuck him. You don't argue with the boss, whether or not she's wrong."

The next day the irrigation water is shut off for the season. I should have known, but I didn't know. Prior irrigating experience came from summers in the Sierra Nevada. That water ran right out of the river. Decades later, I didn't think to wonder about the source of the irrigation water. I just opened the headgate and there it was, until it wasn't anymore.

Side rolls, gated pipes, and ditches gone dry, I head to Disappointment with the dogs, where the creek is but small pools strung together by dry streambed.

JUNE IS USUALLY the hottest and driest month in these parts, and this June is no different—it's hot. Over-one-hundred-degrees hot. The kind of hot where you slip past dozing in the hammock on the cabin's covered porch into true slumber. Where in Grand Canyon you embrace the shocking chill of forty-six-degree water and dunk in over your head, knowing your clothes will dry quickly and hoping your tangle of river-washed hair will cool your neck for at least a few minutes. The kind of hot where on Disappointment Creek I hunt out the deepest puddles, splashing each dog wet to the skin, and splash myself the same way, dipping my sarong into the murky water, grateful for the cool it will give my naked body in the breeze. River girl, desert dweller, I know that wet is the best way to handle heat in the desert.

In my wet sarong, I lie in the hammock. When I stand up and adjust the fabric, I see that my hip and ass are green, the dye staining my skin. I laugh at my green ass, an odd sound in the hushed heat. The dogs don't care.

Thunderheads build behind the San Miguel Mountains to the east, and move toward us, a thick spill into the upper valley, pushing a slight breeze in front of them in their westerly crawl, but it is not enough to ease the heat. I think about going to look for mustangs, imagining them brushed up like the deer and the rancher's trespassing cattle, finding shade in the shadows of piñon pine or juniper. Later they will have to wander from shade to drink and browse even in heat that will linger past nightfall. TJ might feel compelled to find them despite temperature—she's nearly two decades younger than me, kid-less, a camera, a pen, and a hundred mustangs her constant companions. Regardless of season, she's out watching horses.

~~~

BACK AT THE ranch, we sit around the table for the Monday morning meeting and discuss plans for group participation at the Mustang Million in Fort Worth. Andrés's wife and kids will be back in Montana, the kids in school. The wife wants me to buy tickets for them all to fly from Montana to Dallas–Fort Worth to watch Andrés compete.

I say no. The boyfriend leaves the table. "Fuck her," he says later.

It's hot at the ranch, too, tempers building like air pressure, no monsoons in sight. The boyfriend heads to Albuquerque and Andrés and I are going to town for errands. I said no to his kids joining us—there weren't seatbelts enough for everybody, but I didn't express it well. As an afterthought I say, "I'll go get the other truck."

"It's too late," Andrés says. "You hurt them and they won't recover." We head out the driveway and Andrés persists. "They will not get over this. You cannot undo what you did."

"Enough," I say. "Stop."

He doesn't stop. He keeps applying more pressure. I need to move my feet. But I'm driving. I stop the truck, put it in reverse, step on the gas pedal. "I won't do this," I say, backing up the gravel road toward the driveway.

"If you keep backing up," Andrés says, "I'm going back to Montana."

I back right up to his door.

You know what the boyfriend said when he returned to the ranch that night and I told him what happened. But I was the one who felt fucked.

ANDRÉS WANTS TO take the mustang to Montana. Technically I'm responsible for the BLM-adopted horse, unable to transfer ownership until I've had him a year. Andrés has no money.

While he could place in the top twenty at the Mustang Million, the little mustang has rope burns on his hocks from a training session gone badly, and I think he's under too much pressure.

I say no.

By the time Andrés and his family are packed up and ready to go, Andrés says he wants to stay. He has tears in his eyes as I stand at the truck window saying goodbye, his wife openly crying, their lives again loaded into Andrés's truck and trailer. "I'm sorry this didn't work out," I say, and mean it.

Andrés pulls slowly away. This time Howard-Fubar is not in the trailer.

I lead the sorrel mustang to the pasture gate to turn him out with the other horses. His flaxen mane and tail blow straight out behind him and his shiny copper sides blaze in the sunlight as he bucks and kicks and does his high-stepping trot toward the horses that make up our small band, moving his feet toward freedom.

I rename my beautiful bay quarter horse gelding Kua, "back" in the Hawaiian language, or to carry on the back. His is the strength I ride upon; he is the backbone of the dream.

IT'S JULY. TJ comes to the cabin for supper. The blessings of rain follow her, the heat finally broken—first a light female rain framed in lightning then a full-on downpour. From the covered front porch we watch it come, straying drops nourishing our skin, then hurry inside to escape the sheets flung under the eaves by the sudden wind. At the old pine table we eat fruit and quinoa salads, alternating stories: TJ talks, I eat, she chews, I talk, catching up on a week.

She takes a deep breath. "A mare died."

My fork stops on its way to my mouth. "Where? How?" I don't know if she means on the sanctuary or in Spring Creek Basin. I don't know if it matters where.

"In the basin." She looks out the window through water. "When I saw her she had already foaled. I knew she needed help."

Rain loud on the metal roof, I push forward into the story. "What did you do?" What *can* you do with a wild mare miles from any corrals or a road that a truck and trailer can traverse. A mare you can't catch anyway. "Did you see the foal? Is it alive?"

She shakes her head. I don't know which question she has answered. Then I do: the orphaned foal, without the protection and nourishment of its mother, died, too. "I saw them both when the mare was still alive, blood caked down her hind legs, the foal a little dun filly. I called BLM—I knew the mare had to be put down. They couldn't find her. When I found her again she was already gone. I didn't find the foal's body."

A day-old foal wandering alone into death. Rain falls more softly on the roof. My tale of change at the ranch stays put in the lee of TJ's story.

Then I hear the change in the water. TJ heard it a moment before me—the low steady roar—but was polite. I'm not, leaping toward the open door and heading barefoot onto wet ground. The dogs race us to the ledge of sandstone that reaches out above the creek, Cojo standing at the edge. I soak in a small disappointment as I tell him to get back—we missed the first wall of water, which scraped the creek bottom clean and erased the notations of earlier high water.

Now thick, dark, pulsing water pushes up the huge slab of sandstone at the creek's center, crowned with the logjam of last summer's highest high-water mark—a log two-and-a-half feet in circumference but short lodged against a twenty-foot-long tree trunk, smaller branches and sticks of willow woven around them, mud packed into crevices—a huge detritus nest. As the water surges and recedes in a fast-forward tidal rhythm, some branches untangle and get carried away. The oily smell that is Disappointment rises to air.

The rain lets up. TJ has chores to do. I walk with her to the Jeep, my feet now in slippahs. As I watch her head out the not-yet-muddy driveway, its base still absorbing water, I know she is a new friend. I know this because today we did not fill in the talking with the backstory of our lives, focusing instead on the present: mustangs and rain.

I grab my journal and return to the ledge in time to see a new wave topping what's already flowing, pushing forward more branches and debris—water from an arroyo somewhere to the east, its momentum starting farther up and gathering force before reaching Disappointment Creek. The water pillows up my marker rock. It moves under the logjam that stopped its forward momentum last summer, pumping like a heartbeat, each pump a farther push up the rock. The river reaches up and over the huge stone slab but the short waterlogged log does not budge, nor does the trunk. A few bursts of water deposit handfuls of pine needles on stone, nature's pictographs that tell of high water. Sound changes, the intensity softens. The clouds left with TJ, drifting west with the sun.

In the slant of early morning sunlight, the creek with its load of silt is the color of desert chrome. The river has shrunk eight feet in width and dropped four feet down the marker rock, last year's biggest flood still king of this mountain, its logjam unmoving. Upstream, the new high-water marks of summer are carved into banks, new logs and pine needle debris lying out to dry on other rocks, or wrapped around cottonwood trunks and willow shoots, the water gaps washed out, again. In the silt-filled creek, puddles have disappeared in the flow.

Heat fills the spaces between summer storms but does not reach its earlier peak. Disappointment Creek continues to run. In Spring Creek Basin, ponds have filled and Spring Creek itself holds trickles and puddles and seeps. It is enough. The horses have water.

Part III

BASINS AND RANGES

I have watched wasps, whales, their mappings, and have realized their sentience. It is the same with the horses. They have a great intelligence. They require much of me. Part of that requirement is that I am conscious, awake.

—Linda Hogan

10

Spring Wind

Idream I am underwater. Slipping, spinning, sliding, swimming, gliding through water. I can breathe here. The man I'm with in the dream doesn't know this about me—that I love to swim, I am a swimmer, that I can breathe underwater. But the man in the dream is like Harrison Ford and not afraid of anything. He follows me into the water. We partner like dolphins, surfacing occasionally. No fear. Just beauty.

Sometimes in this lone-woman life, I feel it: fear. Not when I am physically alone at the mustang cabin wandering through rocks and rattlesnake country and no one knows where I am— just the dogs and me, the wind and me, the sky so blue against the highest rimrocks, ravens whooshing past such great company that contentment is what I feel, right up until anxiety propels me back to the ranch: animals to feed, phone calls to make, bills to contemplate.

One morning as I follow the creek to the western water gap, needing to check the water gap after a spring rain—cows will be coming upvalley soon—mud oozes over the sides of my Chaco river sandals. I swish them around in the creek, the water from Lone Cone still chilled. As I navigate a rocky stretch, mud slick on Chaco bottoms, I don't hear anything different over the creek's gurgle or see anything new but I pause, feeling it.

At the next stretch of mud, where the undercut of a previous flash flood makes ascending the bank impossible, I step in. I am not the first to travel downstream this morning. I slip my sandal off and hover my foot over the track. Including claws, it's about my size.

One foot sinking into the sludge, the other naked, I glance up the steep brushy slope of the canyon and a chill hits me like wind off a snowfield.

The dogs splash in the creek. No one has sniffed at the tracks. For a minute I follow the story in the mud—an ambling, minding-own-business bear—and then I turn and head faster than I mean to back upstream to the cabin. The water gap can wait for another day.

Used to be I'd go on in the face of fear, tracking a bear or cougar in hopes of seeing the animal; camping on back roads that took me farther from people instead of closer. But I've grown afraid of the mistakes I've made. Afraid I don't know how to unravel them. Afraid when I can't do something—slide a 320-gallon water tank, two inches of water swirling around its bottom, into the bed of the truck—after years of being able to do it all. *It all* still needs doing, and sometimes I just can't. Sometimes I have to suffer not getting the job done.

Perhaps that is the biggest fear: that I just can't do it. Followed by the open hollow fear of not knowing what to do instead.

I do not like this fear. I want to leave it behind like an ex-husband.

I RIDE KUA often. We wander through juniper and piñon pine, some of which is upright and growing but beetles and wind have downed a lot. Kua moves his feet in the direction I point him, stepping over fallen trunks and branches without getting caught. We work in the arena, as well, practicing what Andrés taught us. When I ride Kua we are confident, competent. We can breathe. It's late in the night that fear prevails. Trapped by circumstances I created, there's no way out, nowhere to go. I can't move. Packing up and leaving is not an option when you have horses and cows to feed. It doesn't take much for fear to become another disorder—anxiety a cousin to PTSD.

DETRITUS: CACHUMA, 2013. *These thighs have run. They have swum. They have gripped horses and men. They have held sunshine and rain. Felt the cold and carried it inward, chilling me. Pushed me up off the floor. Pushed down on a calf muscle to a foot and a gas pedal. Stood me up in the stirrups to free the withers of my horse to run, to get me closer to a steer to rope. They have guided one foot forward another back as I changed the paddle from left to right in a canoe race. They have braced me against the bow of the canoe, the frame of my raft as I rowed into rapids.*

These parts of my body are not happy.

They cramp at night but not like charley horses.

Like heroin. As if I'm kicking heroin again every night. On the plane. Driving. Sleeping. Kicking heroin again and again, thighs clenching into silent fists as they fight something, say something, ask for something, and I don't know what.

So I move. I walk. I run.

I INVITE KEN to a Buck Brannaman clinic in Eagle, five hours from Dolores the direct way. Ken tells me he's thinking of coming to work at Cachuma Ranch. He has a baby and is thinking about marrying the baby's mama. I drive to New Mexico to pick up Ken, his horse, little Lacey, and Kathy—eight hours. The next day we drive together to Eagle, eight hours. Kua tolerates this because he has no choice. I tolerate it to help my son and his family.

It's a Horsemanship II clinic—advanced. Some people have been riding with renowned horseman and clinician Buck Brannaman for twenty-five years, others for ten or twelve. No one is riding with Buck for the first time except Ken on Cisco and me on Kua. Several times each day the riders gather around Buck, who sits on his big sorrel gelding or his big bay gelding in the center of the circle. The hub. He encourages questions, answering them at length. I watch, and listen, copy other riders. In Horsemanship II Buck expects his students to know positions and patterns. I get confused easily, going around the arena against traffic for seconds before realizing I've turned the wrong way. I rope like a teamroper, not knowing the hoolihan or backhand, the easiest vaquero throws. Andrés knew them all, and Ken knows many.

Buck tolerates me, is kind, patient. I tell him about my horse, the rearing up and spinning off that led me to Andrés. I tell him I gave the horse to Andrés. I tell him that Andrés rode Kua for months and gave me back a better horse. But we still have issues.

It's day two. Buck sees most everything that goes on in the arena even when he doesn't appear to be looking. "He's a hell of a horse," he says, "but he's a troubled horse."

He's a hell of a horse! I smile as Buck shows me a basic exercise to help Kua loosen his neck, relax the brace. All the horses but Kua and Cisco are pros at this one move. Our horses are rigid. The idea is that Kua has to *not* move his feet but stand still in his rectangle and move only his head and neck when I apply pressure to the snaffle bit, pulling the inside rein toward my hip, holding it firmly, releasing only when Kua yields, turning his head without moving his body until he can see me there on his back and I can reach out and rub his forehead. The idea is that Kua will learn there's another way to handle pressure: not fleeing, but yielding—if the person on the other end is someone he can trust.

Once Kua figures out what I'm asking, he does it readily. When we form a circle around Buck and the horses stand during the questioning, Kua voluntarily bends his neck and turns his head to look at me. He feels safe doing this. He can breathe. It becomes his default mode. I feel safe in the presence of Buck. For once Kua and I mirror the calm parts of each other.

One evening I babysit Lacey so Ken can take Kathy to dinner. When they return, Kathy is shining. She picks up eight-month-old Lacey, hugging her.

"I proposed," Ken tells me later. "A Bob Marley song was playing when I asked her." A Buck Brannaman clinic, a Bob Marley song—a memorable proposal.

On the way back to the ranch—the short way, Eagle to Moab to Dolores—we pass huge mud ponds alongside the freeway where water boiled out of the mountains and canyons so fast little got absorbed into the soil, instead carrying the soil with it. Spontaneous rivers ran over the pavement and detritus lies everywhere, telling the tale. I-70 was closed for a day due to the flooding and debris, the bigger logs and branches and boulders pushed with a tractor off the side of the road.

We stay at Cachuma one night, touring the ranch in the morning. I harbor the hope that they will move here. After turning Kua out with my small band, we haul Cisco and Ken's sorrel to the New Mexico ranch. I am the only one on the last leg, heading back to Cachuma alone, my brain spinning with Buck's teachings and Ken's forthcoming marriage and other possibilities.

Driving into the ranch, no one there but horses, dogs, and cows, I feel the hollow fear. When I walk into the pasture, which has greened up again with the rain, some of the horses come up to me. Maui rests his head on my shoulder. His head is heavy, the weight and warmth a comfort even though I know the discouraging words Ken or Buck would say. Shutting out their voices, I pretend it's a hug.

Kua sidles away when I approach. The sorrel mustang watches me, maintaining his margin of safety. I leave them alone—no pressure. Cojo watches me, too, waiting for me to get back on his side of the fence, where he offers his head. Tears spill into his fur.

The next day I head over the Glade to the mustang cabin. Passing through lush meadows, clean ponderosas, and quaking aspens, the fresh air fills my lungs. Dropping into the valley, I pass thick gray mud piled alongside the bar ditch like winter's snow, and trails of debris show where water crossed the dirt road. New high-water marks scar the creek banks.

At the gate I let the dogs out, except Cojo, sparing his twisted legs the half-mile run. Remnants of puddles mark the driveway and warm-season grasses reach feet high. I do not go inside the cabin, not yet. First, like Cojo, I go to the ledge. He peers down, toenails digging into sandstone. "Get back," I say, as I lean out to see.

The huge logs of last summer's biggest storm, grounded for a year on the wide, flat marker rock below the cabin, have disappeared, the sandstone wiped clean. No fistfuls of debris, not even single pine needles, are left in the wake of high water, the logs lifted and carried downstream like twigs, vanishing into the world of a desert's flash flood like an orphaned filly turning to bone somewhere in the folds of her wild home.

KEN AND KATHY have a simple wedding in front of a spring-fed pond on the New Mexico ranch, the eastern spread of the rain-touched Great Plains a rich green in the afternoon light. Tyler and my mother have come, and Keith, with whom I walk down the aisle for the second time. Lacey is the star, still bald-headed at nine months old with her big blue eyes and toothy smile. Her great-grandmother and her other grandmother and I take turns holding her and changing her and feeding her. When tears fall from overstimulation and exhaustion, I rock her in a living-room chair, back and forth, a welcome rhythm, and am happy when she falls asleep in my lap. Tyler and my mother leave the next morning—such a quick trip for them, for me with them. Keith wants to take everyone to breakfast in town and when I choose not to go, Ken takes it wrong. Or maybe not. But I stay anyway and clean the ranch kitchen, needing that.

TWO WEEKS LATER, I drive to Ken's, pulling the gooseneck, towing horses. The desert still green-tinged from the rains, the prairie grasses at the ranch practically lush, northern New Mexico feels cool, fall in the air. The horses wait in the trailer as I head inside.

Ken is on the phone, pacing as he talks. Lacey is asleep. Kathy looks at me, her large brown eyes showing a question and redirecting from me to Ken, who says, "Okay, yes. Beginning of November," and hangs up.

He turns around slowly. "I accepted the job in California."

Ken was on the brink of bringing his family to Colorado. He'd given notice at the New Mexico ranch. After hearing this at the wedding, Keith told a friend for whom Ken had worked previously. The friend offered Ken a job on a fifty-thousand-acre ranch with hundreds of cows, Ken's dad an hour away. Ken just chose that over my few acres and few cows, over me.

We step outside. Without speaking we unload the horses and feed and water them. The wind has turned cold and my heart is cold and I wish for one second that I had something to take it all away. Back in the house, I behave like a grandmother. When Lacey wakes up, I hold her and rock her. Loving Lacey. Loving my son. He's made the right decision, for him. But that fear, of losing him again . . . *I dream I am underwater. But I cannot breathe.*

~~~

THE MOVE IS a big one. Tyler flies in and Ken and Tyler haul the horses to California while Kathy and Lacey and I tow a trailer full of furniture, clothes, and stuffed animals.

When I get back, I notice that the unused fly rod I gave the boyfriend for his birthday is gone. Searching the house, I see that a bunch of DVDs are missing, along with tools from the barn, some of which were Ken's. The boyfriend has vanished. I want to say *fuck him. Fuck you.* But I am relieved. That he didn't tell me reflects the main issue between us: he doesn't talk. He could be silent for days and then grab my shoulder or hip hard when he got into bed, wanting sex. I didn't talk either, feigning impossible sleep. Maybe worse than that, he said he loved me.

I spend another winter alone at the ranch. But not really alone. I have boarders, horses, cows, dogs. A stray cat I picked up outside a restaurant. Without the boyfriend, I can read in the brief minutes between lying down and sleeping. I still rarely write. I don't recall breathing.

FOR MONTHS I'VE kept Disappointment Valley a secret from my family, finally introducing the idea of the mustang cabin to Ken and Tyler when they come to Cachuma for a winter visit. "It may not make sense," I say, and to Ken directly, "You may be mad at me. But I'm buying this place in a valley just over there."

We drive in by way of Slick Rock Hill, that dramatic country with close proximity to a Utah we once knew. "Tukuhnikivats!" cries Ken, which he did as a kid whenever he saw the tall La Sal mountain peak. I laugh. I *laugh.*

After descending the switchbacks and crossing the valley, mute and leaden in its winter state, we pass TJ's and Ken perks up at the sight of a real ranch headquarters. When I stop the truck at the cabin they do what Cojo and I always do: walk to the edge of the ledge and look down at the creek and across and around, and then they disappear, scampering over rocks like chipmunks, like boys. Like brothers.

An hour passes before they return to check out the cabin. Sitting on the porch in a spot of sunlight, I wait for words, but they don't stop to talk, rushing through the cabin and taking off again like on river and camping trips, them off exploring until a meal called them back.

Later Tyler says, "If this is what you wanted to do, Mom, I'm glad you did it." Ken's silence implies agreement.

NOW IT'S SPRING. Ken and family have been in California for months. Kathy is pregnant again. With Tyler they fly to Colorado for a visit, and Kathy's parents and brother drive up from New Mexico. The ranch house is clean and full of life, meals and granddaughter Lacey shared by all. The days are busy with projects—fixing fence, getting an old Ford pickup to run, lubing the tractor—Ken and Tyler wanting to get everything done in the short duration of their visit.

The last morning it snows half a foot. We camp out in the living room in front of the river-rock fireplace and it feels like family times at the Cojo or at my grandmother's small ranch on Mount Diablo, my sisters and me the granddaughters. That's how I want it to feel. That is the vision I had for this place—a vision that blurred with fear when Andrés left. Now I see it again. And see another quick image I'd had: Kathy on the porch of the old ranch house with Lacey.

Kathy's folks head home and the next day I take my sons and daughter-in-law and Lacey to the airport, the old lump in my throat at their leaving. I wait alone in the truck for the plane to lift off, a habit acquired during the years of the boys traveling between parents.

I jump when my cell phone rings. It's Tyler. "Are you still here?" he asks. An hour has passed since they boarded. "We're deplaning. The door is broken. I told Kenney you'd be here."

I have them all for one more night.

That's when I ask Ken again to come to Cachuma Ranch to help me. "I'm not just saying I *want* you here, I'm saying I *need* you." It just snowed and irrigation is about to start. "It's not that I can't do it—I just can't do it alone. Or, all of it. Or well. I can't do all of it well alone." I'm asking a lot: for Ken to upend his family again, disappointing friends and his father.

"I'll think about it," Ken says.

ON SATURDAY THE water gets turned on—somewhere higher in the mountains where ponderosas shadow the forest floor, a valve is opened and water leaves its manmade holding pen, rushing through cement channels and dug ditches toward something that might feel like freedom. I check the ditch—dry as summer before monsoons hit.

The ex-boyfriend comes to the ranch to get the last of his stuff and to help me prepare for the coming water. We clean the headgate and find the tall metal keys to valves and sort through the thick rubber hoses put away after the last irrigation season, back when Andrés was leaving, and the ex-boyfriend reminds me of everything he can think of about the intricate irrigation system. And I remember he is a rock.

The day peaks at sixty-seven degrees. Sleeveless, I replace the three-part, two-by-four-inch plastic gates in the gated PVC pipe, the special angled tool clumsy in my hands, the ex on the tractor cleaning out a pond, dust rising to the sky. He left the ranch in the fall. Winter was dry, too. He leaves again. This time we say goodbye.

Though I kept the headgate closed, wanting the flow to pass for a few hours, carrying down the line the trash collected in the ditch in the months since it last ran, I go to bed listening, the soft snores of dogs and cat the only sounds. In the morning, I stay in bed a long time.

All traces of yesterday's warmth have vanished, along with the ex-boyfriend's reassurances. Clouds hang heavy on Sleeping Ute and La Plata Mountains. In the vortex of storm I drive to the headgate, and there it is: murky brown water flowing fast through the ditch toward green grass, fat cows, and summer evenings with happy horses. I crank the headgate open, diverting my share into the ranch pipeline, and race the water home.

As the water fills the gated pipe, I adjust the little gates, watching the water shoot out then tapping them closed to trickle size. With my skinny-bladed shovel I work on the "forks" coming from the gates—digging the little ditches that carry the trickles into the field, which might better be called tines as they look more like what stabs your lettuce than what you hold in your hand. The thirsty soil quickly becomes mud.

Wet to my knees, mud tracks on my ass from slipping and sliding, the bend to the earth and shovelfuls of mud hard on my back, I stand and stretch. That's when I see it: the white sheen of hail riding on water spreading out across a field.

The next morning icicles hang from the wheels of the side rolls. Afraid to turn off the water lest a bazillion pipes freeze and crack, through binoculars I watch the neighbors and copy them, letting the water run.

WHEN I GO to sleep during irrigation days, I might count the hours of irrigation water in a field, or I might count horses. While my own horses make a short list, learning the mustangs of Spring Creek Basin is challenging. I categorize by bands, starting with band stallions (which can change). If I can't identify a stallion, I can easily get lost in horses. I have gender, markings, size, age, season, and color to consider (colors also change, seasonally and over a horse's lifetime).

Noting all these details of a horse might tell me who it is. But try identifying a white right hind fetlock on a bay stallion across a mile of undulating turf, grass and the air itself waving in the field glasses, the horse moving among others or standing quite still, facing you across distance, his eyesight and sense of smell far more acute than yours. He would know TJ carrying her camera over her shoulder and her heart on her sleeve as she walks across the basin, and can tell that I am not she. He might move off quickly, or keep facing me forever so that I cannot glimpse that telling hind leg.

Seeking sleep, which usually finds me first, I start with Chrome's band: *Chrome, Winona, Terra, Mariah, Kwana, Jadi, Remy.* In May, the season of spring winds, those seven horses turn to eight.

Moving water one afternoon, I keep seeing images from my Hawai'i life. Pictures of *Hōkūle'a*, the first Polynesian voyaging canoe to sail the open ocean in more than six hundred years. A traditional double-hull canoe sixty-two feet long, she was built to prove a point, and she did it well: a millennia before Europeans sailed away from land, Polynesians had the means and skills to sail across uncharted waters using stars and the signs of the sea to guide them. In 1976, *Hōkūle'a* sailed to Tahiti, the crew using no motor or modern navigational equipment. Water carried them, stars guided them, wind and wave moved them, and seventeen thousand people of Pape'ete greeted them when *Hōkūle'a* entered the bay.

History was made that day, and history changed. And still *Hōkūle'a* sails, carrying hundreds of Hawaiians and non-Hawaiians across the sea. On May 17 she will set sail again, launching a four-year international voyage: Mālama Honua, caring for our communal island, Earth. Many people will sail aboard the mother canoe and others will crew on *Hikianalia*, built to escort *Hōkūle'a* across the different oceans as she visits nations around the globe.

In the irrigation water I see people of the 'ohana wa'a. Just pictures, faces, senses of people I know, people I love. Maka, who will sail aboard *Hikianalia*. Often when *Hōkūle'a* sailed he was crew, and for the time I was with Maka, I often sailed, too, learning the ropes and the sea and newfound freedom as the ocean shifted from separating islands to what connects them. Standing in a field in the middle of Turtle Island, irrigation water flowing past my knee-high rubber boots, my body hums with the excitement of the last-minute preparations before the launch. I breathe it in. *Hōkūle'a.*

As I leave the field, change from rubber boots into cowboy boots, catch Kua and load him into the trailer to drive to Disappointment Valley, I stay aware down to nerve and bone of what is taking place on O'ahu to get *Hōkūle'a* ready for the sail to Hawai'i Island, the beginning of the journey. I'm also aware that, despite impeccable preparations, the ultimate decider of when the journey gets underway is the wind.

Easing down the switchbacks, I thrill as I always do at the sight of that ocean of valley spreading between rimrocks of Dakota Sandstone. In the east the freestanding Lone Cone wears a white reminder that we are still teetering between seasons—we might get rain, snow, or sunshine in the coming days.

Kua chomps grass in the old sheep pens and the dogs sniff for rabbits that might be hiding under the porch. In the morning, dogs secure at the cabin, I load Kua and drive to the BLM pens, my love for this horse as lopsided as Maka's and mine, my heart full enough back then to fill empty spaces. Of all the animals I've had in my life, only dogs love me back with equal adoration and loyalty, and I know how rare it is to find equality of any kind between man and woman, even equality of love. I saw it with my mother and Ed and know that it's possible, and maybe that's enough. Maybe being alone with dogs is enough.

FOR MORE THAN a dozen years, members of the Four Corners Back Country Horsemen rode into Spring Creek Basin to count mustangs, an event that began as a way to help the BLM substantiate its mustang numbers. From its inception, Pat and Frank Amthor organized the event, continuing to do so after TJ became the volunteer herd documenter—horses and numbers now known.

In TJ's Jeep, TJ and Pat will lead people into the basin who are unable to ride, yet want to see mustangs, too. I wave and head off on Kua with the mounted group, feeling as tied to the land as I ever have as Kua's hooves connect with the Mancos Shale soil that floors the arroyos and flats and badlands of the basin, yet I am aware that 3,400 miles away across land and sea, the canoe has started her journey.

We top the first ridge and there stands a gray stallion backed by a pinto mare, sorrel filly, black mare, black foal, bay bachelor stallion, and an unidentifiable (to me) second gray stallion, who snakes in toward the mares when their stallion's attention is diverted, by us.

"That's Seven," I say.

"Yes, seven," a woman says, scribbling on a scrap of paper resting on her saddle horn.

"No, Seven."

The woman repeats, "Seven."

Well, yes, there are seven horses, but, "The band stallion, *Seven*."

The two gray stallions rear up at each other, Seven flashing hooves and fire at the younger stallion, whose legs are charcoal, his belly dappled gray. The mares flee.

"Puzzle and Tesora. Shadow and her new colt, Pitch. Who's

the other gray stallion? And the bay?" The riders ride on, and I'm worried Kua won't stand still enough for me to focus the binoculars I wear like a heavy lei. The mustangs have trotted down into an arroyo anyway, Seven following his mares, the extra stallions following him.

"I can't remember the name of the bay." The riders ignore me.

"I have to tell TJ there's another stallion pestering Seven." Apparently I'm talking to Kua, whom I know well—deep red bay, no white markings anywhere, strong, wary of people, the back on which I ride. My backbone. He's ignoring me, too.

I shut up and follow the saddled, demure, domestic horses. Then, "Copper!" I say, to nobody in particular. Or maybe to TJ, who will quiz me later. "The bay—Copper." No one—neither Kua nor the other riders nor their horses—care in the least. But I do. At night, heading toward sleep, I will see Copper in my mind: a red bay like Kua, both left pasterns white, standing in the shadows of junipers, watching Seven and his mares, waiting.

Hours later we return to the corrals. I leave Kua at my trailer and drive back into the basin alone, wanting quiet time with mustangs after a day of people. At the basin's entry I meet TJ and Pat. Their words spilling over each other, they tell me a foal was born that morning. By Chrome, out of Mariah, the delicate little filly slid from the mare onto a grass sea.

They leave for camp, where Frank is barbequing everyone's supper, and I drive farther in then hike around the east side of Filly Peak in the twilight. There stands Chrome, watching me from a valley fold, completely still but for that long wild mane twisting in the wind. While I love the pinto stallion Corazón for his stout, strong body and big heart, it's Chrome that makes me go weak in the knees. Rugged and fierce and battle-scarred, yet so tender, he grazes nostril to nostril with his mares as his foals buck and play underhoof, his long mane sweeping the ground.

Now he looks from me to his band around the hill, the little, long-legged, dark bay filly standing in the last evening light beside her mother, Mariah.

The wind kept us cool and bug-free while we rode through a beautifully warm mid-May day. The wind launched a voyaging canoe and an epic journey. It guided the mustang mare Mariah to a safe birthing place in which to deliver a foal under the watchful eyes of Chrome. *They call the wind Mariah.* In Hawai‘i, they call the wind makani. And so the filly is named.

To CELEBRATE A year of having the mustang cabin (it's been four since my fathers died), I head to Disappointment Valley on the anniversary of escrow closing. Aspen leaves unfurling to become green mirrors of summer's light, and the tentative green of the cottonwoods along the creek, whisper that winter has passed, yet the cold in the wind and the snow left in pockets on the northern slope of the Glade remind me that we are still at the ambiguous edge of a season.

Gnats, however, have noticed springtime. Small, annoying, biting creatures, they are drawn to ears, eyelids, and hairlines. Beyond their whine, the cicadas are nearly as loud as the creek carrying Lone Cone's snowmelt downstream. Ravens circle the round hill opposite and baby raven heads peek out from a nest in the cliff. Tall, feathering bottlebrush squirreltail, a cool-season grass David Temple nurtured around the cabin, reaches two feet in height—taller than it ever got last spring due to my water gaps and the rancher's trespassing cattle.

The dogs pockmark the red ants' hill that mounds in front of the cabin between clumps of native grasses. Last summer the cattle made huge depressions, from an ant's perspective anyway, and the ants filled the depressions with more tiny boulders from the innards of the earth. Why? How does it serve them, to have their hill rounded rather than cratered? What a feat for their many little feet, filling then mounding a hole the size of a cup or bowl. That they are out now and busy tells me that the coldest months are behind us, at least in Disappointment.

The temperature drops with cloud cover and breeze, which helps thwart the afternoon bug population. A quick trip into the basin gives me glimpses of Makani through the legs of her grazing band members, Chrome off to the side. While many photos of mustangs are of stallions fighting, Chrome shows me that the bulk of their time is spent grazing, watching.

Returning to Cachuma in time to irrigate, I don't guess that my visits to the valley might become even less frequent, that my two dreams—Ken at Cachuma, me part-time at the cabin just being and writing and watching mustangs and red ants—might be mutually exclusive.

I'M GROWING MORE anxious by the day as the ranch bleeds money, the purchases of hay, irrigation hoses, and tractor parts outnumbering the income from boarders and renters. I have too many horses, Ken reminds me each time we talk, the horses grazing the pastures down faster than sunlight and irrigation water can grow grass. Of all those horses, I have only one I can ride: still troubled, still gallant, still afraid, dear Kua.

What happens isn't big. It's small but cumulative. I ride Kua around the ranch, pushing cows from pasture to pasture, which can as easily be done afoot but I like the movement ahorseback. One morning as I dismount to open a gate, Kua spooks. At me. At me stepping down like he did in the round pen at the clinic where I met Andrés.

A bubble of fear gurgles up through my throat as I prop the gate open and remount. Kua spooks again. He doesn't kick or do anything big, just sidesteps and there I am, my left foot in the stirrup, my horse stepping away from me, my body suspended in space, the black-and-white Westerns of my childhood reeling by: foot caught, body dragged. I hold my horse and fear in check the best I can, feeling the burn in my knee and the age in me as I reach up and across space, swinging my right leg over the back of my horse, finding the stirrup, adjusting my seat in the saddle, moving on.

He's a hell of a horse, Buck Brannaman said, *but he's a troubled horse.* That meant, really, that anything could happen.

It becomes predictable: when I mount or dismount, Kua sidesteps. Another rider would handle it correctly—Ken would handle it correctly—even the rider-me of years past would know what to do. But the rider-me of now approaches Kua with trepidation, which does nothing to calm my troubled horse. We are like endless reflections of each other down a long hallway of mirrors that won't quit.

I don't know the cure. Don't know how big the anxiety that befell me when Andrés left has grown. Displaced by not knowing how to do my life, my age, fear fills the territory where answers might grow, like tumbleweeds taking root in disturbed soil.

Not having another horse I can ride, I stop. I step down off Kua and I stop riding.

11

In the Pen

Après all these months of watching mustangs in the wild—Chrome and his mares, other bands, young bachelor stallions, the old solo stallions often hidden in the fringes—I know that for the full story I must see mustangs in captivity. It's time.

TJ, Pat, and I follow the Arkansas River through the Wet Mountains of the Rockies to Cañon City for a tour of the East Cañon Correctional Complex, where a short-term BLM holding facility functions within the federal pen.

Purses, cameras, cell phones, and pocketknives locked away in the BLM field office, we get briefed on prison protocol, instructed not to make eye contact and certainly not conversation with the prisoners, and we're loaded into a van and escorted inside. Only "inside" this part of the prison is actually outside: eighty acres of corrals, barns, arenas, round pens, tack rooms, and offices. While there are men aplenty, from our tour guide, wild horse and burro specialist Fran Ackley, to inmates all around, we are the only women present, and we are here to see horses.

Yet I can't help but notice the men, flashbacks to my earlier life. I might have ended up in prison myself; I just didn't get caught. And here I am, looking at horses and men who did.

Fran stops the van at the outlying pens where the older ladies and gents await sanctuary space like our human elders waiting to get into assisted living. Ages seven and up, these mustangs are deemed unadoptable and kept at the outskirts. Orange-clad prisoners drive flatbed trucks weighted down with half-ton alfalfa bales into the pens. As horses crowd around the hay, the pecking order is easy to see. In the wild, the social structure of family bands helps the species survive, like wolf packs. But wolves are predators, running to kill, and horses are prey—they run for safety. Within the confines of this prison, some cannot run far enough away, the submissive standing off to the side while the dominant geldings and mares follow the feed trucks closely.

Within this prison, there is a social order to the men, as well, one we can't see, their survival also dependent on functioning within that order. Shivering in my down jacket in the February frost, I wonder where I am. At one time a dominant mare, fighting my way through life, after getting clean was I lead mare with Smith and my kids, with Rebecca? What of the times when my nature was buried in addiction or a tough marriage or grief—what then?

Following TJ and Pat back into the van, suppressing the synapses firing in the presence of so many hardened men, I remind myself that we're here to see *horses*. And we do, moving on to the training facilities where inmates who are part of the Wild Horse Inmate Program do ground work with some horses and ride others. Now it's okay to watch.

The younger, adoptable mustangs live near the training facilities and main alleyway—horses waiting for someone to fall in love and rescue them. The BLM has seventeen "off-range corral adoption and purchase centers" and many long-term sanctuaries where mustangs can live out their lives without much additional harassment. This is what these horses face: 1) adoption, where a person pays $125 (more for mustangs in WHIP training), takes the horse to a previously approved facility, and proves over a year that the mustang is well fed and cared for before final papers get signed; 2) sanctuaries; or 3) "sale authority," when older horses or "three-strike" horses (those not adopted after three tries) can be bought outright for $25 and go to fates unknown. Slaughter, at one time a fourth option when horsemeat was shipped abroad or used in dog food, was outlawed in America but not in Mexico and Canada (I checked cans on grocery store shelves as a young girl, insisting that my mother not buy Alpo or any brand with horsemeat). Some mustangs slip under the wire—purchased by kill buyers, they are shipped illegally across borders to a violent death.

Leaving the van and men behind, we walk between pens, the horse smells powerful and comforting in the cold of the story: all these horses removed from their homes and waiting here, for what? Mostly for the feed wagon, or the warmth of sunshine, though some wait to hide again while others wait for some kind of distraction.

Fran shows us hundreds of mustangs. Thousands, actually—2,901, says the handwriting on a blackboard on the office wall. Individual horses stand out as we move between pens of mares and geldings, yearlings and mature horses—beautiful grays, bays, buckskins, duns, roans, pintos, sorrels. With wild manes and searching eyes they burst into movement, racing across the pens, then settle. Some come close to investigate us as we observe them. There are many in between. Many men, as well. I avert my eyes.

Onward to the next pen, our collective hearts heavy. Unlike many of the human inmates, these horses did nothing to earn this fate but be born.

Fran designed the elaborate, mustang-friendly system of pens and alleyways, loading chutes and processing chutes, and managed the facility for nearly thirty years. Tens of thousands of wild horses were processed under his care. He tells us that only a small percentage of horses captured in herd management areas go to adopters and loving homes. And although mustang sanctuaries have popped up across the country, like rainstorms in the desert, more are needed.

We approach another pen. "Three-year-old geldings," Fran says.

Through the corral fence we watch young mustangs sparring like boys, rearing and jabbing with their front hooves. At sight of us they charge away, beautiful in their shaggy winter coats, then trot back, tails and heads high, breath steamy. There are thirty-five mustang geldings in the pen, the muscle and fire of youth rippling through them, and in all that movement, I spy *him*. And, I swear, *he* is looking at *me*.

The voices around me fade. People disappear. Horses blur. A dozen young geldings crowd the fence. The big bay stands back, watching us. Watching me.

TJ says something to Pat. I don't hear the words.

"May I go in?" I ask Fran.

"Sure," he says, trusting that since I know TJ, I also know something about mustangs. Before he finishes nodding I'm climbing the fence, careful, though, to move quietly, to find the liquid motion of my human body. Some horses spook anyway, and thirty-five young, mostly untouched-by-human horses from the high-desert West move through the pen with the power of wild water. I stand in the current, hands up in front of the near horses' faces to slow the flow. Some stop, others pivot away, and a few don't care, crowding me.

Behind the near geldings the big bay reflects my stance—solid yet ready to flee—but I can see his eyes beneath his shaggy forelock: stillwater pools. Calm, inquisitive. His thick coat almost as dark as his black mane and tail, he has a white hind pastern and a white star on his forehead. Around his muzzle and eyes a soft tan glows—even his eyebrows, like a Doberman. But he isn't built sleek like a Doberman, and doesn't behave like one. He's built like a . . . quarter horse. Of course he is. I have loved quarter horses since girlhood.

He watches as I move among the frisky three-year-olds, standing his ground warily while allowing my presence. My breath slows, becoming more surface, careful, *like breathing underwater;* in the presence of power and grace I remember I can do it, *breathe underwater,* breathe in the bodies of the horses in this pen like a huge Olympic swimming pool, *wild horses,* and I quiet my heart to match my breath match my steps so as not to startle him, any of them, in the cold of a February day in Colorado as across the backs of other young geldings he watches me, I feel his eyes, *underwater, I am swimming underwater,* and step by slow step I take three toward him and the other geldings part, giving us room. I remove my glove and in slow motion lift my hand toward him, lifting and reaching through air electric with his brace and breath as he watches me, leaning not *away* like Kua but *toward me.* My hand out, relaxed, palm down, submissive yet inquiring, his neck stretches as far from his chest as it can while his feet stand steady, his nostrils searching the air, tasting for danger, and the mustang's muzzle and my hand enter a space where everything turns liquid like dance and we are, dancing, as he reaches farther and I do, too, and he sniffs the back of my wrist. Warm breath and whiskers on my skin.

When he tenses I feel it, see it, his body taut, quivering, not in fear but with the effort it takes this big animal from the wild flanks of Wyoming to *not* wheel around and run away. To stay. I lower my hand slowly and take half a step back. Take a breath. A moment.

His strong chest leans toward me again, while again his feet don't move, and I have forgotten the other horses in the pen and the people outside as my hand lifts and the muscles in his stout body relax as he reaches still farther with his nose. In movement as slow as my heart, my breath, I lift my hand and turn it so my fingers loosely cup and hold the air between us and I reach with them toward him and I feel it, then, feel his soft muzzle with my fingertips. He accepts the touch—his first voluntary human touch—and the warmth of his breath, his spirit, his gentle nature fills me. When I step back and to the side he moves, too, not away like dear troubled Kua but following . . . *me*. Mirroring my movements. Even with the other geldings intervening, he follows as I step slowly here and there, backward, forward in the spirit-water-air bubble that holds us. He has hooked on.

From the far side of the fence, TJ says, "He likes you," and I feel a smile rising inside, an internal sun drying up any leftover fear. The mustang's mana has remained intact—his prowess and spirit. And I have hooked on.

I don't know how long we dance. Too long, for I'm part of people on tour and we need to move on. I could stay in this pen of mustangs for the next several hours—all night, but for the cold. TJ would stay, too. Watching mustangs is what she does. Watching wild horses is the best medicine, like watching a river or the flames of a campfire burning low in the night.

THE CALM STAYS with me but is tempered with sadness as we drive away from all those horses. In their midst, I felt something either new or very old. We were all children once, or foals trotting freely beside our wild mothers—all those mustangs and men and me were someone *before*. Who was I before somebody's hands changed how I saw the world?

DETRITUS: CALIFORNIA, 1960S. *The geology of my body was discovered not by me and not at an appropriate age but by someone who cared not that my crevices and canyons should remain hidden until I was at least in my teens. Instead the geology of my body was sought and pried and ripped apart by bulldozer fingers looking not for oil in the shale of the plateau but for some gratification of a need, or greed. Same motive perhaps and maybe same men of the oil and gas industry now that rapes these lands but this was my body, my own personal story waiting there to be told. By me.*

Instead those bulldozer fingers prying into the geology of my body found a hidden canyon and made a little uplift of it and pushed and prodded over the mound until the geology of my body erupted in a new height I should not have experienced until so many years later but bulldozers are powerful machines, like men. And I was only five. Or four.

And then older, too, the geology of my body no longer mine after the first time as I sought to hide it from those men who now I watch destroy land and innocence with backhoes and steel teeth and levers and pipes like fingers digging deep into earth, into the geology of the Earth's body when she just wants to be left alone, for erosion to happen like age from wind and water and time, which should be what shapes us as women, as girls, shaped by what we love not hate. The geology of my body would have, should have been shaped by water and sun and horses and dogs and stuffed animals.

TJ AND I return with a trailer. This time I successfully overlook the human inmates as I open myself to the sights and sounds, smells and movements of thousands of wild horses in captivity. While the Cañon City facility is a luxury accommodation compared to some—the horses live in acres-large pens in which they can run and spar and play—it is nothing like the wild backgrounds from which they come. I want to take a dozen, five dozen, home. When we drive off, there is one less horse in that holding facility, one less mustang in the pen.

Hauling horses or livestock you can feel their movements, their shifts of weight, any steps they take. Often a horse not tied will turn completely around and the whole trailer rocks with the movement. I feel the mustang turn a single time as I drive slowly from the prison through town and west along the curves of the

Arkansas River, easing into the turns, careful not to step hard on the brakes or jerk the wheel. On the straight stretches he doesn't move, either.

It's after dark when we pull into the ranch. The dogs bark from their yard but I can't greet them till later. I back toward the pen TJ helped me set up according to BLM regulations: six-foot-high fences, at least twenty by twenty, some shelter from wind, rain, and sun. This pen runs alongside the barn, mostly under the protective overhang of the barn roof, and is larger than twenty by twenty. We're still having blustery cold winds and snow, but I hope to soon expand the pen so the mustang can have more room and more sunshine when it comes. First I have to be able to halter him.

With a flashlight TJ guides me to the post I need to touch with the trailer, closing the gap; the trailer gate will then swing open and be secured to a wing panel. We make our movements in pale barn light and moonlight, hoping the shadows and dark corners won't spook the mustang though horses see better in the dark than humans. We talk in quiet voices as we move about, so he can keep track of us and also, for me, so I might calm myself, for my stomach is busy with excitement and anxiety.

Andrés and the boyfriend long gone, Ken on a ranch in California, me alone at Cachuma with horses, including boarders' horses, and cows, I forged through the weeks of winter, buying and trucking and stacking hay, again and again, forever more hay; breaking ice; plowing snow with the tractor; hauling pick-up-loads of shavings for the boarded horses. I am exhausted, and still not writing much as many cold ranch days I leave the house at eight in the morning and return at eight at night, but I can read at bedtime until the book hits me in the face, reminding me to turn off the light. And here I am, taking on another big project.

Not just any project. A mustang. Although not fresh off the range—he's been in captivity for nearly two years—he lived in those big pens with other wild horses, none of them halter broke or tamed in any way. Other than my fingers on his muzzle and his initial processing, his only human contact was this: every few months the horses get run through alleyways into a narrow chute to the hydraulic tilt squeeze chute, where they get wormed and have their feet trimmed, lying on their sides in the chute with a rope around their pasterns held by men in bright orange while another man does the trimming. It happens in the most humane way possible, and Fran oversees everything, but this is the only human exchange these horses have, this hurry and tilt out of control and toes manicured and needles puncturing skin that is so sensitive it can feel a mosquito land before the mosquito sticks its stinger in.

And now the big bay mustang got loaded into a trailer for the second time in his life and hauled for hours to a facility run by a tired, older-than-middle-aged solo woman who is wondering what the fuck she is doing.

BEFORE LEAVING FOR Cañon City, I filled the water trough, put hay in a large rubber tub, and made sure everything was ready. The Paint colt, Maui, two years old and still the calmest of my horses, stands in the next corral, watching curiously as I walk around fences in the muted light, rechecking gates and panels, and when I'm sure all is safe and secure I unlatch the trailer gate and swing it over to TJ. She ties it to the wing panel and we position ourselves where we can see but won't spook the mustang. I expect him to burst free the way hauled cattle do.

He stands as deep in the twelve-foot trailer as he can. I understand. The geology of my body just wants to be left alone, until I *want you* to touch it.

DETRITUS: MAUI, 2004. *At a slack key concert, hundreds of people lounging on the lawn in front of the stage, my friend spies Maka in a circle of people who have just returned from Kaho'olawe. As we're introduced, I give Maka the aloha kiss-on-the-cheek hello and sit down, turning sideways so I can see him.*

Maka: "eyes"; also "beloved." Maka's last name, Makanani: nani is "beautiful." Sitting cross-legged on the grass, leaning into the sounds of Hawai'i, Maka does not take off his dark glasses. I never see his eyes. But a pair of cheap sunglasses can't hide his mana or his beauty. When "Hawai'i Aloha" plays we all rise, clasping hands and singing. I'm in between my friend and Maka, my hands disappearing in theirs as we lift them toward the sky.

A year later, I stumble into Maka's path on Kaho'olawe. He's been going to the island since the seventies as part of the Protect Kaho'olawe 'Ohana, a group of Hawaiian activists and support-ers formed in 1976 to protest the bombing of Kaho'olawe, which started when the United States Navy seized the island the day after Pearl Harbor was bombed. Target practice continued until 1990, denuding the island, destroying its aquifer, and leaving unexploded ordnance for future generations to handle. The Protect Kaho'olawe 'Ohana sued the navy for violation of religious freedom rights and was awarded monthly access within designated areas for cultural and environmental restoration projects. For nearly thirty years, Maka was on the majority of those accesses.

He's on my first, striding through the kiawe trees toward the beach, several young Hawaiian men in his wake.

And he's on Hōkūle'a, standing at the bow of the canoe ready-ing lines for the docking when she sails into a Maui harbor several months later.

His rascal grin, his twinkling eyes—who could resist? I try, half-heartedly—try to fool myself out of love—but I have hooked on.

One warm Lāhainā evening, after a talk given by crewmem-bers, Maka and I paddle a canoe out to Hōkūle'a, moored in Hanaka'ō'ō. He's on night watch, and I spread my sleeping pad and bag on the deck opposite his but we don't go to them for a long time, instead watching stars that people have viewed from this region for millennia, feeling beneath us swells that have origins before the beginning of time. Hōkūleʻa has traveled one hundred thousand miles over the Pacific, sailing to each tip of the Polynesian Triangle and beyond, and I feel all those miles and years and layers of people with us on the canoe. My life, too, in an ocean that holds the rivers of my past until they return to the mountains as rain. Each drop contains the world's story. Creation, connection. Water, saltwater, blood.

On the water under starlight I can't tell one from the other—sky from sea, this drop from that, Maka's shadow from my own. We tell small stories of our lives, me of the river, Maka of the sea, soft conversation wandering through us like peace. I'm leaning back against the railing, absorbing the presence of stars, moon, and man, when Maka, 75 percent Hawaiian, 25 percent European Portuguese, born on Kauaʻi and raised by his "100-percent-Hawaiian grandmother," says, "Kat, you have any Native American blood?"

I look across the starlit water. Lānaʻi and Molokaʻi rise as shadows from the sea. "It's so far back, there can't be anything left." I take a breath of salty air, and feel my lungs cleansed. Watching the sprinkling of town lights on Molokaʻi's shoreline, I say, "The blood is on my mother's mother's side, of a people who were 'eliminated' in 1910 by order of the New York State Supreme Court, which declared the Montaukett Indians of Long Island officially extinct. But they weren't extinct. They were in that courtroom and outside. Somewhere far in my background a Montaukett woman married a haole man and birthed hapa children, and those children's children had children, and eventually me." I look up to see Maka watching me.

"It doesn't matter that it was so long ago," he says. "You still have the blood." While many will dismiss that faint lineage, to Hawaiians like Maka, unrecognized as a tribe by the US government, blood is more sacred than enrollment in a system that has systematically tried to eliminate them, as well.

Walking up the deck from the bow the second night on the canoe, I see that Maka has made one bed, pushing the pads together on the wooden deck, our sleeping bags upon them, one on the bottom, the other on top. We talk as he fusses about, checking anchor lines, knots, stowing gear. Then it's time. I lie down first, slipping between the sleeping bags, enjoying the warmth, and when he kneels down I open the blanket to him.

A complicated, impassioned man who has dedicated his life to Hawai'i, Kaho'olawe, and Hōkūle'a, Maka loves me as much as he can. For a long time I don't care about his limitations or the lopsided love; for several years, he comes to Maui and stays at my house and together we leave for Kaho'olawe with the Protect Kaho'olawe 'Ohana, boating across the channel in a Zodiac in the predawn, Maka at the helm. Then things change, as they tend to do, and as Maka heads off to Kaho'olawe without me, the foundation of our relationship starts eroding into the sea like that bombed and windblown island.

It's not that I want more; *I just don't want to be* less. *"Maka," I say one morning as he stands near the round kitchen table, teak framing strips of bamboo.*

When I say, "Maka," he says, "Kat?" in a tone that indicates he knows something is coming. He probably almost knows what it is.

"Maka, I'm older."

His large fingers spread over the table. I love those hands, speaking along with his voice.

"Kat, I'm sorry I forgot your birthday." A glance at me; a hand waving at the past.

"Maka." I love saying his name, hearing him say it, the k *near the back teeth, above the throat. "Maka, it's March. My birthday is in December. Before Christmas."*

"I forgot Christmas, too?" He looks at me, takes me in, his eyes dark and deep and naked. But I have to i mua, go forward.

"I love you, Maka. I have loved this time with you. You being here whenever you are. I haven't minded storing all your stuff."

Maka collects things and my closets are filling. "But I see that now I am just a storage unit."

He looks out the window past the lychee tree, to the gulch and the ocean beyond.

"I don't want to be a storage unit anymore, Maka. You have to move your stuff."

He looks back at me. We almost smile at each other. He takes a breath, releases it, and says, "Today, Kat?"

I laugh out loud. Go around the table and hug him. He's heading to Kahoʻolawe in the morning and won't be back until Sunday. "No, Maka, next week's fine."

I pile all his stuff inside the front door—four truckloads, five years' worth of stuff. All Maka has to do is load it up and take it away. Easy.

Maka makes it even easier.

As I hold my father's voice in the phone for the last time, from my wall of windows I watch Maka walk to the edge of the gulch and look out across the ʻāina to the sea. We don't share the aloha kiss goodbye.

FOUR YEARS LATER, the mustang stands still in my trailer for what seems like ever as TJ and I wait. Finally he steps hesitantly toward the wide opening, reaching his head out to peer into the palely lit night, his weight and body anchored solidly to steel. He backs up into the shadows where we can't see him but I can hear his breath as he searches the new smells. Minutes later he moves again toward the opening, standing at the edge of safety. Leaning. Listening. Learning what he can of this new place before he enters it. Receding into the trailer's depths.

Us waiting, watching, me wondering what to do. "Just wait. Let him do this on his own time." TJ's voice calm, guiding.

He eases forward again, the floorboards echoing his steps. He sticks out a foot, testing the water, pulling it back. Again the hoof comes out, touching the ground before retreating. I want to laugh. It's so *cute*. He's so *natural* in his investigations. A wild horse trying to figure out what is safe, safer—the trailer or the unknown. This time when he places a foot down on the earthen surface of the ranch he leaves it there for seconds. Feels through his hoof. Withdraws it. Then again at the edge, he steps into his new world.

It took half an hour for the mustang to come out of the trailer. I'm stiff with cold. We close the gate to the pen and the trailer door quietly while the mustang circles, smelling the hay, the water, the corners, calm little Maui. We watch. When he settles into eating, nose to nose through the fence with Maui, TJ leaves. It's after midnight.

Showering for warmth, I sleep briefly, wake early, and hurry outside to check on my new mustang. He watches from the far side of the pen as Maui comes right up to feed. I stand back, giving the mustang room, but don't leave right away. Just stand and talk to them both.

Later, cattle moved to a new pasture, all horses fed, greenhouse watered, dinner picked, I open the trailer door and sit watching the mustang and Maui from the edge where the mustang's feet lingered before breaking through fear into a new life. He and Maui eat side by side, the required six-foot-tall panel between them, Maui content to just eat and be calm. Too gentle, Ken says, Maui has followed me into the house. Now here he is, still a baby yet solid as a tree.

Listening to the simultaneous chewing, the smell of moistened grass hay spiking the soft evening air, the stray cat purring under my hand, dogs resting—everyone is relaxed, content, even me.

The next day I clean out the trailer and back it into the depths of the equipment barn. At feeding time I bring a stool and my journal down to the horses. There's no one at the ranch to see me writing and reading to my mustang.

Again the peaceful munching, back teeth grinding sideways, fronts cutting off the excess, lips drawing in the stray wisps of grass hay. The mustang nuzzles deep into the tub, searching for prime leaves of alfalfa—dessert mixed in with dinner, any kid's dream. And this, my dream. Reading aloud so that he gets used to the sound and presence of me, I hear in my voice that wistful girl of yesteryear who sat in the back row, farthest from teachers, closest to windows, daydreaming. Then she wrote.

She wrote stories of wild horses galloping over hills she had not seen, open rolling prairie rising and falling across the pages, the horses wild yet gentle to her so that she rode bareback among them astride a buckskin mare. Or a black stallion she called Night Wind—I have that story still, its pages charred from the fire that burned down my mother's house, me in college, my books and journals and stories packed in a box in my younger sister's bedroom.

How is it that more than forty years later I hear her voice as I sit before a munching mustang, his chewing and sweet breath and occasional soft blowing bringing forth the girl in me? The dreamer in me? Is it just peace that does this, pulling me from the chaotic current of my life into the flatwater between rapids, or do I have in this horse a reason to sit still and write that is important enough that I am actually writing? Or is writing still just dreaming in a different form?

As I WATCH the mustang adjust to his new place, I ache for what he's lost. Maybe he was too young when captured to remember the details but clearly he is innately different from my other horses, except the mustang Andrés picked out, both mustangs like Kua, quick to move away from anything potentially danger-ous. Which is me.

I go into the mustang's pen to clean it and feed and water him. He stands in the farthest corner. Gradually we work toward one another. Soon I can rub my hand along his neck, both of us ready to spring apart. When I can touch his shoulders, back, withers, chest, legs, and face with confidence, I bring a rope halter into the pen. He stands still as I rub it along his neck, over his withers, down his front legs, back up toward his throatlatch and ears and jaw. Rubbing it along his face even, letting the loose rope of it touch him everywhere.

One morning I open the halter, reach behind his ears for the headstall, slip the noseband up over his nose, release it. I do this several times and then for several days until I'm brave enough to slip the halter on, pull the headstall down, thread it into the throatlatch, and fasten it with a flat knot. The mustang does nothing, or nothing new or different. He tolerates. I brush him and rub him all over, and run the lead rope over him as I did the halter. One day I halter him and step away, holding the rope. He turns toward me, takes a step, and follows me around, hooking on just as he did when in prison at Cañon City.

TJ keeps asking his name. While I have considered other options, I've known from the beginning the only choice I wanted to make. His eyes and body so big and brown and beautiful, so of the land, of place, of the 'āina that birthed him, raised him: Maka. Eyes. Makanani his whole name: beautiful eyes. Beautiful beloved.

12

MIGRATION

ONCE UPON A TIME MY LIFE WORKED THIS WAY: I'D HAVE one dream followed by another—visions or pictures of things I wanted to do, places or houses in which I wanted to live. I'd have the picture, do the footwork, and more often than not the picture happened.

It started as daydreaming when I was that schoolgirl sitting close to the window, riding clouds as if they were horses.

DETRITUS: CALIFORNIA, 1967. *Ever since I was little I wished on my birthday candles for a horse of my own. I'm twelve when my mother says she'll match what I earn. I do extra chores and save pennies and dimes and nickels and iron shirts for her boyfriend whose hands wander a girl's body as if they don't belong to the speaking part of him. The horse is a big sorrel quarter horse-Thoroughbred–Tennessee Walker gelding. His lope is like riding a pillow. I can breathe there. Mostly I ride him bareback, and that's how you really get the feel of a horse. Like moving through waves underwater, the motion of the ocean around your whole body—we flow like that through green pastures, jumping downed oak trees, loping along the lane. Somehow my mother manages the board, single mother of three daughters selling her wares at weekend craft fairs, but guilt does not keep me home and when I trade that* gelding for a quarter horse filly at the Sierra Nevada ranch, the filly's stride takes me away.

I'm alone in a field of dried grasses, bridle over my shoulder, walking down the valley to catch Tirade. Dew loosens the smell of sweet earth as my feet move toward the horses waiting broadside for the sun to appear, the ponderosa pines rising to red, white, and Douglas fir on the steep mountainsides around me. I feel myself growing smaller with each step, as if I am no longer a normal human being walking but simply a being, a critter, an element that holds no more and maybe less significance than the grass I'm crunching underfoot. I'm just me—not me as defined by family or men—and in my smallness I feel the greatness maybe the way a deer does or a deer mouse, creatures that inhabit their realms without question. I am just me in the presence of the greater, and by the time I get to the end of the field I doubt my ability to ride, so small have I become. But I grab a handful of black mane and swing up onto Tirade's back. Her sides warm between my knees, we move into a lope, snaking behind the other horses who buck and fart and run as a band up the meadow toward the barn, me right there with them, that feeling of smallness and connection staying with me until I am in the presence of people again.

THIS THING ABOUT *wanting* has guided my life. It's not like window shopping or watching those shows on TV that Rebecca started to watch, confessing that she bought a four-thousand-dollar diamond necklace she didn't want and couldn't pay for. It's not like lust, either, though I have certainly lusted after some places and men. Want is a voice inside me. A shimmer, a tremor of excitement. Recognition that resounds within.

One day I stopped at a yard sale in Haʻikū. The house was hidden behind a thick hibiscus hedge, which shielded it from public scrutiny. I went upstairs to look at furniture. The room was big and open with a wall of windows and I thought, *I want to live here.*

I called my father in California the moment I saw a For Sale sign pop up in front of that hedge. His wife had died of cancer two years earlier and he was considering moving to Maui. My older sister was visiting at the time; along with our mother and Ed and a realtor friend we went to see the property. Two houses. We entered the bigger house first, stopped short by the view. The whole place was like old Hawai'i—what we knew in the sixties. Soon I was living in the house with the wall of windows.

Some leavings also started this way. What if I moved *there?* I would decorate that life as if it were a house, which I would also decorate, creating something from nothing, putting a painting on a blank wall for color and shape. Like writing fiction—it starts with an idea, a feeling, a picture. A shimmer, when it's right.

Fear when it's wrong.

There were times it didn't work so well. Or maybe it did. In the Sierra Nevada in 1997, I found a small house on the river—inexpensive, away from people, near water. The owners wouldn't consider my offer. I offered more. Getting homeowner's insurance would be difficult—the house was in a floodplain. Then there was a problem with easements. I said to the gods, "Why are there all these problems? Should I or should I not buy this house? Please give me a sign." I pictured large cursive words on a banner towed behind an airplane. No banner, no plane, but the next day the river flooded, running right through the house, taking out doors and windows, its high-water mark the silt on the windowsills.

Still in the Sierra Nevada, I needed work done on my well. The well man pulled the pump and fixed it. A couple of days later, he got sick. A friend from Flagstaff was visiting when the well man did the work. From my house she drove to Seattle where she got ill, groaning alone in a motel room. I also got sick, grateful for once that the kids were with their dad. We did not learn what we'd gotten sick from, though the well was the common denominator.

Supposed to work a Grand Canyon trip (as a swamper—a grunt-person), I had to tell the river company I couldn't make the launch at Lee's Ferry. "Maybe I can hike in at Phantom?" They said okay.

I stayed in bed three more days, hydrating, eating what I could, and set out. My friend had returned to Flagstaff—if I couldn't make the hot, nine-mile descent to the bottom of Grand Canyon to meet the rafts, I'd go to her house.

Either way, I had a two-day drive ahead of me. Usually those long drives clear the cobwebs from my brain and clarity moves in. Not this time—I'd been too sick. Reason enough not to go down the river or even drive but I throttled down the back-side of the Sierra Nevada anyway, cruised along 395 through Owens Valley, stopped at the prohibited waters of Owens Lake to splash my face and hair and top—a cheap form of air conditioning—and rolled down into the Mojave, past Las Vegas, to St. George.

The closer I got to the Colorado Plateau, the better I felt. At last I reached the Arizona Strip, climbing the grade to the Kaibab Plateau and Jacob Lake, descending through limestone, driving across House Rock Valley along the length of the Vermilion Cliffs.

Passing the familiar lodges, I turned left toward Lee's Ferry before the old Navajo Bridge (the new one not yet built), and wound down toward the river. There's a break in the rocks where the Paria Riffle shows, and my heart surged when I saw the river bouncing and sparkling along down there. I drove to the put-in, put my feet in the achingly cold water, brought the river to my face, wet my shirt and hair, wondered what I should do. Called my friend from the payphone at Marble Canyon Lodge, heat already drying my clothes.

"Well?" she said.

A hike to the bottom of the canyon would be *hot*. "I don't know."

She'd heard me say this a hundred times before. This time was no different—she was steady with patience.

"I don't know if I should go, if I'm strong enough. It's hot."

"Did you go to the river?"

"Oh, yes. I had to. When I caught that first glimpse, it was as if the river was smiling at me, saying hello."

She paused, giving me time. Then, "And you felt how?"

I could feel how I felt all through my body—tingling with excitement. Chicken skin, and not from weather. *I'm at the river.* "Happy?"

"Are you going down the river?"

"Yes?"

FOR DOGS, JOY takes corporeal form in the tail. For me it's a *rightness*, a *knowing*. Like looking into the face of my newborn. Like being with God, sitting on a rock somewhere talking.

IN HAWAI'I, CLARITY was everywhere, water a conduit. "I want to sail on *Hōkūleʻa* out to the middle of the ocean where I can't see any land." Two months later, I was on the canoe; many sails later, I was on a canoe in Micronesian waters, no land visible anywhere.

I want to go to Kahoʻolawe. I did go, at least twenty times.

Maka the man. Ten years later, Maka the mustang.

But there was a gap. I lost the pictures, the ability to see.

Does a broken heart cancel out joy? That's what happened to Rebecca. Joy magnet through our youth and even our bad-girl years, when her mother died Rebecca didn't bounce back. Together we would still giggle the way we did in sixth grade when we got kicked out of the room for disrupting the class, but when she was alone her world turned grim. There were moments of the old Rebecca, though. The day after Obama won the 2008 election (six weeks before she overdosed), her phone message said, "He's smart, and he's fine," and in a roll of afterthought, "and he's got good policies!"

Maybe Rebecca's death foreshadowed what was to come: I didn't go from lost to found, I went to more lost, leaving not only Maka but his Hawai'i, Maka the big teddy bear into which I stuffed my heart. Flattened by loss, my ability to read my na'au went to shit. I moved to New Mexico to hold grief inside me—or to escape it. Only with Tyler did I feel comfortable sharing it. I knew that Ken, living on a ranch on Colorado's Front Range at the moment of decision, closer than ever before, wouldn't ask me to.

Confusing the Rio Grande rift with the Colorado Plateau was the first (and perhaps most embarrassing) mistake I made. As grief and an injured knee shrunk my life, drought grounded the rio and we both sat mired in dysfunction. Surgery and pregnant monsoons helped us. The river flowed again. My knee healed before my heart did and I found myself on a borrowed gray gelding cowboying beside Ken the way I had with his father through the years of our marriage, Ken and me riding side by side through the shortgrass prairie or apart across distance, coming back together like currents in a braided river.

Meanwhile, I hooked on to Andrés. When Andrés left, my life was of horses and fear.

Andrés left and I had horses and work to do and just me. I forgot the picture of Kathy on the porch of the old ranch house with Lacey. The boyfriend restored the house, built in the 1880s, fortifying the rock foundation and tying in an upstairs corner that was supported from below by a kitchen cabinet—work that needed to be done, though I thought I was doing it for me. For an older me, actually, thinking this might be my older-woman home. Me thinking. Perhaps that was the problem. Instead of just feeling, allowing the pictures.

Kathy and Lacey on the porch.

Then again, perhaps the picture is not always what *I* think I want, but what is whispered to me: *Move to Colorado and he will come.*

KEN TOLD ME he was fixing a broken pipe on the California ranch when he thought, *I could be doing this same grunt work on a ranch my family owns.* Irrigation season half over when they arrive, he, Kathy, and Lacey move into the big house. I live in the old house. I have kept the ranch going but am strung tight with anxiety and exhaustion. We wade into this new relationship carefully—working together as a family.

Tiny Kathy large with pregnancy, granddaughter Lacey racing everywhere, I wonder if they will stay because they want to, or if Ken will move on to a real ranch to cowboy in the boot tracks of the five generations before him. To follow his own dreams instead of forcing himself to wear mine. One day, as he drives me to the Durango airport, he tells me of cowboying jobs he's seen online. He's only been at Cachuma a few weeks. He wants to make a bigger difference, he says, than he can with our small herd of cows, but he doesn't know what he will do. I want to support his decision, whatever it is. When he drops me at the curb and drives off, we have no answers.

I'm going to Oregon for a writing workshop with Wendy Beth, the trip planned and paid for months before I knew Ken was coming. I catch him after he's recrossed the Animas River on his return to the ranch. "We're grounded," I say, cell phone to cell phone. "The plane that's supposed to take us to Denver is broken. There aren't any more flights tonight."

As we head back to Cachuma through a canyon of ponderosas lifting toward timberline, we continue our conversation about what Ken might do: adapt his dreams to our small family ranch or go on with his own growing family to his own life. And what I might do if he leaves.

The next morning, fed up with phone calls to airlines trying to figure out how to get to Oregon, I throw my bags in the Subaru, say goodbye again, and feel better for having made the decision to drive before I even hit the two-lane highway. With nearly a thousand miles ahead of me, I'll miss the beginning of the workshop but will still meet wilderness writer Gary Ferguson and see Wendy Beth and later my older sister.

I drive 815 miles that day-into-night, up through Utah, across Idaho, into Oregon; sleep not in my car but in a motel in Baker City; and arrive at the workshop at noon the next day. Wendy Beth and Gary Ferguson greet me with huge hugs. I belong. After lunch, other workshoppers crowding into the narrow shade of the ranch house with a writing assignment, I lie down in the back of my faithful Forester, noting that this is the first time I've gone prone in the middle of an afternoon in well over a year. I paid for this privilege. Drove 946 miles for it. And now, away from the activity of the ranch long enough to write, the knowledge that what I am writing is shit does not help my guilt.

Among the questions Ken asked as he took me to the airport to not fly to Oregon were these: *Will you sell the ranch if I go? Where will you go next?* Followed by, *It's almost time for you to go anyway. You never stay.*

DETRITUS: MOAB, 2000. *In a white Chevy pickup bearing the red-dirt patina of southeastern Utah mud, Brooke Williams drives his wife Terry and me out of our Utah valley to the winter-quiet town of Moab, where we pluck new neighbor Jeff Foott off the sidewalk out of the blustery wind. He and I get to know each other better as we squish into the Chevy's back seat beside a large box of mail, Terry's daily intake.*

Dining at one of the few Moab restaurants open in winter, the four of us pass questions around with tortilla chips, and the newcomer—newer in coming to the area than me—and I discover that we were born in the same Berkeley, California, hospital. We agree that Berkeley seems a long way off both in distance and time, and moving becomes the topic of conversation.

Foott moved around for a few years, settled in Wyoming for a couple of decades, and is just relocating to Utah.

"I've only moved three times in my life," Terry says.

The waitress stops to light a candle before taking our orders, giving me time for a quick calculation: a fifteen-year-per-place average.

"Including changing houses, I've moved over thirty times in forty-five years," I say. Easy math, even for me: an average of every year and a half.

They look at me as if I've just grown a beard. I am equally perplexed. I don't know people who lived in the same place for as long as fifteen years. Except my mother and Ed. My sisters and their husbands. My father and his wife. Even Rebecca. The list grows, the three people with whom I'm dining adding to it.

Brooke reaches across the table for my unused coaster, turning it over and drawing a rough map as he asks my course. The map grows into a sort of angular spiral of the West, with Hawai`i out there on the side.

"Why?" Terry asks, her jeweled eyes bright in the candlelight. "Why did you move all those times?"

"Were you running?" Foott says.

Our quesadillas and chili rellenos arrive and Brooke sets the coaster map aside. I think about the different places I've lived, the U-Hauls and highways and long night drives, the friends I made, what I left behind. About desert air at two in the morning, cocaine on a tiny mirror, a cat jumping out the car window at a freeway gas station and coming back like a dog when called. About what it feels like to wake up in a new state.

I gaze into the dark beyond the big windows, and back into their faces. "Sometimes I was running." They look at me intently,

*as if my answer matters. "Running from, running to. In twelve-step
programs it's called a 'geographic.' Geographical cure."*

*They like that, but it doesn't answer their questions. I don't
have a better one. Moving is just something I've done, like school
or marriage or drugs. "Maybe I was looking?"*

"For what?" Terry says.

"I don't know. Maybe I'll know when I find it?"

TRUE TO FORM, a few months later I left that trio of friends and
our beloved Colorado Plateau valley and river for the only other
home I'd ever loved as much, this time moving far out of U-Haul
range. Hawai'i became the fourth state I lived in in five years.
Four states, five years, six towns, seven houses. Once on Maui I
moved only four times, the houses all in Ha'ikū, within a mile of
each other. A record.

When I look at the coaster map, which I pocketed before leaving the restaurant, I see two patterns: the pathway spiraling out
from Berkeley to include areas west, north, east, and south of the
hub, and the phenomenon of returning to places in which I'd lived
before. I didn't just make sentimental visits; I went back to stay.

And yet, staying is what I seem unable to do.

WHEN I RETURN from Oregon I find that anxiety has trickled
down and become Ken's, as well. The cat disappeared, scared off
by the new dogs. The irrigation water ran out, as it does every year.
We buy some cow-calf pairs and Ken finds a place for our growing
herd for the rest of the summer. He sells a horse. I sell a horse.

Kathy nine months pregnant, our lives are on hold. I get the
call in the early morning and jog down to Ken's house in the dark,
resting on the couch until Lacey wakes up. Three months shy of
two years old, she thinks Lucas, named for a horse of Keith's, is
a funny-looking doll nuzzling into her place in her mama's lap

at the hospital. Lacey and I go back to the ranch together. Life is still on hold, but here's my granddaughter beside me, my grandson on his way home.

Ken and I build up the woodpile, preparing for winter. We look for bigger leases, to run more cows—the work and livelihood we both understand. I slip out to the mustang cabin to write then shut it up for the season, turning off the water and draining the pipes. Mice move in. Tyler comes to Cachuma for a month, staying with Ken and his family in the big house, its cement floors frigid. Each time little Lacey falls, she bruises. Nobody is quite happy.

I don't know what to do. I can't just get in the Subaru and drive 946 miles away and away forever, or look out at a prairie sky from the daybed in the Forester and have it all okay.

I give Kua to Ken and spend time on the ground with Maui and Maka the mustang. Ken reports the different jobs he sees online. I tell him he should go. I don't want him to go—it's winter, not the best time to leave your mother alone on her ranch even if it is the bed she has made. We cut and split and haul wood and buy and stack more hay, trying to keep people warm and animals full. Spring will be the time of change, I figure—with irrigation starting, me trudging through the mud with heavy, smelly rubber hoses tucked under each arm.

I can't see a good time for Ken to leave.

In the spring we switch houses, the wooden floors of the old house more welcoming to toddlers. I'm not eager to go to the big house—too big for just me, its old-barn-wood interior too dark for my psyche—but grandbabies come first. Even so, I watch with a touch of sadness as the new paint in the old house grows grubby with fingerprints, the spruce floors chafed and worn by feet other than mine.

On the other side of the mountain the cabin awaits—the cabin and mustangs and freedom. I just can't see how to get there.

~~~

DETRITUS: COLORADO RIVER, 1995. *Forty-one years old on my first Grand Canyon trip, I sit in the rowing seat of an eighteen-foot yellow raft loaded down with river gear, the oars in my hands. The boatman coils up the bow line, pushes the raft from the ramp, and jumps aboard. It's his job to row the big rapids, mine to bail, but he is letting me start on the sticks.*

Dropping the blades into the water, I take a stroke, feeling biceps and triceps at work as I pull, feet and quads pushing. The raft glides toward the current; another pull and the current catches and I pivot the raft around, turning into the flow. Water ripples over rocks and shooshes along the canyon wall. The dry air smells so clean it hurts.

Where the Paria enters the clear blue water of the Colorado, the incoming water is thick and gray from limestone canyons miles away in Utah. At first the strikingly different colors run side by side, the line of differentiation growing hazier as the Paria pushes farther into the current of the bigger river. The merging waters create the Paria Riffle, and in the flatwater on the downstream side of that first little bump, the whole river runs another color—no longer clear blue or murky gray but a mix of both.

Like the Colorado, I have had clarity and I have had mud and I am still running.

13

THE LONG ROAD

THEY SAY IT STARTED IN MY YOUTH, BACK IN THE FIFTIES when Coppertone turned white people bronze. I didn't like yellow but I liked that billboard photo of the yellow-haired girl in her yellow two-piece, her puppy tugging at the bottoms and revealing her tan line.

In my forties I succumbed to the practice of applying sunscreen to my face every morning. "Why, then, is it my face that now suffers?" I ask the doctor.

"Because of those early years," he says. "We didn't even have *sunscreen* then, just . . ."

"Coppertone?" We both laugh, this before he starts cutting.

The nurse practitioner explained the Mohs procedure carefully during the biopsy appointment three weeks earlier: they cut out what they can see, take it to the lab in the back, check for more basal cancer cells, and if the flesh is clean they stitch me back up and send me home. Since she said it can take all afternoon if they have to keep cutting, I brought a chapter to work on.

Waiting for the numbing to take hold, I look at the pages, and when the doctor and his assistant enter the room I place paper, purple pen, and glasses on my lap. The assistant turns on a bright light, puts double-stick tape on my face, and presses sheets of blue cloth-paper to the tape, leaving a hole not for my eyes but for the incision that's about to appear on my forehead.

I can hear my skin resisting then yielding to the doctor's knife, the tug and release. If you've gutted an animal, you know what I mean. If you've cut fabric, you also know.

"In what genre do you write?" asks the doctor, perhaps guessing how aware I am.

"Literary fiction and nonfiction." My standard answer.

"What are you working on now?"

I take a deep breath, try a few words, and quickly discover that I prefer hearing my voice to the scalpel. As the doctor continues cutting, I explain the plight of America's wild horses, and talk about advocacy groups and the BLM, how we need to work together. I tell him about PZP, how it works if you use it and doesn't if you don't, and about TJ, her long days in the field tracking mares she needs to dart because in the long run those darts keep mustangs free.

Time to take that piece of me to the lab. The assistant turns off the bright light and pulls the blue paper from my face, placing a fat bandage on the brow above my left eye. "Would you like to watch TV?"

I don't watch TV. I'd rather read, or go into worlds I make up, where my characters can work together or fall in love. I can make people get clean or get cancer and heal and I can kill off only the bad guys. I can even make the BLM use PZP in all the mustang territories it manages.

When the doctor returns to tell me he got it all and to stitch me up, he has a different assistant with him. I ask if I can look in a mirror. They glance at each other. She gets the mirror. The hole in my head looks like a bullet wound.

The new assistant asks what I'm working on.

"I've just told the doctor all about it. He won't want to hear it again."

Instead, he tells it. Needle poking and sinew tugging at my skin, the doctor explains about the numbers of mustangs in the wild and in holding facilities, how advocates and the BLM are using PZP, how it works . . . if it's used.

"My father's a vet," the assistant says. "He'll probably know about PZP."

"Good," I say. "Not enough people do."

During a night of throbbing pain and poor sleep despite Tylenol, I remember the one thrill of the day. In the doctor's office, my entire life there in my face—ocean and rivers, horses and cattle there in my face—I could hear beyond the knife the doctor telling the story of America's wild horses. Mustangs had an audience for a day.

It's fall and my truck is home after five weeks away. Not me-away, the truck away, living at Gary's Repair in Mancos for five weeks and a day.

The 2004, four-door Toyota Tacoma was feeling a lot like home before its extended visit to Gary's. A 2,875-mile road trip will do that, especially when you have a dog with you (Reed only, this time) and you sleep in the bed of the truck as far from people and lights as you can get on dirt roads going nowhere you know, nowhere you've been before, but hopefully somewhere that will surprise you in the morning.

Going to Oregon for the second summer in a row to meet Wendy Beth for a writers' conference—the drive premeditated this time—I pulled off beside the Snake River after logging eight hundred miles. As I considered the best angle to park for sleep, a lifted pickup drove bright and loud toward me. Reed and I left quickly. But the hour was late and my back and butt hurt and my eyes were more closed than open so when I passed through what looked on the map like a town, I searched the three buildings for a motel sign and of course there wasn't one.

Soon afterward a BLM campground sign appeared. I am loath to camp in campgrounds, but out of desperation I drove through the place and realized that these campers were hunters—body bags hanging from trees clued me in. Not that I dislike hunters, I just don't like them in packs, so I drove on up the dirt road, wanting to be able to pee beside the truck in the middle of the night, that middle coming on fast. Finding a sheltered place near a large ponderosa, I stopped, smelled the familiar caramel, and heard running water nearby.

Predawn we awoke, too cold and too early. Walking to the water, flashlight in hand, I saw it wasn't a big river, so I found a place to stand with my feet braced against rocks, dropped the flashlight and my clothes on the bank, and bathed. In graying light I redressed and crawled back into the sleeping bag to warm up, Reed curled near my head. Moments later two ATVs roared, the drivers in camouflage accented with hunter orange. Then a pickup went past, and a school bus. The town with three buildings that weren't motels apparently had houses and residents in its vicinity in addition to its campground and hunters.

Reed and I returned to the river. It was full of flotsam, thick foamy stuff piling up behind rocks and riding into eddies, invisible earlier in the flashlight's pale beam. But beyond the dirty water, pines and firs rose up the sides of the canyon, and large granite outcroppings appeared. Despite the questionable residue on my skin, my best ex's promise of a road trip's magic in the morning came true.

A couple of hours later I saw mustangs, which made me late to meet Wendy Beth—hard to be on time when you're driving a thousand miles for the date; harder still when you're me and mustangs show up in your path, but that's a later story.

Leaving my older sister's house days later, I found an obscure dirt road in Nevada with no hunters or school buses or human beings anywhere nearby when I awoke. Just big sagebrush, piñon pine and juniper, and willows in a draw. Which maybe meant water.

Reed and I followed the trickle to its source—a spring near

old mine shafts and an old mine shack complete with plank bed hinged to the wall. And granite, which surprised me, because I imagined Nevada predominantly basalt.

Back on the road, I spotted mustangs—not hard to do in Nevada, that much I did know—and I drove down another dirt road and traipsed through more sagebrush to get closer. This is also another story and I must get back to the truck. Which I did, with a camera full of photos and most of the day's drive ahead of me while most of the day had already passed. And the night ahead was not one in which to truck-camp but to drive through to home.

I drove. Stopped to pee and for gas only. Sometime after dark, we reached the San Rafael Swell, a good place to stop and stretch and look at rocks in the moonlight. Around eleven thirty, one last stop to fuel up eight miles before the Utah-Colorado state line, fifty-nine miles from Cachuma Ranch, I did the unthinkable: I bought a gas station hotdog. So rarely do I do this that it's remarkable. Gas in the truck, gas in my stomach, soon I'd be home.

Crossing through the intersection of 191 and 491, I picked up the tempo to twenty-five—you do not speed in these Mormon towns—and leaned forward to take a bite of the hotdog.

Even as I bent to the dog I saw the shape of the deer to my left. Saw her enough to know she was a she and that she was three-legged, her gait like three-legged Bow's. I hit the brakes and the hotdog went flying along with everything on the passenger seat and no doubt Reed in the camper shell and then so went the deer. I saw her on my left but hit her with the right front corner of the truck—her compromised momentum and my foot on the brake pausing us for one second before we collided and there she lay, the hotdog's catsup and relish on the dash and my hands and the steering wheel as I pulled over and fumbled for the hazard lights, which in the six months of owning the truck I hadn't used.

The three approaching vehicles did not stop.

In the mess I found my phone. "I was eating a hotdog," I said to the dispatcher. "No, I'm okay. But not the deer. She's not dead. She needs to be shot." I didn't cry. "She had a broken leg before I hit her."

I waited with the deer for the cops. Her breathing even, eyes open, she was not, I was sure, seeing stars in the midnight sky. She didn't fight, just lay there as I touched her neck and shoulder and examined her left hind leg: broken above the hock, bone and blood dry, the skin shriveled up at the edges. She'd been living like this for a few days at least.

Two young Mormon cops arrived—they'd been chasing stray cows at the nearby fairgrounds—and were much nicer than those who have given me tickets in the past. Without saying fuck I told them about the hotdog—*stupid fucking hotdog* is what I wanted to say—and they just kept being nice, telling me to get back in the Toyota when one of them went out of sight. I didn't, though, and after the pistol fired I watched as the doe lifted her front end and thrashed her head and succumbed. Reed stood panting in the bed though the danger had passed.

The truck made awful grating noises but the men said I was safe to go on, so I limped out of Utah and turned onto the first dirt road I came to—not to find a place to sleep but to call Wendy Beth in Oregon, hoping that with the time difference she might still be awake. She was. My breath came out in a sob. I cried the rest of the way home.

Really it wasn't the hotdog's fault. Or mustangs or old mines or a last breakfast with my sister before beginning the drive the day before. The doe was doomed to die. She just hadn't done it yet. The timing was such that I would have hit her with or without the hotdog.

Except, that's not true, is it? If I hadn't pulled that stupid fucking hotdog from the bin, laid it in its bun, lathered it with catsup, sprinkled it with relish, stood behind another late-night customer to pay for it . . .

~~~

AFTER FIVE WEEKS and a day the truck has come home. The dogs are inside with me by the fire. The deer is still dead, and for that I am grateful—her suffering stopped when she met that bullet, though her path toward death began with the first vehicle she hit before she hit mine.

You see how I've shifted the blame?

But I cannot do so here. I put down my pen to go out with the dogs—six dogs as I'm watching Ken's three in addition to my own while he and Kathy and the kids are at Kathy's folks for Thanksgiving. I'm driving down from the upper barn in my freshly repaired truck, five of the dogs loping alongside as they often do, Cojo inside the camper shell. Unbeknownst to me, Ken is driving his family down the other dirt road. Later he tells me he saw the Toyota and dogs at the barn but wanted to get the kids to the house and out of car seats so didn't stop. So while I was running into his little dog Peanut, or she into me, his one- and two-year-old children were reentering their home, their parents unloading suitcases.

No hotdog in hand, no tiredness to blame, just carelessness and recklessness colliding—not paying attention enough on my part and some quick urge to see what was on the other side of the road on hers. They say there are no accidents but as my hands feel the life lifting from Peanut's little body, I want to believe otherwise.

She ran head-on into the tire—she's hit but not run over. I rest my hand on her side but don't pick her up until she's finished dying, then I wrap her in my sweatshirt and set her inside the camper shell. Scrunched up near the cab, Cojo looks from Peanut to me. He smells Peanut, blood flooding her mouth. Water from my eyes. Cojo has seen me cry before. He's been with me eight years. But dead Peanut is a first.

I don't know Ken's home.

Maybe if I knew I wouldn't have wailed so loudly.

With the living dogs sniffing at other smells along the way, I drive slowly down to the houses, shocked to silence when I see Ken's rig in his driveway. I drive past, down to the barn, where I text Ken: *Call me.*

He doesn't.

I text again. *Now.*

"What's wrong?" he says, as soon as I answer.

"I killed Peanut."

Sorry is a small word to utter in the face of this, but I am. Still. Deeply, beseechingly sorry.

THAT LITTLE BLACK-AND-WHITE Chihuahua-pug-Jack Russell terrier lived in Ken's lap, on the back of his chair, *in* his bed, between the covers for God's sake until Kathy moved in. Peanut slept *on* my bed when I visited in New Mexico, and in Colorado she started spending nights with me again. Maybe the kids were too rambunctious, or Ken's lap wasn't big enough for all. I let her stay. I loved her, though little dogs like Peanut are not my preference. But she was *little Peanut.* And she adopted me. Who was I to send her home? Although ultimately it was me who did so.

Lacey did not ask about Peanut that night or the next day or week or month. Maybe not telling her was bad grandparenting but I was a wreck, unable to reconcile what I'd done. Lacey didn't ask; we didn't tell. Ken buried his precious Peanut beneath a grandmother juniper, slabs of sandstone fit together like puzzle pieces over the top to keep the coyotes from digging before the freeze set in. It was the beginning of another hard, cold winter, the next face surgery for basal cell carcinoma two weeks later, the day before Lacey's birthday. I didn't even see her on her birthday, though our houses are only two hundred yards apart.

~~~

AFTER THE NIGHT in the truck with Reed in Oregon and bathing in a filthy river, I drove west along Highway 20. Just past the town of Burns I saw the Bureau of Land Management's Burns District Office, central to the management of Oregon's mustangs. Someone inside suggested I go to Oregon's Wild Horse Corral Facility three miles west.

A banner by the highway told me a big adoption had taken place that weekend—horses were rounded up by helicopter, trucked to the facilities, and auctioned off. I drove up the dirt road slowly. Stopping at the office, I asked questions of the BLM employee at the counter. These mustangs were off the Kiger Herd Management Area; the ones remaining in the pens were either awaiting transportation to their new lives or unadopted.

"We don't use PZP," she said when I asked. "The herd is too small. PZP doesn't work on small herds."

"How big is the range? What is the AML?" Appropriate management level. The BLM loves acronyms.

She told me the Kiger HMA is 36,618 acres, with fifty-one to eighty-three adult horses allowed.

"We use PZP in our herd management area," said I, "which is 22,000 acres with a carrying capacity of thirty-five to sixty-five adult horses. We haven't had a roundup in five years and won't need one anytime soon. Because of PZP," I added.

"People want these Kiger horses. Buyers come all the way from Europe, Germany, to adopt them. The top stallion just sold for nearly ten thousand dollars."

A wild horse from the wilds of America's West transported to Germany in the belly of an airplane so it could breed and produce more horses when we have tens of thousands of mustangs in short-term holding facilities available for adoption—what could I say? Besides, I was trying not to piss her off. "So the Bureau of Land Management is in the business of breeding horses?"

I sensed our conversation was over when she turned her back to me.

I drove the dirt road around the perimeter of the pens slowly, the circle designed so viewers can see without leaving their vehicles. The pens were large, mostly without shade, mustangs arranged by gender and age: stallions together, open mares together, pregnant mares and mares with foals corralled together. "Quality animals with dun factor coloration and Spanish mustang characteristics are returned to the HMA following gathers to maintain the core of the breeding herd," says BLM literature. The dun factor was evident: these mustangs were mostly bay dun, red dun, and grulla, and, like the Spanish horses brought to North America in the 1500s, compact and stout in stature.

Stallions sparred for seconds—rearing, wheeling, kicking, striking—then lowered their heads to the feed troughs. Foals lay in the shade of their mothers' bodies. Some horses ran to a far corner together, turning and snorting at what spooked them (me). Most were destined elsewhere, due to color. Stopping to click my camera, I wanted them all and wanted them free.

IN BETWEEN THE writers' conference and visiting my sister in Ashland, I wanted to see mustangs in Oregon's dry, high-desert mountains. First I needed to find a place to camp for the night. Taking a gravel road up Steens Mountain, where I knew mustangs lived, I wound into the darkness. At the end of a rough side road, Reed and I went to bed.

Too soon morning spread before us—no river but a big view of hazy distance. We poked around a manmade meadow looking for tracks (later I saw signs that talked of reclamation from juniper invasion) before bumping back to the main road up the mountain. Stopping to glass a canyon for mustangs, I watched a couple hiking to the summit spook up a Rocky Mountain bighorn ram with huge curls, who came flying directly at me. When he saw Reed he veered away. My heart struck rib bones.

Down the far south side of Steens Mountain: horse poop in the road! We got out and walked. More sign in the trees—tracks and stud piles—but no horses. Morning turned toward afternoon. I had to head out. My sister was expecting me.

At the base of the mountain, right beside the road: a pinto band of fat, calm, Oregon mustangs. Like our Spring Creek Basin band of ambassador mustangs—*Chrome Winona Terra Mariah Kwana Jadi Remy Makani*—these wild ponies were used to seeing people and vehicles, colts stepping behind mares and the band stallion, the others barely moving as I got out to photograph (my telephoto lens not nearly as long as TJ's) then left them alone.

Hours later, I arrived at my sister's, my little detour costing five hundred miles.

NEVADA HOLDS 83 of the BLM's 177 wild horse and burro herd management areas. Highway 50 goes through the heart of mustang territory, as do most of Nevada's few thoroughfares. I didn't have to look for horses. They were there. I just had to decide which dirt road to take.

I don't know which it was—unmarked, between two towns about a hundred miles apart, I turned south instead of north, that's all. Drove on a rutted road until I spotted a band a mile away. Parked in the shade of a lone juniper and walked out toward them. At first they didn't notice me as they searched for blades of grass beneath basin big sagebrush. Through binoculars I could see they were thin, not at all like the Kiger mustangs in the pens or the Steens Mountain mustangs at the base of the mountain or our mustangs at home.

In Nevada's basin-and-range topography exists those prominent geologic features—basins and ranges—and little water. The Great Basin encompasses a series of endorheic basins in which water flows inward without escape other than through evaporation or drainage downward—it collects into lakes or vanishes. Not necessarily a preferred place to be a mustang, but they don't have a choice.

When the horses spotted me, the band stallion, a lean, lanky bay, separated from the band, neck arched, head high, stepping high, snorting through the desert air as he trotted toward me, his breath resounding in my chest. His cremello lieutenant stallion spooked away, looking back at me, and didn't come closer. I sat down right there on the dry, hard-packed Nevada soil. The band stallion kept coming nearer, nostrils flaring, gathering data then sprinting away, his band at the far edge of his movement. In this way he circled me, using up precious energy. To just stand up to leave would have alarmed the band even more so I stayed still, as nonthreatening as I could make myself.

The lieutenant stallion and two mares drifted south, browsing more than grazing, and the long-legged bay stallion lowered his head to feed though his eye was still upon me. When they moved far enough off, I stood and walked away, checking over my shoulder. The stallion watched my retreat but by the time I made the mile back to the truck and let Reed out, the band seemed to have forgotten me.

The BLM says the herd management areas in Nevada are too big to administer PZP programs. They *are* large. But there were only eleven mustangs in that band, including five mares. Clearly they were not used to someone squatting in their midst but if a person were to do so a few times it's likely the mares would get close enough to dart. TJ didn't just walk into Spring Creek Basin one day and start shooting mares in the rump with her darting rifle. She worked for it.

The other women who dart, and the few men, work for it. In Colorado's Sand Wash Basin Herd Management Area, which covers 157,730 acres and allows 163 to 363 mustangs, the Sand Wash Advocate Team partners with the BLM. The team, comprised mostly of women volunteers between TJ's age and mine, traverses the mesas and ridges within the 246-square-mile HMA to document, dart, and assist with bait trapping. It's not that Nevada's herd management areas are too big, or Oregon's too small, it's that the BLM has to be willing to develop focused PZP programs and enlist volunteers—people who know the terrain and the horses, or are willing to learn.

TJ's idea: get the ranchers to help. They often know the terrain best. But the BLM has other ideas.

It's complex. My story is simpler. I drove, saw mustangs, friends, my sister, drove more, and saw more mustangs.

Then the deer. Then Peanut. Then my face.

KEN DRIVES ME to Durango in the morning on roads covered with ice and snow. After the first cutting, I call mustang friend Pat in tears. The roads have cleared enough that she and Frank drive in and Pat joins me in the doctor's office for the cuttings—five total, but she's a nurse. The hole on the end of my nose grows to the size of a quarter. I don't ask for a mirror. Frank stays in the waiting room with Ken. Frank leads us to the hospital for the plastic surgery necessary to cover the hole. He and Ken go out and get food. They go out to fill prescriptions. Pat and Frank stay at the hospital with Ken until I'm released after ten p.m. We've all been there for more than twelve hours. If that's a way to measure friendship, I can tell you they are my friends.

When I explained to the plastic surgeon and anesthesiologist that I am a drug addict and asked them not to use narcotics in the drip, the surgeon looked at me sternly. "We will use what we need to use to make this easier," he said, "on you and on me." I went to sleep, he stretched my cheek over my nose, I awoke, and pain came later, not immediately like with my knee.

Both eyes black and my whole face distorted with the swelling, for two days I took the prescribed pain medication—even my pillow hurt my face—and then disposed of the pills.

I missed Lacey's birthday, Lacey only two hundred yards away, me looking as if a billy club met my face and feeling as if it were true.

Lacey's birthday, December 16. The same date Rebecca died. Already years away.

14

Grounded

I FALL OFTEN. LIKE, DOWN. LIKE ALL THE WAY TO THE GROUND. Six times in one week, I fell: three while snowshoeing, one on ice, one being bumped by spooking horses, Kua and Maui startling when snow slid off the barn roof.

Then I fell while holding my grandson. We both hit our heads. I tried so hard not to fall all the way down with one-and-a-half-year-old Lucas in my arms, and not to drop him, that later I was stiff in weird places. He was okay. My head hurt and my face felt strange, as if my scars had loosened, and my leg is still indented where it got caught in the tines of the tractor, which are what tripped me. Or, my focus on something other than my feet tripped me. Age tripped me.

Lucas is okay. I said that already, but it's important. Fear is secondary: Ken's when he saw me on the ground holding his baby, who was crying mightily. Mine during the fall, after the fall, right now. I could have seriously hurt my grandbaby! Hurting me is okay—I do it all the time. But Ken's words: "This is why . . ." and the unfinished sentence. . .

Ken worries, watching me. Tyler, too, whether he's at the ranch or hears the stories later. For me fear permeates the *now* part of the story—hitting Lucas's head on the two-by-four leg of a workbench (hitting mine on the steel tractor)—the anxiety of aging, or anxiety of overwhelm.

When I complained to my bio-father about getting older, he would say, "The alternative isn't much better." My classic line, when I tell this to people, is, "He would say, 'The alternative isn't much better,' and then he died."

He did. He died of complications of a stroke eleven days after the stroke struck him.

It's not that I've led a fearless life. I simply faced each fear and dove in. Until the deaths. I was fifty-four, fifty-five. Feeling fear and pushing into it as always. Time kept ticking by. One day at a time I got older, and suddenly six years had passed.

A person can do a lot in six years. And I suppose I did.

For a while I had some horses. I'm down to three, or two, depending on if Ken takes Kua or Kua stays with me when Ken goes. Ken will go. We just don't know when yet, or where.

Meanwhile, I still do not have a horse I can ride. I do not push my fear up onto the back of a horse I own. Not Kua, who is too much horse for me. And Maka and Maui are still "colts." I am sixty-one. I don't want to start colts. Though we do a lot of groundwork, I don't want to put the first saddle or first ride on them. Because I am afraid. So, shame as well as fear. *No shame*, they say in Hawai'i, or *no need feel shame*. But I do.

This is when I would say to my father, "I don't like getting old," and he would say . . . you know what he would say. And then he died.

I TALK TO my cousin Nancy, who also experienced three deaths close together, and she tells me there's a thing that happens, according to therapists: a particular fear seeps in—fear of one's own impending death. Of course we live knowing we will die, but when those around us drop boom boom boom, we start expecting it. Like, any day.

I tell Nancy I'm afraid my sons might find me cold and naked in the morning. Nightgowns and pj's are so confining—I feel trapped, bedcovers and clothes twisting around me in the night—but worrying about the naked discovery, I start wearing nightgowns, and debate about underwear.

I forget to ask Nancy how long the fear will last.

It's SPRING. I'm working with Maka the mustang. We're alone in the big round pen. Maka has grown into a dark bay hunk of gorgeous horse. No one who sees him believes he's a mustang. I lift up his thick black wavy mane to show them the BLM freeze brand that marks him as once wild and free, then captured.

People don't know the beauty of mustangs.

More than sixteen hands at the withers—unusually tall for a mustang—and weighing thirteen hundred pounds, his feet are seven inches across. Salad plates. His hip and hindquarters and knees are huge. So is his heart, or so I think.

I'm in the center of his circle; he's in a rope halter with a lead rope twelve feet long so he has room to move his huge yet graceful body around me. I have a turquoise flag I got at a Buck Brannaman clinic (TJ got a purple one)—a long pliable metal rod with fabric at the tip that flutters and speaks but will not hurt a horse.

Maka is smooth and easy in his trot around the round pen, loping the same way, watching me with the inside eye, one ear pivoting out as he monitors the whereabouts of Maui, Kua, and Ken's family's little mustang Don Quixote, who roam through the junipers in the pasture that adjoins the round pen. Maka can see over the seven-foot fence. He needs to focus more on me. I stop him and turn him back, first the hind, then the front, like in Buck Brannaman's DVDs and clinics, and send him around the circle in the other direction.

Maybe the horses outside the round pen are running around with the weather, but I don't really know—watching my big beautiful mustang, my world has shrunk to just him and me, my heart pounding love through me hard enough to crack my ribs. Like all young girls, I want this horse to love me back the same way. Yet his outside ear stays focused on the outside horses, and I know he is divided.

I keep him circling, asking his body to bend around me, his attention to focus inward. He curves in his slow trotting circle, so graceful in his size, the rope loose between us except when he turns his head to monitor the other horses and I give a quick jerk: put your attention in here.

When he does, I stop him. Not through the rope but with my body—a single step back, my forward-pushing momentum withdrawn.

He stops his trot and turns toward me, first his hind, then his front, his back feet stepping over each other and then his forefeet taking a step to align him, butt to the fence, head to me. I walk to him.

I think I walk to him to rub his forehead, to pet him, reward him in my human way. Touch. Words. My heart swollen with love.

I think I step to his right, his neck bending so he can look at me, and I don't know what I was going to do, I don't remember, I only remember being close to his big brown chest and heart and eyes, the reasons for his name, Maka like the man, Makanani, beautiful eyes and heart and spirit, my focus so inside the small circle I have made of him and me that I do not have any consciousness of the world beyond the bigger circle of the round pen.

But he does.

Something I will never know happens. I think I hit the ground and sit upright in seconds but when I look for him he's at the fence forty feet away, not heaving with frightened breath but standing calmly, the lead rope stretched out in front of him as if he's ground tied. He looks at me, at the lead rope, hip cocked, resting.

Does this tell me the passage of time between the tackle of his chest and me sitting up in the dirt? I don't know. Won't ever know.

I try to stand. Bad idea. So I sit there, knowing I hit my head or my head was hit and I cannot stand and my ears are blocked of sound and my vision soft as I search my brain for answers. What to do. I sit in the dirt of the round pen for a long time, the small gravel marking my palms as my hands support me. I cannot stand. I breathe. In, out. Maka does not move. He knows that if he does the snake of the lead rope will whip around his legs, biting him. I know that if I move I will tip over.

I'm on my butt, legs crooked in front of me, one arm supporting me. Maka's big chest or shoulder knocked me back and sideways. Or, I fell back and sideways. I sit crookedly and think I want to lie down. But I cannot. *Call Ken.* Cannot. Don't have my phone. I can't find my shades. They are behind me, launched off my face with the impact and lying several feet away. I cry a little. The flag is in front of me, probably dropped when I dropped. My body doesn't hurt (yet), but my brain won't focus. Fuzzy eyes, fuzzy brain.

I know I cannot sit here forever. Since I cannot call Ken, I have to go to him for help. I know that much: that I need help.

I sit for a long time. Eight minutes, ten. And then I roll over and with my hands push myself up, knees to standing. Get my shades. Do I pick up the flag now, or later? I don't know. I walk to Maka. Pet him. Do something, lead him in a circle? Put something between the wreck and turning him out with the other horses. It is a small something. I don't remember it.

Somehow I stay walking, leading him. He follows me like the big puppy he is, or can be, to the heavy gate of the round pen. I remove his halter, not wanting to risk him jumping free out the gate with me still holding on to him. I rub him on the shoulder, I think, or neck. I don't know I smell of blood, don't know I'm bleeding; I only know I am living in two realms, dreaming while aware of my actions, undoing the halter, opening the gate. He stands there, unsure. I step to his hip, slight pressure, and he moves out through the gate before the other horses crowd in.

I think I close the gate. I don't remember picking up the flag but it is in my hands with Maka's halter. I think I manage to push the other heavy gate open and closed, and I'm outside the round pen. I know the way to Ken's. I know how far it is. I doubt walking.

And there coming down the road is my friend Mary. She is visiting from Alaska and has gone on a walk. She looks like an angel, her silver hair haloing out with the wind, her arms moving like wings. She catches up to me, and passes, her walk brisk. I step slowly, one foot in front of the other. I cannot speak. She slows, matching my deliberate pace.

"Are you okay?" she says. I feel her peering into my world.

Later she will tell me I said no. I don't remember. But if I said no then I was not okay, because usually, still, I push through the thing that hurts or scares. Usually I *am* okay.

We keep walking and then there's the shade of a thick juniper and she sets me down. I don't know that I need shade as the afternoon is chilled, but somehow it makes sense. A line in the dirt road between sun and shade and I'm on the shady side of the line.

"I'll go get the car," Mary says, and asks directions to the house, which I manage to give. But I don't manage to think *Go get Ken.*

Her rental car comes back and I'm sitting in the road in the shade. Mary waits for a second before realizing that I cannot rise. She gets out and helps me up and into the car. I think we talk about the hospital, and finally I say, "Get Ken." She drives back down the road and finds Kathy who gets Ken.

He takes over. Together they put me in the Tacoma and find my purse and Ken drives us to the hospital while Mary calls ahead. I am already in an altered world. I saw Angel Mary walking down the road. Now Ken floats us to the hospital.

They help me into a wheelchair. I cannot walk on my own. But I'm not hurt; I don't hurt. I don't know I'm bleeding—no one has looked at the back of my head to see the gash where I bleed into my hair, into the collar of my down jacket, which I don't remember putting back on, blood in the Navajo hand-rolled silver necklace I wear, turning it pink. Blood in my shirt. I only know I'm floating. Dreaming in the other world while talking to people in this one—this hospital world.

They take three CAT-scan photos. Put seven staples in my head, closing the three-inch gash without shaving my hair. Sometimes I think I'm lucid—I'm glad they don't shave my head—but when I try to tell Ken and Mary and the nurse and doctor what I'm seeing, I can tell by their faces that lucid I'm not. I'm in an altered space, not one I know despite the many altered spaces of my past.

Angels Ken and Mary take me back to the ranch. They make scrambled eggs for me. Mary washes my bloody neck. Ken goes home to his family and I dress for bed and climb in, already dreaming. Dreams I won't remember. But they have colors. And horses. Rainbow horses.

I DON'T KNOW when it will start but I know it will: their fear for me. Tyler calls with it in the morning. Even TJ, who lives in Disappointment Valley full-time, driving and hiking and riding all over, mostly alone, mentions it: *What if you were at the cabin. Alone. Seven miles away. More than an hour to medical help once I find you.*

Tyler asks if he should tell my mother. No, I say. She will worry more about me.

In the hospital Ken looked at the gash. "It's clean," he said. "No gravel or dirt from the round pen." I could feel him looking at the back of my head. "It was Maka's hoof," he decided. "He knocked you over and his hoof struck your head as he went by."

Maka's big, salad-plate hoof. I don't know how to doubt it but I don't want it true. My big beautiful mustang boy spooked, that is all. I was in his way, that is all.

I am fine now, a week later, staples removed, brain healing.

I am fine now, a month later, having rested my brain and body for weeks. I have not yet worked with Maka again. I am still a bit wobbly, and nauseous at times.

Two months later, I am really fine. No longer fuzzy, confused, I can stack hay bales, calve out cows; we're getting ready for irrigation to start. We have horses—a dark bay, a red bay, Ken's buckskin, the grandkids' grulla mustang, and a palomino Paint—rainbow horses. I am looking for another—ranch-broke and wise in the ways of cattle and taking care of a rider—a horse that a kid or a woman in her sixties can ride. Because I am not ready to be grounded just yet. Because I still love seeing my world from the back of a horse—a broad world of redrock and rimrock and juniper and piñon pine and basin big sagebrush and those native grasses that thrive in this desert despite hardship.

Because I want my life to change. I want the alternative to be better. Better than fear. And that is all.

Part IV

AFTER / *PEDOGENESIS*

And the trails I ride are new
Even though I've made the circle many times before
For they change with every season
And with every shift of light
From the summit where the clouds fall to the sweet, valley floor

—Dave Stamey, "The Circle"

15

WHERE SCIENCE AND MUSTANGS MEET

IN DISAPPOINTMENT VALLEY, WE LIVE AT THE EDGE OF THE
San Juan Mountains, which comprises this western edge of the
Rockies; the edge of the Colorado Plateau, which spreads south,
west, and north of here; the southwestern edge of the state of
Colorado; the northeastern edge of the Four Corners area. We
live at the edge of piñon-juniper woodland, the ponderosa pine
forest beginning just feet higher up and building to mixed coni-
fer and aspen, and then that edge: timberline, where trees stop
and snow or alpine baldness begins.

Being at all these edges really means we're at the heart of it all.

From the ledge of Dakota Sandstone in front of the mustang
cabin, I watch Disappointment Creek flash and flood and trickle
through the seasons, setting in motion this confluence of place.
At its source on the side of iconic Lone Cone, the creek runs
clearly. Downstream a few miles, the creek often runs steel gray,
silt mixing into snowmelt as the current gathers runoff from
side drainages, or it may run browner if Ryman Creek is on the
rise, bringing snowmelt down from the Glade. Disappointment
Creek carries whatever it can to the Dolores River after meandering through lower Disappointment Valley, collecting more
salt and silt.

The Dolores carries water released from McPhee Reservoir and whatever spills from seeps and drainages it encounters on its way to the Colorado River over there in Utah. Major silt contributor to the Colorado, the Dolores River is guilty mainly by its association with Disappointment Creek.

This is a desert of thrifty not fertile soil. It is alkali, salty, dry. Puddles leave white bathtub rings. It grows cacti, bunchgrasses, and salt desert shrubs—greasewood, fourwing saltbush, shadscale, snakeweed—which need minimal water to survive.

This valley, like other valleys of the Paradox Basin, is made of salty Paradox Formation with additional rock layers on top. Though deposited under the influence of geologic law—originally horizontal thanks to gravity—the layers later deformed with pressure and time. They squished like my old Therm-a-Rest, which, when it bears my weight, sinks in the middle, the pressure escaping to the outer edges where the air finds weaknesses in the seams and either balloons or leaks out, leaving the middle of my sleeping pad as flat as the valley floor. Given that Disappointment Valley also runs along the axis of a syncline (a U-shaped fold), its lower elevations are courtesy of squishing and folding.

Today spring winds suck all moisture from soil and skin. Disappointment Creek runs downcanyon under a pushy upriver wind. Soil blows back upvalley, Utah into Colorado, Arizona into New Mexico. With less ground cover more soil blows. Perhaps overgrazing should be the new outlaw of the old West.

Instead that outlaw seems to be mustangs. Horses that also live at the edges of things—the edges of good grazing land, of military test sites, of towns expanding into wild horse terrain. The edges of wilderness mapped and managed by government agencies. Natural edges of cliffs and ridges, and edges created by arbitrary lines drawn on paper and traced across the landscape with barbed wire. Somehow wild horses, as oblivious of their impact as a desert river, have riled ranchers, the Bureau of Land

Management, the media, the public. While their inclination is simply to survive, they have become an innocent threat. They are hated by many, loved by some, and misunderstood by most.

Some mustang advocates recognize that too many horses on these harsh yet tender desert lands can damage the terrain irreparably, and that removal of some may help more stay wild. Other mustang "advocates" say freedom for all, not grasping that with no predator but man (because men have killed too many predators), mass starvation is a tragic possibility when herd numbers grow beyond what the land can support. "Remove the cattle," they say, overlooking more practical and attainable solutions.

In 2016, with nearly fifty thousand mustangs and burros in BLM-owned or -sponsored short- and long-term holding facilities in the West, the word *slaughter* started making the rounds. Some supposed advocates voted to slaughter those horses in holding—tens of thousands of mustangs.

WHEN *THE HORSE Lover: A Cowboy's Quest to Save the Wild Mustangs* is fresh on the stands, TJ and I go to Farmington, New Mexico, to hear H. Alan Day talk about the book he wrote with Lynn Wiese Sneyd. Day's Mustang Meadows, the first government-sponsored wild-horse sanctuary in the US, was started in the late 1980s. In partnership with the BLM, Day and his crew ran 1,500 unadoptable (as deemed by the BLM) mustangs on 35,000 acres of South Dakota prairie (through which ran a Spring Creek that actually flowed). After three years of horses thriving on Mustang Meadows' prairie grasses, the BLM told Day to sort off seven hundred horses, saying they were now adoptable. While Day didn't find out what happened to those mustangs, he was aware that horses were bringing eighty cents a pound at the sales yard—maybe $650 per horse, or upwards of $450,000.

Next the BLM told him to gather twenty-five of the thinnest, oldest horses. A rep went to the ranch to look them over, and ordered Day to euthanize them all. Meaning, shoot them. Though he was paid less per head per day than it cost the BLM to keep horses in holding, Day was under contract. He talked to his foreman, his conscience, the horses, but in the end he had to do what the government demanded. In a pen of twenty-five horses, some scarred or one-eyed, some thinner than others, all in their twenties, he did the unimaginable, dropping them one by one.

At the book signing, Day says to the small crowd in the Farmington public library, "We've got to stop the problem at the baby-making end of things."

After his talk, TJ gives him a big hug and introduces herself, in that order. "I volunteer with BLM," she tells him. "We've been darting with native PZP for four years now." I watch their heads nodding as they talk, in complete agreement that PZP is the most humane, commonsense answer.

The BLM has tried to control population by mustang removal. So have ranchers in the past, when mustangers captured and sold wild horses to slaughterhouses. Now ranchers sue the government to remove wild horses so the horses won't threaten cattle numbers and bank accounts. The difference in the numbers of mustangs living in ten western states and the numbers of cattle in those same states is sobering, but only to advocates.

SITTING AMID SMOOTH rocks and prickly cacti on the hump of a hill in Wyoming's McCullough Peaks Herd Management Area, I count sixty-five mustangs in one group—bays, grays, sorrels, blacks, and pintos; stallions' bands, bachelor bands, and some outlying stallions. Two foals (not in the count) romp—a bald-faced colt born to Miley in March, and a week-old brown-and-white pinto. Miley is the one horse I can identify, a black sabino with white stripes down the sides of her pretty face. Near her a trim old battle-scarred bay stallion fends off suitors.

From the draw below me a squawking, scolding raven appears, lights in a dead cottonwood, then flies up and circles above, constant noise. Another raven shows up. Together they drift, their voices puncturing the wind, which is at my back, carrying my scent directly to the horses. I rub my hands and wrists with aromatic fringed sagebrush for my own pleasure, knowing it won't camouflage my human smell.

The mustangs watch me but I am not that interesting, sitting with my journal on my knee. They shift focus to TJ, walking northward, her camera already attached to the monopod. She's moving in closer to the herd for a better angle of light, backdrop, horses.

The noisy ravens circle the sky. Meadowlarks sing. Mustangs relax, dozing in the sunshine. Many look fat and shiny while at home our mustangs are still shaggy and somewhat lean after another rough winter. With the low-grade wind I can almost forget the highway is there, though between wind and ravens' calls I hear the occasional vehicle. At the far edges of this mustang world rise snowcapped mountains: the Absarokas to the west, Owl Creek Mountains in the south, and Bighorns to the east. Cloud shadow blankets the earth, bringing chill. Otherwise this is T-shirt weather. In Wyoming, in April.

TJ works her way closer, though she's still more than a football field away (this HMA posts that you must maintain a distance of three hundred feet from the horses). Through binoculars I watch a bay stallion groom a sorrel, lips and teeth moving up and down the other's neck. Mama-mare Miley grazes while her colt naps. Two stallions race across the hillside at each other and posture, rearing, boxing, heads snaking in toward the other's throat, then drop to all fours to graze.

With the cloud shade and downshift in temperature, horses start to move a little more—naps interrupted. Some pick at green shoots of cheatgrass or last year's stalks of galleta and alkali sacaton. The bald-faced foal is up, the pinto foal nursing. I don't see any yearlings but I'm keeping my distance, not wanting to crowd the horses or invade TJ's photographic space.

The cloud passes and warmth and noisy ravens return. As mustangs stretch into the sunshine, their bands become more apparent. Seven bachelor stallions have circled up—their heads in the center, rumps out, tails swishing. Another band faces south. The next band, all pintos, grazing. I leave my seat amid glacially polished stones to perch in pebbled soil. The raven pair flies silently off. A tick crawls across my jeans. A second has found its way under my pant leg and onto my skin, looking for a place to burrow in. I remove it and move again.

As we leave, I pass beneath another dead cottonwood, a large nest woven into its high branches. The ravens return to circle their nest, quiet with the wind. TJ tells me she saw mustangs mating. Others lay down as she sat with her camera. I don't tell her about the ravens.

We continue driving south on the return leg of a 1,930-mile round trip through the high desert—southwestern Colorado to Montana and back. We spent the week with mustangs and mustang people—full days of travel, horses, and PZP training at the Science and Conservation Center in Billings. There as student, I wanted to learn everything I could about native PZP. And through instructor Kimberly Frank (who is record keeper and bookkeeper, runs the zoo contraceptive program, darts mares, and is a loving mother and grandmother), TJ (Kim's assistant that week), and Robin Lyda (now retired) in the lab making PZP, I did learn. Kim, Robin, and PZP practitioners like TJ collectively carry forth the message of PZP for former senior scientist Dr. Jay Kirkpatrick.

My one regret: I did not meet Dr. Kirkpatrick in person.

On December 16, 2015, "Dr. Jay," as his students fondly call him, died of a sudden bout with cancer. That was the birthday of Lacey's that I missed due to the skin cancer removed from my face. That was the seven-year anniversary of Rebecca's death.

TJ went through PZP training with Dr. Jay in 2010, bringing PZP to Spring Creek Basin in partnership with the BLM in 2011. From the day I sat in TJ's heated truck when Andrés and I were helping the rancher move his cows up Disappointment Valley, I have known Dr. Jay's name, beginning an email correspondence with him that focused on mustangs, PZP, and writing. He helped me with an op-ed that was published three weeks after he died. The last email from him came on December 7, after he'd read my final draft. "Nice job Kat," he said. In the throes of stage 4 cancer, he died nine days later, committed to the last day of his life to the implementation of PZP programs in every wild horse herd in America, and in other populations around the world: urban deer, bison, elephants, zoo animals.

He faced much criticism for his work. He got little fanfare for his successes. Yet those who worked with Dr. Jay are as dedicated to his mission, and to him as scientist, conservationist, animal rights advocate, and friend, as he was to mustangs.

"Why?" I ask TJ as we drive south. I have seen videos of Dr. Jay, his round face, round eyes and eyeglasses, smile, and dimples like Maka's when he grins enough to melt this girl's heart. Dr. Jay exudes warmth and intelligence. Compassion. I want a hug.

"He was just *kind*." TJ's eyes tear up. She does this when talking about mustangs or Dr. Jay. A young filmmaker who wanted to make a documentary about PZP caught her tears on camera. I have seen them many times—driving and talking, like this; watching mustangs in the basin; speaking publicly about the wild horse situation and PZP. She cries, while my passion can turn to anger.

There is a rare anger in TJ, too. When that filmmaker edited out everything she said about Dr. Jay, she was furious. I remind her of that, and she starts in. "Without Dr. Jay, we wouldn't have PZP to use in slowing reproduction in wild mares. His reproduction work wasn't just 'important'—it was the absolute key to every goddamn thing I do for this herd . . . what everyone else who uses PZP does for *their* herds. His work was *beyond* 'important.' It was life-changing—for me personally, and for the horses who owe their continued wildness to PZP."

We both know I am the choir, but I don't mind her rant.

THE 109,814-ACRE MCCULLOUGH Peaks Herd Management Area is a living example of Dr. Jay's vision. In 2011, under the management of Tricia Hatle, wild horse specialist at the BLM's Cody Field Office, the Science and Conservation Center and mustang advocacy group Friends of a Legacy began a PZP program on the well-documented McCullough Peaks mares. Within five years the herd reached zero population growth, vastly different from "zeroing out the herd" (which means the BLM is actively making a herd disappear by rounding up and removing every last horse). Spring counts in the McCullough Peaks HMA show that foals on the ground balance the winter mortalities that inevitably occur in the rugged mustang deserts of the West.

Unlike other herd management areas in Wyoming, no grand roundups will be scheduled anytime soon in McCullough Peaks—like a raven pair protecting its nest in the high branches of a cottonwood, the McCullough Peaks mustangs are free to protect their own without threat of imminent removal. This is true of herds in Challis, Idaho; our own Spring Creek Basin; and other herd management areas in the West in which the BLM is working in partnership with volunteers to utilize PZP.

Dr. Jay Kirkpatrick is the beginning of the PZP story.

As DR. JAY tells it, one day in 1971, the year the Wild Free-Roaming Horses and Burros Act was passed into law, "into my office walk two cowboys—sweaty headbands, stuff on their boots... and one asks, 'Are you the reproductive biologist here?'" In response to Dr. Jay's "I guess so," one of the cowboys said, "Can you make horses stop reproducing?"

At the College of Veterinary Medicine at Cornell University, where Jay Kirkpatrick earned his PhD in reproductive physiology, emphasis was on getting horses to reproduce, "and at the wrong time of the year," so he was surprised and intrigued by the opposing idea presented by the two men.

At the time of the execution of the Wild Free-Roaming Horses and Burros Act, the government estimated seventeen thousand wild horses on rangelands managed by public lands agencies. The two "cowboys" in Dr. Jay's office, Ron Hall and Gene Nunn, were at that time the BLM's wild horse experts for the Pryor Mountains, which bridge the Montana-Wyoming state line. They explained to Dr. Jay that while the act had horses at its heart, management parameters had not been built into it. They predicted that in ten years, "We're gonna be in big trouble"— those seventeen thousand horses multiplying to sixty thousand. "Only way we're gonna get anywhere with this is if we figure out how to control reproduction," said the forward-thinking Hall.

With his good friend from Cornell, John W. Turner, Jr., whose PhD was in endocrinology and zoology, Dr. Jay started studying wild horse behavior in the nearby Pryor Mountains Wild Horse Range. They developed and practiced several approaches to fertility control before scrapping a fifteen-year, hormone-based research program to start anew. With immunologist Dr. Irwin Liu from the University of California–Davis, they shifted focus to immunocontraception vaccines.

For some species, certain antibodies interfere with the reproductive process, impeding fertilization. With a vaccine using the ovaries of pigs butchered for breakfast sausage, bacon, and pork chops—porcine zona pellucida—Turner and Dr. Jay started inoculating mares within Assateague Island National Seashore off the coast of Maryland, where National Park Service legislation requires that wild horses remain within protected lands and that numbers be controlled. Twenty-six mares were darted that first year, in the same way TJ does it today—firing a dart across distance into the mare's rump—and the following year not a foal was born. In time the partnership between the Science and Conservation Center and the National Park Service revised the program to allow each mare to foal once, and today the population continues to sustain itself.

In 2011, forty years after the Wild Free-Roaming Horses and Burros Act passed, decades after cowboys Hall and Nunn met with Dr. Kirkpatrick, about 1,600 mustang mares running wild in the West—a fraction of the mares—were injected with native PZP. In 2016, Priscilla N. Cohn, PhD, associate director of the Ferrater Mora Oxford Centre for Animal Ethics at Oxford University, said that PZP was being used in more than thirty wild horse management areas, helping to "reduce the need for inhumane and costly roundups and warehousing of horses." That year, PZP was also used on seventeen African elephant reserves, urban deer in four states, the bison of Catalina Island, and eighty-five species of ungulates housed in zoos.

WHEN I FIRST met Linda Hogan, she volunteered in a rehabilitation center for injured birds of prey. I already knew the care and love she gave to a stanza, a line, an extension of her love of earth and wildlife, but in her presence I felt the kindness emanating from her. No wonder a rescue mustang found her and walked by her side until Linda took the little mare home!

Like Linda, and my friend Wendy Beth who fosters rescue dogs while she finds them new families, Dr. Jay was an advocate for life. With each dart of PZP (which has a 95 to 98 percent efficacy rate) injected into a mare, a conception does not take place. A fetus is not made and born into a life of possible stampede by helicopter followed by noise and bright lights and bad smells and pain and being quartered far away from family. And then living in holding until some old woman like me takes him home, if he's lucky, or he goes to a sanctuary like TJ's, if he's luckier. If not, he stands around in a pen like those mustangs east of Susanville, and you and I pay for him for the duration of his life. Maybe you didn't want a horse. Well, you and I have thousands of them.

I took birth control pills in my late teens and early twenties. I wanted not to conceive, not to come face-to-face with an unwanted pregnancy and all that might mean—from considering abortion, to adoption, to unwed motherhood, or, maybe worse, marrying someone I didn't love.

Consequences to wild horses are similar. What Dr. Jay and his colleagues came up with, and TJ and others are implementing, saves bands and herds from separation, loss, death. And saves the government (and us, as taxpayers) millions.

Don't get me wrong. I adored my own babies. I love each foal born into Spring Creek Basin. I love every wild-born foal I see or know is there. I love their bands, whole herds. And I love the land that sustains them. The soil, vegetation, wildlife, water.

Using PZP helps protect all of that.

Because of one man who reached out to colleagues and spent forty-five years figuring out, making, and administering PZP. Before his death, everyone out there darting went through training with Dr. Jay, and now, like me, with protégé Kimberly Frank. We are trained, certified, and entrusted to do our part.

Today, even without its founding leader, Dr. Kirkpatrick, the work of the Science and Conservation Center continues, Kimberly Frank at the helm and TJ and others in the field. The biggest challenge we face is how to encourage the government to establish native PZP programs in more—most—*all*—of our wild horse herds.

BEFORE WE LEFT Montana, TJ and I made a detour in search of another mustang—the sorrel with flashy white markings that

Andrés selected for the Mustang Million. TJ went with me last year to deliver him to Andrés in Montana. This time we stopped the car at the base of a hill and the mustang lifted his head straight up out of the grass to see. Fat and sleek, he looked more like spring than leftover winter, the irrigated pasture grass serving him well. Like the bay stallion in Nevada, head up higher than anyone else's, he followed us with ears and eyes, listening, glistening, flaxen forelock and mane highlighting his new-penny coppery sides. A healthy, well cared for mustang. A relief—one Nevada mustang at home in Montana.

AFTER HOURS SPENT with the McCullough Peaks mustangs and also visiting the Pryors, we keep driving farther, longer, TJ navigating as we pass through the folds of Wyoming. Past dark we get a motel room and walk to the store, which is closed. Deciding to eat apples and trail mix instead of going to a restaurant, TJ sits outside in the cool evening writing on postcards while I flop on my bed and think. I don't write, not yet.

We rise early, and drive.

Stopping in a tiny town to mail the postcards, TJ sees a cowboy hat she likes on a "real cowgirl"—a woman in a pickup with dogs, parking on the road to run in and get her mail. "I might actually consider wearing a hat like that," TJ says, adjusting her Texas A&M visor. I crane my neck but the real cowgirl is gone.

Strands have come free of my braid and tickle my face. Nostalgia fills my stomach. Despite inheriting the genes, and wearing them, I never felt like a real cowgirl. I rarely wore cowboy hats and felt like an imposter when I did, even though Keith and I ran cattle and raised two little ranch boys and a lot of calves and cowdogs. I wasn't like that woman I didn't see in the truck. Wasn't born and raised on a ranch like my grandmother. I was born in Berkeley like my mother, younger sister, and other grandmother, three generations of women on my mother's side born in the same Berkeley hospital—there's story in that but it doesn't make me ranch-raised like my grandmother, like my own kids.

I like this town, though, and the picture I see: picking up and moving here and becoming part of something big like Wyoming. Like Laura Bell in *Claiming Ground*, or Gretel Ehrlich in the earlier *Solace of Open Spaces*. I know the quick fantasy is not real, not for me, anyway. I would always be an outsider, and possibly the only soul in the state feeling the Bern. What startles me is the picture of moving—the first I've had in the four years since leaving New Mexico for Colorado. Is it time, my year-and-a-half attention span no longer overridden by treks between horse ranch and mustang cabin?

Searching the broad valley bottoms and distant hills for mustangs, I realize we're near where Tyler and I camped years ago with Smith and his fiancé on the Popo Agie River, Smith and twelve-year-old Tyler fly fishing while I drove into town to make plane reservations to get to Kenney, whose thumb had come off.

I text Tyler. He remembers. Where were we living then? I ask. Must have been Moab, he texts back. Memories blur like the landscape.

In Lander we get gas and our bearings. Sort of. We know where we're headed but aren't sure how to get there. We drive south through winter-white aspens and snow clinging to the northern slopes of the Wind River Range, the highway elevation greater than seven thousand feet, the aspens barely beginning to bud. It's almost May. We top the final pass and head down toward another mustang desert: Great Divide Basin.

There are signs of the BLM but no BLM signs saying anything about the herd management area. We choose our entry, guessing that a cattle guard marks a BLM boundary, stopping to examine our map, trying to locate ourselves in the bigness of off-highway Wyoming. Off-asphalt Wyoming. We're on Wyoming dirt, as in dirt road, but where? Oil and gas roads crisscross before us. We pick one leading into—we hope—the herd management area from which my mustang Maka was removed. I want to see his birthland, his relations.

From graveled miles to ridged and washed-out dirt road, TJ driving, we scan the terrain. An endorheic drainage basin, Great Divide Basin is huge, dotted with rounded and plateaued hills, few trees, some sagebrush. We spot two mustangs in afternoon shadow—a stallion and mare at the base of an uplift. We're not close enough for photos or to see colors other than dark, even through binoculars. We watch for a moment, and move on.

Pronghorns stir the views by the dozens but for a long while the only additional activity is our vehicle moving along and the change in the slant of sunlight. Even stud piles are scarce. After another rough stretch of winter ruts misguiding tires, we sight a band of horses far across the dusty valley floor. Maybe two bands.

I want out of the car. I want to venture closer. I want to see horses—Maka's distant relatives—up close. I want to walk. I want TJ's photos. I want a lot.

"There's not enough light," TJ says.

It's true, I know. But I want to see *mustangs*. We've driven a long way for this.

"We don't know how far we have to go before we hit pavement."

Also true, well over an hour already on this rough road that maybe we see on the map. If we're correct, there's more unimproved road in front of us than behind us. We have lots of fuel and a spare tire, just not enough daylight.

My eyes strain through binoculars. Even counting these horses is difficult through dusk and distance. Seven, including one foal? "Okay," I say, yielding to TJ's more pragmatic approach to driving toward dark on eighty miles of dirt road we don't know.

She resumes the crawl across the desert. Before we leave the herd management area, we see another small, hazy band. "That makes fifteen horses," I say, "total."

I recount mustangs and refigure mileage as we drive toward the speeding lights of Interstate 80—the first sign of other vehicles in three hours. Eighty miles of dirt road, seventy miles of which were within Divide Basin HMA. Three hours, seventy miles, fifteen horses.

What we can't fathom is how this 778,915-acre herd management area (562,702 acres of which are BLM public lands, the remainder of these "checkerboard" lands being state or private)—high desert that can "support between 415 and 600 head of wild horses," according to the BLM—has "too many." In 2014, the BLM removed 527 horses, which left just 91 mustangs in Divide Basin HMA (again according to the BLM), well below the allotted number. And yet two years later the BLM says it needs to remove more.

Ninety-one mustangs left after the 2014 roundup explains our low sighting. But it does not explain a leap to too many mustangs running wild. We saw fifteen horses in seventy miles of "the big empty," as people refer to the Red Desert that holds Divide Basin. It certainly felt empty to us. Full of sky and pronghorns and sagebrush and space, empty of horses.

BACK IN SPRING Creek Basin, TJ's black Jeep dips and surges through deep, impossible ruts, heading northwest on an infrequently driven and rarely maintained dirt road. This was a year of late spring rains, May offering nearly an inch of rain each week to this dry corner of Colorado. In the basin rain fell in such a way that most of the ponds filled. We're hoping there's water enough in the northwest pond to draw horses.

Despite our good spring, summer monsoons are tardy, and heavy, smoke-filled air fills the hot afternoon. We spent the morning with our BLM herd manager, Mike Jensen, with whom we work closely, looking at exclosures and former transect sites, identifying grasses, planning a field study to assess mustang impact on this desert ecosystem. When the others left, TJ and I forged deeper in—we couldn't be so close and not look for horses.

There are four herd management areas in Colorado, and one herd area. In Nevada, where more than 80 percent of the state is public land, the BLM manages more than forty-five million acres, fourteen million of which host herd management areas. Mustangs are a desert land issue—and this is one environmental issue for which scientists like Dr. Jay have found a solution. The only problem is getting government agencies to plan and to act, endorsing and *using* PZP.

Same with bait trapping. In some wild horse habitats, bait trapping—drawing horses into a trap over time, using hay, minerals, or water as bait—is being used instead of helicopter round-ups. Although mustangs will feel fear when the gates close and they realize they're trapped, it is a gentler approach than being terrorized by helicopters.

TJ and I wrote a bait-trapping proposal for Spring Creek Basin and presented it to our BLM field office with the backing of local mustang advocates. For four years the proposal meandered through government processes. Finally, in 2018, bait trapping was deemed an acceptable alternative to helicopter roundups in Spring Creek Basin, though helicopter roundups are still on the list of options if bait trapping "doesn't work." We believe that, like PZP, bait trapping will work if you use it; however, we won't need to bait trap anything anytime soon.

SPRING CREEK, FOR which the basin and herd management area are named, is the one drainage inside the basin that carries water over distance, but it runs only when rain falls in a certain area of Mancos Shale badlands in the upper valley. I saw it run once, gray-black water charging down the previously dry streambed, standing waves forming and falling away as logs and stones pushed along by the sudden river made dams and then water broke through, again and again. Violent and lovely, it would have swallowed my truck whole.

Even with the somewhat predictable monsoons, Spring Creek rarely runs and is not a reliable source of water for the horses. And these mustangs are fenced away from Disappointment Creek. In years past, catchment ponds were dug to water cattle, strategically placed to corral into waterholes the runoff from certain drainages. Some years there is just not enough water, and a discussion may ensue about hauling water in for the horses. Sometimes the BLM uses water hauling as argument for zeroing out the herd. The first time I heard a BLM employee actually say this in reference to Spring Creek Basin, I sputtered, "You can't fence horses off a natural water source and then condemn them for not having water." But, they can.

The Jeep tops a rise and we're greeted with a vision of mustangs on the skyline silhouetted against a backdrop of smoky haze. Every time I see these horses I have the same visceral reaction: quickening heartbeat, involuntary smile. Tail wagging. Sometimes tears follow. There may be a scientific explanation for this like there is for how even a forced smile makes you feel better, but this simply feels like happiness. Mustangs in the wild = joy.

TJ stops the Jeep. We glass the hillside. A dozen mustangs linger on the horizon: three bands and a lone bachelor stallion. We tank up on water and iced tea before leaving the Jeep. Though we don't have to walk far for a closer view, we might be away from the vehicle long enough to get good and thirsty. I bring my backpack with more water, an apple, my journal; TJ carries her camera, her monopod over her shoulder, a second camera strapped to her back.

While my intention is to write down everything I sense and see, I am usually so distracted by the mustangs themselves that I take minimalist notes—names and brief descriptions for later identification. *Duke. Tall bay, Roman nose, star.* Unnecessary documentation as TJ's camera and brain contain far more information than I can possibly absorb, but I am still learning these horses. Later I will close my eyes, see the mustangs again, and try to identify each one.

We move closer. The horses stay still, watching us—because it's TJ. Does this make them not wild—that they recognize TJ and therefore don't race off, that they tolerate me because I am her shadow? The dilemma is that to save their wildness, TJ has to move among them. Like band stallions and lead mares, she is necessary for the survival of this herd.

I sit amid clumps of blue grama, galleta, alkali sacaton, and Indian ricegrass. There's not much cheatgrass—later I will ask our herd manager why. Cattle have grazed this country, sheep before them. Pronghorn, mule deer, and elk season here still. Mustangs have been in this valley for at least 150 years. At an exclosure earlier in the day, someone noted the amount of winterfat within and without the fenced piece of desert. "The winterfat is coming back," he said.

When TJ's employer bought the ranch that is now the sanctuary, a permit to graze 326 animal units on adjacent public land for three winter months for ten years was included. The new owner did not wish to graze cattle—he wanted the Spring Creek Basin mustangs to have that feed for themselves—and he worked with the BLM for several years to close the allotment. With just wild horses and wild ungulates grazing and browsing, and with the help of quiet heroes like TJ, her boss, herd manager Mike Jensen, and Dr. Jay, the desert that is Spring Creek Basin is recovering.

TJ curves around the hillside, conscious of angle and light. To her back the rim of Spring Creek canyon shows. One-seed junipers and piñon pines dot hill and arroyo but there's no shade near the horses. Something else is missing, as well.

Foals. The fillies and colts of springtime.

Of the up-to-sixty-five adult horses we're allotted in Spring Creek Basin, we're at about sixty. There could be twenty foals on the ground, yet we have only two: one before us napping with his mama in the heat, the second miles away on the far side of the basin. More could come this year—the mares are fat from the good spring rains, pregnancies possibly disguised. Even if we have the expected three to five foals, we will not reach maximum capacity. There will be no roundup in the teens, or even in 2020 or 2021—no mustangs from this herd management area heading toward short-term holding at Cañon City's East Cañon Correctional Complex where, if not adopted, they would begin a forty-nine-thousand-dollar lifetime sentence in captivity.

In 2011, with eighty-two mustangs residing in Spring Creek Basin, including thirteen surviving foals (eight died), the BLM held a helicopter roundup and removed forty horses. Under Dr. Jay's tutelage, TJ started darting Spring Creek Basin mares that year. When foal numbers dropped, the BLM permitted TJ to dart ten mares, and what we see before us—one colt nuzzling his dozing dam—is the result of a successful PZP program.

PZP does not cause abortion or harm mare, fetus, or nursing foal in any way, though a mare might jump from the sting of a dart in her rump. The dart quickly pops out, is retrieved from the grass or bush that caught it, and checked to make sure the PZP was injected. Mares are not vaccinated every year; a selection process based on genetics, age, and herd and habitat health indicates which get the dart. Mares continue to cycle normally, with no disruption to herd dynamics or psychology (which spaying or gelding would alter completely). Stop the darting and the mare can conceive again.

Some advocates oppose PZP, seeing its use as human meddling. Which it is. But we've already meddled—ponds dug into desert soil to catch water, fences preventing mustangs from accessing natural water sources used for generations, "free roaming" no longer allowed.

Introducing PZP into a herd management area is the wisest action the BLM can take for horse, habitat, and the American public. With fewer horses born, fewer roundups happen, and more years pass between removals—saving money. Fewer horses are traumatized and fewer unnecessary deaths occur—saving lives. Fewer horses taken to holding facilities equals fewer taxpayer dollars spent. Including the dart, PZP costs about thirty dollars per darted mare per year. Most darters are volunteers like TJ, working for mustangs not wages. Native PZP is an inexpensive, humane, science-based management tool that needs to be used.

Fertility control with PZP has slowed herd reproduction in Colorado's Little Book Cliffs and Sand Wash Basin, Wyoming's Pryors and McCullough Peaks, and on other great expanses of land across the West.

On three hundred thousand acres in Nevada's Virginia Range, comprised of private, state, and BLM land, 3,200 wild horses fall under state jurisdiction. In 2019 and 2020, 1,215 mares were darted with 2,560 fertility-control treatments (primers and boosters)—because of a cooperative agreement between the Nevada Department of Agriculture and the nonprofit mustang advocacy group American Wild Horse Campaign. Documentation and support comes from five local wild-horse organizations and fourteen volunteer darters, trained by the Science and Conservation Center. This is what we need: cooperative agreement between civilian and government organizations, and hardworking volunteers.

In 2021, it will be ten years since TJ started darting, and ten years since there was a roundup in Spring Creek Basin. That is a record—this is the first BLM herd management area to go a decade without removing horses as a direct result of a partnership between the Science and Conservation Center, the BLM, and volunteers working "at the baby-making end of things," as Alan Day prescribed.

The public has presented other solutions, opposing and dramatic: reinstate slaughter practices, or do nothing at all. Equally terminal ideas—death by a stun gun or death by starvation. And the government is on a kick to spay mustang mares. More costly to the taxpayer, more traumatic for the horses, and irreversible, spaying mares leads toward the ugly and possibly ultimate government goal of zeroing out the herds.

Horses, whether they were reintroduced to the Americas in 1493 or some were here all along, are here now, just like the rest of us. They have roamed much of the West for the last five hundred years, and for millions of years before that. We don't have the wherewithal to control human population, homelessness, or hunger, but with a thirty-dollar injection, we can make a difference in life on the range.

Aspen. Bay stallion. Raven, pinto but barely, white patch on her left side. Kootenai, Raven's lifetime friend.

The next year, Kootenai disappears. She is just . . . gone. A memory floating above the trees.

The following year, TJ finds Duke's body—*tall bay, Roman nose, star*—the desert turning him to soil and bone.

16

LUNAR RED

THE COVERED FRONT PORCH OF THE MUSTANG CABIN FACES the bend in the creek below, the Dakota Sandstone cliffs opposite, and views of the Glade. It offers summer shade, protection from boisterous monsoons, and dry winter storage for firewood, and hosts a barbeque of Ken's, the hammock, and the small, hand-hewn picnic table at which I write when cold or gnats do not chase me back inside.

Today TJ and I sit on the utilitarian back porch—an uncovered square of wood planks planted at the back door, closest to where I park, so that groceries and loads of laundry have somewhere to land other than dirt while I unload more stuff. Because it faces west, I don't sit here often in summer, but when TJ drove up I met her here and we sank into conversation, our backs to the logs where shade lingers. She's here for a late lunch but the heat holds us still.

The expanse of Disappointment Valley unfurls in waves of distance and heat, La Sal Mountains rising up beyond, snow still lingering at the summits. The road, unseen from here, runs parallel to the east-west fence I share with mustangs. Beyond the fence a tall rim of burnt-charcoal cliff also trends east-west.

Lone mustang stallions have appeared against the skyline for moments as they wandered the sparse bunchgrasses growing on the rim. I have seen bands meandering out of a fold in the random hills just to the east, to graze the greasewood plane or shade up in junipers. I have even seen mustangs from my bedroom window.

I live here for that, for the isolation, for the story told by water and its dramatic changes through the seasons. All things here are seasonal—propane, my backup heat source, gets delivered in May and October, about when the red ants come out and disappear. Mustangs change coats and colors, and sometimes bands, with the season. Elk move back up into the high country come spring. In winter coyotes get bushier, mountain lions stealthier. In summer, heat dominates.

Cattle are moved with the seasons. Each spring and fall, I redo the water gaps so the neighbors' cattle don't trespass. The only sheep in the valley are the desert bighorns reintroduced to the redrock layers near Slick Rock, visible more often in summer before monsoon season, the Dolores River their main water source then. Of our species, hunters mob here in October and November, villages set up among piñon and juniper, huge RVs and herds of ATVs altering the landscape visibly and audibly for weeks. We wear blaze orange during hunting season when we ride, check fence, or go out to see mustangs. It's the only time of year more than two or three vehicles a day travel our dusty road.

TJ stands up. The dogs stir at her sudden movement. "Mustangs," she says. "The pintos."

I search the northern distance—a hump of land that rears and drops to the road, beyond that the fence and Spring Creek Basin. I find the pinto band dappled in juniper shade: stout Corazón, his mares, this year's sole foal, and a lieutenant stallion. I've not seen mustangs from right here before and wouldn't have but for TJ's younger, keener eyes.

Corazón's band was the first of the Spring Creek Basin mustangs I saw, and here they are, hanging out along our shared fence, maybe, like us, waiting for rain.

~~~

WATER IN THE desert is dicey. Not much falls from the skies and often when it does it arrives in a rush. We two-leggeds live here among the many desert species, some branches of which evolved here while others migrated or were introduced, like cheatgrass, by our species. We make the choice to be here—one of the few species that can move water (like beaver), we can turn on a tap or drive a pickup with a 320-gallon water tank in the bed or order up a 4,000-gallon load of water. That water ensures our survival. It allows us to stay. We alone among all species on earth can make this choice, although if we continue as we are this will change.

In the absence of rain comes prayer. *Homo sapiens* are likely the only species to partake in this act, as well, which has to do with thumbs and language, I suppose. I ask quietly, in an internal voice, for rain. *Please.* We need it for the land, the native plants, the pronghorn, elk, mule deer, mustangs, mountain lions, bobcats, black bear, coyotes, foxes, desert bighorn sheep, mice, kangaroo rats, pack rats, bunnies, birds, and bugs. Selfishly I need it so the catchment system fills my cistern, and for my spiritual cistern—*please.*

As the summer days pass without rain, Disappointment Creek drops lower and TJ's water worry increases. Nine miles of creek meander through her ranch—the only other natural water source for the sanctuary mustangs is one murky spring. She has a well that pulls up alkaline water no human can touch. Her horses drink it—those who don't mind coming close to the barn and house—though they prefer the creek, its water saline and silty but banked by coyote willows not buildings. For her personal use, TJ has water hauled in. Someday her boss may install a catchment system for the house, but his priority was water for the horses. He put in the well.

In the herd management area that is geologically a basin and bureaucratically a designated, fenced area in which mustangs are allowed to live, one might guess, following the fencelines, that the HMA was designed more for human and cattle convenience than for wild horses. The mustangs are close to Disappointment Creek—surely they can smell it—but they cannot get to it. They cannot drink from it. Fences turn them away. So they are dependent on ponds or dirt tanks or whatever you call them, depending on where you're from. In addition to the ponds, there is a catchment system—two fenced acres of thick black plastic aprons spread over sloping ground to collect rain and snowfall, with filters and underground pipes at the low end that connect to a twelve-thousand-gallon metal tank, which can be filled with purchased water when drought threatens, as it does each summer.

Along with the BLM, David and Pati Temple and other volunteers installed that catchment system in the late 1990s. In 2016, we installed a second one, a collaborative effort between the BLM and volunteers including David Temple, Pat and Frank Amthor, TJ, my sons, and me. After several hot workdays we had water capabilities on the south side of the basin. I call it Chrome's catchment, because his band frequents those rough, scrubby hills. We need rain to fill it.

On the back porch, TJ and I shrink against the cabin as the world spins and shade recedes. Below us the creek runs in a low, steady flow, minus the muscle of spring. We got those crazy and wonderful rains throughout May and the first June weekend, which totaled more than four inches, turned our desert green, raised the level nicely in the back ponds of the basin, and filled my two underground cisterns. After those surprise rains, June was as dry as it usually is. Now it's late July, and still no rain. I trust that monsoons will come sooner or later, top off the ponds, and fill the basin's catchment supplies, but if the creek goes dry, TJ's sanctuary mustangs are dependent upon a single spring and humans hauling water.

Wild horses used to have access to the creek up and down the valley. Like the bear, deer, and elk, during the hot months they would go into the high country to graze lush meadow grasses and drink from springs and natural pools, this before the government decided how many cattle could live in designated areas of the West and where to entrap the mustangs they found after 1971. Now if no rain comes and the catchments don't fill, water may get hauled to the wild horses, as well—five hundred dollars per four thousand gallons of water, money advocates will donate to help the horses.

Shade gone, we go inside to eat. Each day for the past two weeks the temperature has pushed—or passed—a hundred degrees. As we sit in the living room side of the cabin's kitchen-dining-living room, plates on our knees, the cabin darkens, clouds moving in from the east exactly that fast. I startle when thunder booms and lightning strikes the sky—a PTSD reaction that has not lifted with time. The dogs crowd my feet. Cojo wants my lap.

TJ and I look at each other. Is this it—our first monsoon of the season?

A few raindrops splatter on the metal roof but no downpour follows. The clouds drift off to the northwest. Thunder grumbles in the distance, echoing our disappointment.

It's after five, the sun still well up in the sky, the evening holding the day's lingering heat. "We still have time to go into the basin," I say.

"It'd be a quick trip. Three hours of good light left."

TJ leaves first. I'm in a flurry of my own storm as I gather journal, binoculars, dogs, and water, always water. Hiking boots and a sweatshirt already in my truck—the latter in case of a drop in temperature and hoped-for rain—I follow TJ's dust to her house, where she grabs her camera and binoculars and jumps into my Tacoma. Clouds crowd the northeast line of mountains; directly to the east, the horizon is hidden in cloud shadow; in the west, La Sal Mountains shimmer with sunlight, those last pockets of snow sparkling glitter.

We cross Disappointment Creek, which looks half the size of what was passing below the cabin. I have a lot of bedrock and so far, even in the driest, hottest weeks of summers past, that rock has held puddles connected by the tiniest trickles. The sanctuary's miles of creek run through the soft Mancos Shale of the valley's bottomlands and the water is known to disappear entirely. Hence TJ's worry, and my quiet alarm—the creek has dropped significantly since I was last this far down valley.

As we head east across the sanctuary toward the basin and the clouded mountains, lightning flashes on the far perimeters. Thick, purple-dark clouds rim the basin, rim the whole eastern world. Long sheets of rain blow across the distant edge of the valley—the longest rain-hair I have ever seen bending in the wind like Chrome's wild, wind-rolled mane, the ends reaching down and brushing the land. From sky to earth this long hair floats and above it, backed by black clouds, a rainbow appears. It starts at the northern rim of the basin. Brilliant colors arc above the rain-hair, vibrate against the dark eastern clouds, and reach to the south.

"It's touching your cabin," TJ says.

"It's embracing the horses," I say.

Four years ago I did not know that the mustangs and I would be neighbors, sharing a common fence. I did not know TJ, or that we would also become neighbors. Spring Creek Basin and the BLM herd management area were unknown to me, as well. I was just wandering up a dirt road in the fall. A road that led to somewhere I didn't know. To some future life I hadn't yet imagined. It led me back to my heart.

Which is right here, beneath a great canopy of color. We cross the cattle guard into the basin and soon we see Chrome and his band, heads lifting to inspect my truck, which is not TJ's Jeep. I stop the Toyota to watch the sky, to watch Chrome's band, all shades of gray but for the one buckskin mare, to watch Chrome. Way off in the dip toward Spring Creek canyon and its dry creekbed, two bachelor stallions graze, a stallion and mare even farther away. Behind and above them on a curve of earth, three bands drift until they have seemingly merged into one, all this beneath the colors of a rainbow. Who could ask for more?

And yet I've seen more. On a supermoon night in September 2015, the moon in its perigee phase, closest full moon of the year, an eclipse happened that turned the moon red. A friend and I were out to see mustangs, TJ separate from us, walking with her camera to get the best light behind a band of horses—Hollywood's band—but before us—right in front of my friend and me—stood Chrome. Tall and ropey with muscle and that long wild mane, Chrome the gallant, the gorgeous, ambassador of the basin, dominant stallion with the biggest band and longest mane ever, watching us as the moon rose red behind him.

Red moonlight flooding the basin, washing over Chrome.

My friend turned to me, wiping at a tear. "I'm crying," she said, as if surprised.

TJ and I drive on into this rainbow eve and the rainbow shifts in the changing light, thinning at the edges and then above and fading into sky as the shades of the horse spectrum of colors replace it, from the lightest gray (white) to black and everything in between: dun, buckskin, red bay, pinto, sorrel, dark bay. The horses beckon us in for a closer look. No rain has touched the ground so we keep going.

"Have you been on this road since the creek last ran?" TJ asks. I know she means Spring Creek. Amazing to us, that one early June rain caused it to run. I have not been deep into the basin in my own truck since then. "I moved boulders to make the crossing possible," she says, "but it's still a little rough."

I'm not worried. We round a bend. Something glints silver in the lowering light.

"There's *water*." A shared burst of recognition and awe.

"Water in Spring Creek," TJ says. We envision puddles.

I make the last turn, dropping toward the creekbed, preparing for the four-wheel-drive bump and grind over boulders and the push up the steep far side. But "It's running!" one of us says, and TJ's out the door before I stop the truck, running, herself, toward water.

I complete the stop, let the dogs out, and walk to the edge of the cloudy, swirling water of Spring Creek. It's not the charging rush of a serious flash flood but a thick, steady flow—water that follows a course of eons as it slowly carves the canyon downstream, Dakota Sandstone eroding and carried one grain or pebble at a time toward Disappointment Creek and the Dolores River and then the Colorado.

TJ, seated on a rock, stares into the water. I give her a minute but the dogs don't, racing up and down the soup of this desert river just come to life with rain.

On a nearby hill, a line of mustangs assembles, one wild mare or stallion after another: the little dun, Hollywood, and his two range-wise mares, Alegre and Houdini, Houdini white with age, followed by Houdini's daughter and a bay mare who looks almost gray, her sides caked with mud from a roll in a pond. More mustangs arrive, standing side by side on the crown of a hill against the clouds and sky of this great basin, looking down. At us? At the dogs playing? Or at the water itself?

Back to the truck for my binoculars, I sit sideways on the seat of my Toyota, feet propped on the running board, elbows on my knees to steady my vision, and watch as mustangs lift over the rise and join the line.

I'm watching wild horses while witnessing Spring Creek run.

TJ remains on her rock as the light fades. Even though this water will mostly go downstream, it will leave holes and pockets and then hoofprints of water and the horses will drink along with all the other wildlife of the basin. Right here, right now, in this piece of desert, there is water.

~~~

No rain falls on us and the road back to TJ's is dry. She has forgotten something and follows me the seven miles back to the cabin. At my gate, I feel the ground soft under my slippahs. The soil looks smooth. The earth springs with smells, sagebrush and greasewood and fourwing saltbush, fresh, sharp. Driving again, I feel mud gripping the tires. Puddles mark the road.

We hear it as soon as we step from our vehicles—loud, pulsing water. I leap onto the back porch to grab a flashlight, leaving wet tracks on the kitchen floor, and lead the way through prickly pear and claret cup cacti to the cliff ledge, the dogs just ahead of us, Cojo's toes at the edge. I tell him to get back as I step closer and there's the river, wild with water. Even in the dim beam, moonlight hidden in cloud, we can see the rush and surge of fast water, rapids forming, my marker rock completely submerged.

I don't realize I'm shouting my joy, the way TJ cried hers. "Look," I yell over the roar, pointing to a log rushing downstream; "Look at that," fierce water pushing over stone; "Look there," peering over the edge into the crashing darkness. "Oh the smells," as the pungency of thick, sediment-rich water collides with the sweet scent of wet sage.

Standing safely above the mayhem, we watch for a long time. The river does not fade in movement or strength or sound. Suddenly TJ says, "You bolster my spirit."

She says this to *me*. I haven't bolstered anybody's anything, I think, other than a few men. "No," I say. "*I* don't. It's *this*," my hands arcing rainbows over the river, the valley, night clouds covering horses, lives that live dreams.

Later in the night, with a better flashlight, I go out to look at the river. Marker rock still submerged, a log flies down the thick, steely current. The flow has not yet begun to ebb.

The river changes through my sleep. In the morning two new large pieces of driftwood sit atop the wide flat stone in the middle of the river, the water fallen, the drainage once more a creek in size. Deep chocolate mud and bent coyote willows line the banks. Below the cabin a huge slab of sandstone that has been working free of the bank that held it for unknowable years tilts more vertically, the roots of sagebrush once growing at the rock's crown now hanging in air.

"You bolster my spirit," I say aloud to everything I see: roots and rocks and ravens, cliff and creek, the cleansed earth, water, sky. I say it to the air, the breeze, the wind. To new clouds forming. I say it to mustangs. To water in their desert. I say it to the powers that make rainbows and bring sons home to a mother's heart.

It is a simple prayer. Not *please* but *thank you.*

17

THE BONES OF US

A LL THAT'S HERE IS HERE IN PASSING: RAINBOWS, A HUMAN life, the wind. The one-ton slab of sandstone in the middle of the creek, a million years in the making. The creek itself.

It turns out water is not everywhere. It can be as scarce and fleeting as a late spring snowflake melting on stone. As love. As life. Water may leave a mark or a memory or it may never touch down but remain as virga, wisps disappearing on the horizon. It is as fragile and tender as Ed dying. As a mustang's survival. It must be watched over and cared for.

Cojo has lived with his pieced-together front legs for nine years, twice as long as predicted by veterinarians. For the eight years I've been his, he ran and played and followed me everywhere, his tail and silly grin and one-up, one-down ears expressing his happy nature. But his pain has grown with the years and when he snarls and bites at me as I lift him from his bed and carry him to the door to go out to pee, I hear again the language of endings.

Ken has to put his buckskin gelding down. Cisco should have many good years left but he crippled a hock one year and a hip the next, living free of saddle and spur in our pastures until one morning a third leg came up lame. A horse cannot have three lame legs.

Two weeks later I ingest some of Ken's courage and call the vet. When she arrives, Cojo is on his bed in the bed of the Toyota and he comes forward to greet her, tail wagging. I sit on the tailgate and he lies down with his head in my lap. I can't speak, just my fingers in his fur, and he's okay until the vet rubs alcohol on the vein. Cojo quickly retreats deep under the camper shell and looks at me with the most betrayed eyes. I climb in and pull him to me and hold his fifty pounds in my lap and soon he relaxes and the needle goes into the vein as smoothly as I could still do it and a tranquilizer settles him before the other drug ends him and that's it, for Cojo.

For me it's the beginning of another big emptiness but in the first hour without him my older sister calls and Wendy Beth calls and TJ arrives and goes with me to the place of cremation where I carry my sweet border collie–Aussie cross to the door one last time.

SITTING NEXT TO Tyler on a plane to Alaska, I tell him about Cojo. He says, "So that's what's wrong." I nod and look at clouds that cover the world below like the fog my sister and I watched on our first flight to Hawai'i, and on many flights since. This time I'm headed to cold.

Cold scares me. I theorize that my body neglects my extremities due to low blood pressure, and my fat insulates not, despite what people claim—instead the fat gets cold and the cold creeps inward, slowly wrapping my body in hypothermic chill (I don't know what thinner people experience, having not been one). So when my application for a *summer* residency at Denali National Park and Preserve was answered with an invitation to go as *winter* artist-in-residence, I panicked first, said no second, and only as a third thought, thought to be grateful.

"Really, no," I said to the park people, explaining my cold phobia. They told me the residency started on the vernal equinox, coercing me gently into discussion: at that time of year, nights and days are of equal length, spring tiptoes to the edges of things, bears and hordes of flies and people are not out yet, and they would loan me snowshoes.

My mother said go. My older sister, who visited Denali when her daughter worked there, said no—she knows how cold and I interact.

My younger sister said, "This is an important opportunity."

I dreamed of bears—a sow and five cubs—probably black bears though the sow and two of the cubs were blond. I have not seen a grizzly. Or a brown bear, as I would hear them called in Alaska: all grizzlies are brown bears but not all brown bears are grizzlies, they say.

Ready to decline the offer, not because of a bear scare in the night but because of the cold, I called the program coordinator. "I'm cold in Colorado right now," I said, the woodstove ablaze, the propane backup heater glowing.

"Denali is a dry cold," he said.

I told him I regretted to decline, because, using my younger sister's word, "What an opportunity." But I'd applied for summer. For the light and water and wildlife of Denali in summer. *That* made sense. *That* is me.

"It's a huge honor," I said. "Thank you." *A cold time of year, winter.* But there would be moose. Maybe a bird sighting or two.

He said, "The wife of one of the Park Service employees saw a lynx in a spruce tree just the other night. She watched it climb down face-first."

A *lynx*. It had paused for a snapshot. I found the photo online.

"I can bring someone," I told my mother.

"Whom would you take?" she said, though she knew.

Even Tyler had doubts—he has learned how to stay warm on the snowy slopes of California and Colorado but he's still a Maui boy. When I called him to say I was going to decline, he surprised me by saying he wanted to go. And so I said yes.

~~~

WE HAVE FIFTEEN miles of Denali Park Road available to us and the few winter visitors, snow and a gate at Savage River stopping deeper entrance into the park (summer tour buses have access to ninety-two miles of Park Road). The road curves with the contours of the land, following frozen waterways we cannot see in the cleavages of hills and depths of snow, and passing through white spruce and black spruce forests that open to a broad valley amid these rounded hills, backed by mountains everywhere.

Denali shows herself in a wreath of saucer clouds the first morning, Tyler's camera clicking away while my mouth gapes open. Day and night, we wander up and down, gasping at wildlife, views, sky. I call my mother to tell her about the aurora borealis. My mother has longed to see it for herself, but at eighty-something she thinks that might not happen. "It's like seeing music without hearing it," I tell her. "Like an orchestra without sound. Waves of chartreuse building and fading. Purple edges floating in. Visual music in the sky. And like live music, it's gone the moment it's made."

In daylight I do not tire of watching, through binoculars, moose eating. A moose's upper lip, all muscle like a horse's, grasps the narrowleaf willow branches and pulls a single branch down between both lips, stripping it of dry leaves. I want to touch the velvet muzzles of mooses like I do my mustang's muzzle.

Nor do I tire of watching winter's herds of caribou, fifteen or twenty antlerless animals blending into the carnal landscape, their legs dark brown to black like tree trunks and the rich earth that shows through in places in March, their throats white as sunlit cloud, their sides muted and ribbed like last year's willows.

We look and listen for wolves. Watch for lynx. See a rabbit—a snowshoe hare. And a willow ptarmigan. Both as white as Denali snow—winter survival for the small and the meek. For me it's wearing baselayers. Several.

Denali shows herself in full splendor, not a cloud, saucer

or otherwise, touching her. For a long time we just watch, even though we don't know this is the last time we will see her.

The residency includes spending four days in a century-old "primitive" cabin—woodburning stove for heat and cooking; kerosene lanterns; no running water, ever, the outhouse as frigid as its surroundings. The literature says I can pee outside, to the north of the dwelling where visitors venturing off the Park Road to see the historic cabin might not see the yellow snow. And that is seriously good news. At C Camp at park headquarters, where we've been staying, also without running water, the nightly treks in pj's and down jackets to the communal bathrooms across the way are taxing on ice and snow. We have curbed our water intake.

The literature also instructs me to engage the visitors who want to see the old cabin. We're all here to experience the national park—if talking to the artist-in-residence is part of their Denali experience, make it a good one.

By the time the four days roll around, Tyler is so enamored with aurora that he chooses not to stay in the small space of the cabin with me, deciding instead to stay at C Camp and continue wandering the midnight road, the only person in Denali chasing the northern lights in the middle of the night at the tail end of winter in Alaska.

He drops food, gear, and me off and I watch him leave. As the flashes of his new, ocean-blue, supremely warm down jacket disappear between the branches of white spruce lining the trail, I find myself gasping for air.

Stepping inside the hundred-year-old cabin, I close the door, the space instantly shrinking around me, the dark wood walls, low ceiling, and small windows with their close views of tree trunks wrapping round and round my chest and throat. *Breathe*, I tell myself, *just breathe.*

The old Alaska cabin should feel no different than my mustang cabin at home. But it does: smaller tighter darker.

I close the door to the historic cabin and there are no dogs. None inside with me. None outside. At the mustang cabin, there are three dogs with me on the porch, in the creek, in the truck, walking, sleeping, their beds a fortress around me. When I get home, I'll be short a dog. Through the loss of Rebecca Dad Ed, through moving and leaving and moving and losing, deaths and births—there for all that—*Cojo*. I lean on a ladder-back chair, panting. Sinking. The other chair empty. The bed catches me. In Colorado, alone, I am not really alone.

I almost cried in front of Tyler, who was torn about leaving because he could tell I was trying not to cry.

Tyler is the best part of this trip, the flash of his ocean-blue, supremely warm down parka better than sunlight, moonlight, caribou, the wolf howls we aren't hearing, if we heard them. Even Denali-the-mountain. The beauty of his smile, his giggling laughter, his excitement over the details of Alaska large and small, his obsession with the northern lights, his email with photographs to his grandmother, *Aurora fucking borealis* the subject line—*Tyler*. The trip would not be the same without him. Except for the part at the old cabin without him.

Fuck bravado. I'm in Alaska with Tyler and if the cabin is too small too dark too confined for both of us, I choose my son.

But I cannot leave. He has the car, will show up sometime tomorrow to check on me. Will want to leave again. Will I stay another night? To prove something—to whom? Good grief, I know I can stay away from people for days, weeks. But without dogs and without views and without snowshoes and knowing Tyler is miles away without me—I do not want to stay so bad I can taste it, them, my own tears caught in my throat.

Something else creeps in. It's sneaky, an itch under my skin.

A LOT OF drug addicts don't make it. They hit a wall in recovery and it turns them back. Or they hit a hole, a cavern inside that floods with all the feelings they think they can't handle. Something emerges, floats to the surface: want. *I want these feelings gone; I'm afraid they will devour me.* In treatment programs and twelve-step meetings we're given tools and repeatedly taught how to use them. But sometimes the want to escape that frothing, foaming, flash flood of feelings is stronger than anything. Tools get washed away like debris. If we're not careful, we can get sucked into the mayhem.

This may not be unique to drug addicts or people who have lived through abuse; I don't know. If I was ever not a drug addict, it was long ago—before I turned fourteen. If I was ever unabused, it was long ago—before I turned five, or four. I have spent years trying to find a place to put pain and anger. While the anger spikes occasionally, the pain seems cumulative.

I still have the tools of pen and paper. I use them. Twenty-four years clean, I still need those tools.

Sometimes they're not enough.

ADDING LAYERS, I step outside the weathered cabin. I'm going to hike to timberline, which is low in Alaska. Barely past the outhouse, I sink to my thighs in snow. Turning in the other direction, I head across Denali Park Road, half of which has been plowed clear of last night's snow, and skirt the parking lot, afraid a rental car full of talkative tourists might pull in. When I find a mushers' trail veering off through a gap in the willows, I follow it.

The mountains of the Alaska Range surround me—backed in the west by Denali in cloud, mountains dominate the 360-degree horizon. With spring inching into the park, dark outlines of ridges poke through snow cover, and some south-facing slopes are textured with alternating white fields and patches of dark soil. White spruce, trunks brown and branches green, further texture the lower slopes, and in the bottomlands the narrowleaf willows grow.

Biologists in a helicopter reported seeing a wolf pack disemboweling a moose somewhere out here. Wind sings around my ears as I scan the white spread of valley. I'm cold then too hot and keep walking along the snow trail, stopping periodically to search for camouflaged caribou, moose in the willows, wolf tracks—anything. But it's just mountains and me and cold wind blowing, and then I hear something different. Not a howl in the quiet of snow but the sweet rush of water freed from ice and heading toward spring.

Soon I'm looking down at water as clear as a Sierra Nevada stream, rare in my part of the West. It slips over polished pebbles as it meanders along, sweet, sweet water, water I want to put to my lips. But I don't, because I'm bundled so tightly against the cold that I see myself spilling into the stream if I try to bend over. I just stand there in the middle of a valley in the middle of Alaska in the latter part of my life, watching, listening—to water, to wind, to the breath of life in this north country.

Returning to the mushers' trail, I hear the snowplow grating along. Running is the motion of our ancestors, like migration, like fifteen hundred caribou moving with the flow of water winter and summer, summer and winter. The snowplow clears the other half of the road, so people can move.

In the old cabin, night falls around me. I build up the fire in the woodstove, warm a can of soup, and endure the squeeze of walls and chest and heart. Reading and writing by lantern light, reading more by headlamp, I know I don't want to do this again. Denali is a national park—beautiful—sheer utter complete total beauty—to be shared.

In the morning, sitting in a round of sunlight on the little porch, I hear voices and jump up to hide in the cabin as I did the day before each time people approached, and then I see a flash of ocean blue. I'm holding back tears when Tyler appears around the twist in the trail, and behind him, Sara Tabbert, woodcarver, the artist part of our artist-in-residence residency. They walk up together, chatting and laughing, and Tyler hugs me and then I do cry, damn it. And confess that I don't want to stay another night.

Sara already spent her four days at the old cabin, plus an extra one, not wanting to leave. Her days were warmer and she worked outside and my stay happened after a storm, days and nights colder again, and she cross-country skis and I didn't borrow snowshoes because before the snowstorm hit we didn't need them.

"You don't have to stay," Sara says. "It's *your* residency. Spend it how you want."

We visit inside the cabin, the door open to the freshness of outside, and I ignore the cold for a luscious hour of people and companionship and camaraderie, and feel like *Northern Exposure*'s Joel Fleischman deciding I like being around people, after all—even, for him, Alaska people. Tyler helps me pack and we shut up the cabin and drive back to C Camp, and Kevin, ex-boyfriend of my niece who worked at Denali, joins us for dinner at 229, the restaurant where my niece worked, where Sara Tabbert carved the background of the bar and even the beer taps, where everyone knows Kevin and stops at our table to say hello and we're seated next to the musher whose dogs were attacked and killed during the 2016 Iditarod and I want to tell him about Cojo, but I don't. Wanting to is enough—wanting to talk to a stranger.

We sit for hours in the warmth of wood and good food and Sara's carvings and Kevin's friendship with us and with all these people he knows because he is part of something in Alaska, part of the world that spills out of Denali National Park into the lives of the people who reside within the great circle of that grandest of mountains, Denali.

The next day Tyler and I venture beyond park boundaries again to see more than the fifteen miles of Park Road. We stop at the Nenana River, which carries some of Denali's thaw north to the Tanana. Though still frozen along its banks, the river rushes with runoff, high-water marks of previous years showing its massive muscle and force in whole downed trees stranded many feet above the present current. Kevin told us he almost ran the river at forty-thousand-plus cubic feet per second. He said he watched the raging water and turned away. His friend ran it solo. Sometimes the adventure just isn't worth the risk, Kevin said.

Tyler spots Dall sheep high up above the river. No vehicles on the road, for a while it's just Tyler and me with seventeen Dall sheep white against the gray shale cliffs of the high canyon. When one jumps to a new height from which to browse vegetation we can't see, we hear a rock fall and bounce its way down toward the river—a single stone spinning through time, changing the earth in its small way, and we are the only two-leggeds in the world to witness it.

The risk in saying yes to Alaska was nothing like the risk of running a river at dangerously high water, but for me it was big. It wasn't just the cold—it was travel that wasn't a road trip and being among many humans when I am a recluse at heart, a cat content to roam at her own pace and whim, watchful, elusive. But I am also part herd animal, like caribou. Like mustangs. My band may be small and of mixed species, but I belong.

It's RAINING THIS first day of the third week of hunting season. Heading out to meet TJ and Pat for an early Thanksgiving dinner at TJ's, I find hunters parked at my gate, and then I see someone's cows on my property. Cattle have been drifting down from the high country and collecting like water near closed gates they want to go through because they know their way to winter forage and it's time.

My water gaps are good. The fence must be down somewhere. I open my gate and ask two truckloads of armed men in hunter orange to move out of my driveway and then I go after the cows, me afoot, them faster. It should take minutes but takes two hours and I am wet, muddy, and still mad when I get to TJ's. But I got the cattle out and the fence fixed.

Exchanging hugs with TJ and Pat, I offer my flustered excuses. They don't seem to care. In fact, they seem rather solemn. "I didn't want to tell you in an email," TJ starts, "since I knew I would see you. . . ." I look from her to Pat. *The mustangs.*

"Chrome is missing," TJ says.

WHEN I LET them go, Cojo's ashes and bone fragments will lift and leave like all else, even the ranch for which he was named, but for now they rest in a wooden box on a windowsill near my bed. Perhaps you could call me sentimental. Or stubborn (many have), holding on to Cojo and a bit of Rebecca as if within their ashes lives part of their beings—holding tightly against the winds of time and change and development and death the remnants of life, even though I know that, like magic and shit, evolution happens. What evolves is often built on what's eroded, the detritus that remains after flooding becoming the foundation of soil rebuilding. Even disappointment can birth something new.

We never found Chrome. Or Chrome's body, his bones. His band—*Winona Terra Mariah Kwana Jadi Remy Makani* and then *Piedra Aurora Buckeye* and *Barranca*—blew apart in the great wind of his absence, and the mayhem that followed his disappearance in that third week of hunting season lasted for months as stallions—even two-year-old stallions—*babies*—vied for his mares. Chrome was the hub and when he disappeared the wheel fell apart, spokes everywhere. The 2016 election took place days after Chrome's disappearance and that wheel of our world fell apart, too. As TJ and I sat on rocks at the crown of Round Top, searching so hard with binoculars for Chrome that my eyes and head hurt, watching stallions and mares racing every which way, a truck full of hunters on a middle road chasing a band, we looked at each other. "This is it," I said. "This is what's coming." TJ nodded.

In Nevada in 1998, three young men, two of whom were marines, all buddies since high school, shot and killed thirty-eight wild horses. For a mess of reasons, the trial fell apart, but shortly afterward it became a felony to shoot a wild horse in the United States. Still, there are additional documented instances of horse slaughter that didn't occur in slaughterhouses. Shooting for "sport"—just to watch something die—happens.

We'll never know if that's what happened here, but our suspicion in itself is telling. Horrific stuff occurs every day, condoned and even perpetrated by the powers that be. That we are witnessing accused and confessed misogynists sworn into power is unthinkable, and real. Harming a child, selling her body or using it for one's own perverse pleasure, is unimaginable to me, and yet it, too, happens every day. I can't say that damaging a child and abusing or killing a mustang is the same crime, performed by the same men; what I know is that both permanently scar the psyches of the innocent, victims and family bands shattered.

Mustang mortality also happens naturally—death at birth of foal or mare is not unusual, nor is death at old age, though we have half a dozen elders in Spring Creek Basin who continue to surprise us each spring. Death by accident or illness also happens, the causes of which are often unknown.

Dr. Jay Kirkpatrick once told of a mare on Assateague Island. "I found the carcass of an old friend of ours," he wrote. "It was M4. She was twenty . . . I briefly laid my hands on her neck—touched her—it was something no man had done during her twenty years. She died less than a mile from where she had been born. She had never been captured, rounded up, immobilized, or otherwise harassed. For a few moments," he said, "I lost sight of the fact that I should have been celebrating her life and not mourning her death."

Dr. Jay is right: Chrome lived and died free. That is what matters. And yet I keep hoping to see him trotting up over the ridge, pausing at the edge of the basin to scan the scene before him—*mares*—then galloping toward the horses, his long tangled mane aglow with sunlight or moonlight or rainbow light, his pounding hoofbeats matching my heart.

TJ FOUND THE grulla quarter horse mare online. We went to see her in eastern Wyoming, twenty-six miles shy of Nebraska. TJ comes from a military family and has moved almost as much as I have. Today road trips curb her wanderlust (and mustangs fix everything else), and we have gone on many trips together, all for horses: Buck Brannaman clinics. Meetings about mustangs, with advocates or BLM. To wild lands to see wild horses. To prison to release captured horses. And nearly to Nebraska, twice—to meet the grulla mare, and to bring her home.

The first time riding her in Disappointment Valley, TJ on one of her quarter horse mares, I was a mass of nerves, but Savanna didn't care. She is eager to see her surroundings, to do whatever work is ahead. I have ridden her into the basin, behind cows, roping calves, in a circle around Buck Brannaman. Savanna is a willing participant, moving her feet while mine hang at her sides, my hands learning to soften as I ask her for a "soft feel," as Buck says—applying pressure and releasing the second she yields.

My mustang Maka kept growing—it's a long way up onto his back. Because of a reaction to vaccines that nearly killed him, he was started even later than I intended, and he learned how his size and strength could serve him—he has bucked a couple of men off. *Usually the adventure is worth the risk*—I have lived my life that way.

Now maybe the learning means more than the thrill. A respectful fear grounds me around my big mustang despite my reluctance to yield to safety and age. I'll likely not ride him, and that is okay. Though he is not *free*, he has a band and many acres on which to roam. And loving an animal, even a human animal, for who it is, not what it does, is a good practice.

Perhaps the love I want is simply that: kindness without pressure. Perhaps that's why I'm single. Not everyone understands a mustang.

LIKE SO MANY of us, Buck Brannaman suffered the fragmentation of childhood abuse. In every clinic he talks about the horseman Ray Hunt, how Buck studied the ways in which Ray communicated with hands and legs, how horses moved in response. Buck found a leader in Ray, and instead of carrying forward his own father's violence, over the years he has fostered a great gentleness within himself. His horses respond to the slightest whisper of his hands.

Men could learn from Buck, too (and many do)—as TJ says, here is a man who teaches cowboys to cuddle their horses. I hope those men apply the gentleness and patience they learn to women and children, as well. The world desperately needs this.

Like Buck, I have grown to know my own PTSD better—what triggers it, how it shows up in my body, how to stop it before it strikes out. Troubled Kua has helped—watching how he behaves when the pressure is too great, showing him ways to handle the pressure he feels. And mustangs have helped. Watching them in the wild—how they live and survive, the role family bands play—and watching them in captivity after they have endured the trauma of helicopter roundups and trailers and men. Some learn to trust humans despite that trauma, standing still while TJ pulls cockleburs from their manes. Others never will. Either way is okay.

As a friend said after meeting TJ: If we could only learn to give the kind of love another needs instead of the kind we want to receive . . . and that is what TJ does.

Like mustangs, TJ and Buck have been my teachers. Perhaps they, not Andrés, were the leaders I sought—helping me find my way out of lost. Once on the road, it was mustangs I followed, mustangs who showed me the way home.

When I told Wendy Beth I would put Cojo on the edge of the ledge upon which he was so fond of standing, she said, "He moved with pain all those years—now he will be free." It's the time of snow flurries and spring winds—a mixture of seasons— and I'm not ready to let him go, even a year later. Perhaps I will release him in summer, when he will drift more slowly away, some of him sure to rise like ravens in an updraft and fall back like rain to the creek below, which he loved, which many years ago, before dams and drought and the siphoning off of good rivers, might have carried his floating fragments to the Dolores and then the Colorado and eventually to the sea, which he also loved.

The way Tyler does, and Tyler's mother: oceans and rivers our home.

And for me, and for Ken, and for Cojo and Tyler, too, also this land.

I still don't know what's right to do and wrong. Maybe never knew, even when I thought I did. Ken and I are building a ranch together, with Tyler's help, and although mother and son fight with the energy of two hurt people, we persist, our cow herd slowly growing.

A section up the road from the mustang cabin shows up for sale, cheap—it has a Nature Conservancy easement that forbids hunting. Despite years of cattle rummaging through it, the riparian area is thick and healthy with Fremont and narrowleaf cottonwoods, silver buffaloberry, Utah serviceberry, and coyote willows. Steep, rugged hills rise above a mile and a half of Disappointment Creek to a sagebrush-and-winterfat basin. More negotiations take place, this time with Ken and Tyler at my side: owner carry, years, cows, prayer.

Getting a survey proves challenging—the last survey recorded in 1892—but I don't take that as a sign. Or if I do it's a sign that I love this valley, its wild horses and wild water, geology and stories and time. If the neighbors' cattle trespass—and they will—well, it's the West out here in southwest Colorado, this fence-out state. Old laws remain in place while cattle roam.

My kids have embraced this strange gray valley of desert scrubland and Mancos Shale badlands and alkali soil-and-silt bottomlands and rimrocks of Dakota Sandstone in wind-sculpted hoodoos and cliffs and fins. With no ocean here, Tyler will come and go following winter swells and spring runoff and avoiding summer doldrums, but the land will stay. And, for now, Ken will stay, raising grass-fed-and-finished beef to feed his family and the local community, our Criollo cattle a throwback to the old cattle of Spain, which arrived in the Americas in 1493 on the same boats that brought some horses home.

FOR YEARS BOXES traveled with me to be stored in closets, contents forgotten, hiking boots and winter gloves to be rediscovered in some future life. Likewise, I have hesitated to unpack my heart. Yet here at the mustang cabin my heart swells like wood in the rain and I've released pieces of my past to make room for spring winds, summer storms, and wild horses. Like the geology of this Colorado Plateau valley, here my lives of land and sea reside—what is left after the sea recedes, the floodwaters pass: the bones of me.

The river girl thrills at the sound of water rushing by beneath cliffs from which canyon wrens sing; the cowgirl draws in the smells of cowshit and sagebrush and smiles as her mare moves in response to her hands and legs, or stands still as she dismounts to open a gate; the Maui girl remembers, pulling summer clothes from a drybag, the challenge and cushion of the sea. My Hawai'i clothes fit me here. As do Wranglers, cowboy boots—even cowboy hats—and river gear. All that's missing is the junky.

Despite loss—indeed sometimes because of it—my life has been fluid, liquid motion. Like a wild horse or wildcat I go, see, feel, and grow just by moving my feet. My home has been sea, a saddle, the river, a road—they all offer movement. In that movement, I have found wild. And in wild, I find me.

Breathing Chrome's air, I found me again.

I didn't have to possess Chrome. Nor do I have to possess each place I love. Alaska is not for me to decorate or move to or own. Perhaps I have learned how to visit.

Twenty-something years ago, I heard William Kittredge say that people in the West moved a lot, and I have followed that map, moving ever onward, a mustang on the run. But wild horses, like a river, don't always run—they pool and eddy out, standing around swatting gnats, nuzzling each other, nursing, napping in the warmth of the sun. Just *being*. No longer do I need adrenaline-fear or the dopamine felt after. Joy can come with being still, watching the world before me—mustangs, cows, red ants, my grandchildren. Mustangs taught me that, too.

Today maybe all I need to know is that I *can* go—as long as I know I can move my feet, I will be okay. A whole being made of fits and starts, bits and parts. I can fracture and I can mend. Like troubled Kua, even in fear I have strength. That strength picks me up, gets me dressed, and feeds me through the tough times. Where I end is anybody's guess, but I dare to guess this much: it won't be with a needle hanging from my arm.

COTTONWOOD LEAVES BACKLIT by a morning sun that warms my naked knees, my bare feet planted on a slab of red sandstone,

Cojo the dust in the breeze, the dogs wait for me to begin the day. But the day has already begun. I am writing to the sounds of moving water. And *right now*, as my flesh meets the bare bones of the earth, skin to sandstone, I feel myself home.

Maybe I have learned how to stay—for a while. It's as simple as one day at a time.

Yet *staying* may be like *waiting*. And life isn't about waiting. It isn't even about hurting. It's about living—moving from one moment to the next as gracefully as possible, the way wild animals do. If we're not graceful enough, life is about learning to become more so. To make better choices. To be of service. To follow the guidance of spirit, to love and to trust, and to see that there is an ocean out there that reflects the sky. In it we are drops, or stars.

And some of us are wild horses.

Epilogue

SKIN

FACED WITH A DILEMMA, I SPEAK WITH MY YOUNGER SISTER, who has just visited. She says two things: Maybe you should stop thinking of the acquisition of Cachuma Ranch as a mistake. Because look at all that's come from it. You're there with your kids and grandkids. Nuff said. And then she says, "Go outside. Sit still or move or whatever you need to do, but go outside."

"I have to break ice for the cows," I say, forgetting I don't need a reason to go.

Passing the refrigerator, I'm stopped by a magnet that holds a Lacey drawing of a pinto pony. The magnet, which my big sister sent me in the throes of the Standing Rock battle, shows an abstract woman with long dark hair that streams into water, words centered above her: *Defend the Sacred*. I stare at the refrigerator.

And go outside, even though I have my answer.

After breaking the crust of ice that formed over the creek in the night, the dogs and I climb a steep hill of Mancos Shale, where I sit in silty soil warmed by the sun. We call this Scoop Hill, because one day beneath that juniper Ken found an ice cream scoop lying in the dirt—steel with a rubber-coated handle, from the forties maybe, the bowl of the scoop much smaller than those of today. Near the next juniper I saw flakes of chert, not washed down, as many are, because this is the crown of the hill. No, some hundreds or thousands of years ago someone sat here chipping a chunk of chert into an arrowhead, leaving flakes behind to tell the tale. And in the last century, someone had a picnic up here—with ice cream? Not likely. Maybe used the scoop as a shovel and left it behind, hundreds of years passing between artifacts.

Sometimes we can't read the story detritus tells as easily as pine needles spread in a wave across a slab of sandstone in the middle of a creek. Sometimes we can.

From this hill I see it as clearly as cows coming to water: Rebecca was the before; the loss of my fathers, the ridge; mustangs are the after. With my sons and grandchildren, our horses who share ancestors, and Criollo cattle that share their story, I live in land I love by a creek I love, because of mustangs. And I have dogs.

My mother moved to a retirement home that offers her redwoods, walks, company when she wants it, and the solitude every writer needs. A friend of hers, from the era in which they were both potters going to craft fairs, moved there first, because her husband died first. Once when I was visiting, the friend said, "It takes eight years."

"What do you mean?"

"It took eight years before I stopped thinking of Hew every day." Now she remembers him often, and the decades they shared are a big part of what shaped her, but she is no longer motivated by what's missing.

After Alaska, the missing became less acute. And I realized Rebecca had been gone eight years.

My younger sister reminds me that it doesn't matter if my reasons were misaligned when I got Cachuma. It brought my boys back. It gave me Ken. And with two simple words she also reminds me that there are people in the world who have known me even longer than Rebecca and Ed and my father.

"Go outside," says my little sister, and I do.

WHAT DO I seek when my thighs need to walk and my eyes need to see and my skin needs sunlight and bare and air to breathe? When my feet need the earth, the rocks in the riverbed, pine fluff on forest floors, Mancos Shale mud heavy on my boots as I walk and walk and walk myself back into a body that holds memories of drugs of love of sex and birth and pain *oh the pain* but if I keep walking up a hill so steep it burns and the breath I need doesn't come and I am a child again, pressure on my throat, air wanting in, wanting out, *breathe*, I say, and I do I can I will until I don't anymore, ever—if I keep walking, I will get there.

So I walk. And, walking, I find something in this body, in this rhythm, in the roll of the land beneath my feet. It is old.

Bare feet feeling the ʻāina, the land, whether it was red dirt or white sand, the skin between the earth and me, the sea and me, not clothes and shoes and hats but my own epidermis.

My feet knew freedom and my body knew freedom as I swam and swam and swam in an ocean that carried me like my horse in the middle of the mountains when I rode and rode and rode without saddle without blanket just me in cutoffs and my thighs in horseflesh and the sweat of us as we raced down the field toward the river and my legs knew freedom and my heart knew freedom and I wrapped them around the boymanchild I loved and found freedom there, too, in love in lust in that old, old act of skin on skin in skin and *that's* what I seek, walking and living in sunlight and moonlight and starlight—the skin of the earth and the skin of me touching.

There are people who still that live close to the land, whose food comes up through the soil and water falls down from the sky, whose breath is fanned by ravens' wings and life means moving within the realms of weather. They know the flow of water, of cows, of wild horses, like TJ, my cowboy son, my river friends, my surfer son. Like me.

Some of us still know our bodies as biology. We are animal. We ovulate and breed and conceive and birth; we bleed. We love, we mourn, we fight, we lose and we win, and winning does not matter. Living matters. Staying alive matters. Water and grass and soil matter. Wild is as simple and as old as that.

It is a gray mustang stallion with a mane to his knees rearing up over a light buckskin mare and joining her for moments, her legs spread apart to bear his weight, too, her tail aside and her vulva winking as he grips her neck with his teeth and her sides with his knees and he enters her, thrusting their whole future into her again and again and she holds it even as he recedes, withdraws, and drops to all fours. He looks over his band and resumes grazing. He can breathe.

He may mount her again in minutes and by nightfall estrus has passed and the band has moved to the shelter of junipers if it's cold or they continue to graze into moonlight with the contentedness of basic needs met.

That is as simple as it gets. And as wild.

It is old, so old.

It is renewal.

And older.

It is beginning.

ACKNOWLEDGMENTS

My gratitude spreads in ripples outward.

Thank you to the nonfiction editors at *High Desert Journal*, Charles Finn, Joe Wilkins, and CMarie Fuhrman, for polishing and publishing versions of "Lunar Red" and "Grounded"; and to the editors of the following: *Contra Viento*, *River Teeth*, and the IAIA student anthology *Sonder*, for giving light to essays from which several "Detritus" emerged; *The Southwest Anthology: The Best of the Writing Programs*, for "Fubar"; the National Park Service, for posting "An Outsider Inside Denali National Park and Preserve," which in part became "The Bones of Us"; *High Country News*, for publishing the op-ed that evolved into the chapter "Where Science and Mustangs Meet"; *Southern Indiana Review*, for "Sundance"; and to the American Wild Horse Campaign, for first publishing some of the mustang tales included herein.

Mahalo nui loa to Joy Harjo, for permission to include lines from your poem, "The Creation Story." To Dave Stamey, for use of a piece of "The Circle": thank you!

Mahalo also to the faculty and students of the low-rez MFA program at the Institute of American Indian Arts: to Linda Hogan (and her BLM mustang, Misty), thank you, for all of it; Chip Livingston, wise council, always; Lidia Yuknavitch, heart-thudding gratitude for my year with you; and to Elissa Washuta, Melissa Febos, Pam Houston, and Toni Jensen, who looked at the details; Jon Davis, for inviting me in; and to fellow creative nonfiction cohort graduates Ginger Gaffney and Ina Leonard, for helping smooth some wrinkles in the earliest drafts; and to Ina, for laughter and Alaska and always. Also to Mary

Kancewick, for a stable arm, and Anita Roastingear, who asked about my dogs.

To all the dogs, cats, and cows who contribute daily to the smiles in my life, and to the horses—wild and otherwise—for life itself.

To the women of Torrey House Press—our leader, Kirsten Johanna Allen; the kind and impeccable editor Anne Terashima; creative director Kathleen Metcalf; and Rachel Leigh Buck-Cockayne and Michelle Wentling—thank you mere words. Hugs would be better. Meanwhile, thank you!

To TJ Holmes, for mustang days and mustang years and all else.

To Pat and Frank Amthor, who have my back.

To mustang women Suzanne Roy and Grace Kuhn of the American Wild Horse Campaign, for all you do on the frontline; and to the women on the ground: TJ Holmes, Stella Trueblood, Connie Wagner, Aleta Wolf, Marty Felix, Billie Hutchings, Tricia Hatle, Ada Inbody, Kayla Grams, and the many I haven't met, and the men, too, like the late Dan Elkins, working with PZP to show that it does work, if you use it.

To Kimberly Frank and Robin Lyda of the Science and Conservation Center, for carrying forth the brilliance, passion, and legacy of Dr. Jay Kirkpatrick, and to Dr. Jay himself, for the horses.

To "BLMers" Mike Jensen and his crew, for our productive and ongoing partnership in Spring Creek Basin; and to David and Pati Temple, Chuck Greaves, and Lynda Larson, for creating the mustang cabin.

To Rebecca Lawton, for friendship spawned nearly thirty years ago when I first read your work, rivers and kids our common ground, and the hundreds, possibly thousands of pages we have exchanged since, including these (thanks also to you and your brother, Timothy Lawton, for the geology lessons!). To Wendy Beth Oliver, for your constant friendship, and Trish

Homburg, for accompanying me on the search for the right place, and to you both for the laughter we shared. And to the lovely Colorado writer Laura Pritchett, for your brilliance, your books, and for cheering me on in the homestretch when my legs tired and I faltered.

To my ʻohana: my mother, the writer Helen Park Bigelow, my sisters, Terry Tobey and Peg Pierce, and my cousin, Nancy Park, who have known me longest and love me still, and who listened to, read, and supported me through many versions of *Desert Chrome*; and to Kathy, Lacey, and Lucas Lausten, who help make Cachuma Ranch feel like home. To best ex Scott R. Ellis, for being that. And to my ʻohana Hawaiʻi, in the canoe and on the island: aloha pauʻole.

To those behind the artist-in-residence program at Denali National Park and Preserve, for giving me a pivotal moment in Alaska. To the Ellen Meloy Fund and its annual Desert Writers Award competition, for honoring this project as a 2016 finalist, and to Ann Weiler Walka and Mark Meloy, for friendship beyond. And even farther beyond, to Ellen Meloy—for your love of place, your enduring words, your humor and friendship, and your ongoing guidance. And while we're out there, to my fathers Robert Bixby Green and Edward B. Bigelow, for the many years of challenges and love. And to Rebecca: *You are still my friend. You will always be my friend.*

This is where I would give the greatest honor to the man in my life. Alas, there is not one. There are two. To my sons, Ken and Tyler Lausten, who have tolerated a mother who moves a lot and writes a lot, often about them: Please don't read certain pages. Beyond that, the story is yours, along with my heart.

ABOUT THE AUTHOR

KATHRYN WILDER's work, cited in *Best American Essays* and nominated for the Pushcart Prize, has appeared in such publications as *High Desert Journal, River Teeth, Fourth Genre, Sierra,* and many anthologies and Hawai'i magazines. Wilder is editor of *Walking the Twilight: Women Writers of the Southwest* volumes I and II and author, with Redwing T. Nez, of the children's book *Forbidden Talent.* A past finalist for the Ellen Meloy Fund Desert Writers Award and the Waterston Desert Writing Prize, Wilder holds an MA from Northern Arizona University and an MFA from the Institute of American Indian Arts. She lives among mustangs in southwestern Colorado.

TORREY HOUSE PRESS

Voices for the Land

The economy is a wholly owned subsidiary of the environment, not the other way around.
— Senator Gaylord Nelson, founder of Earth Day

Torrey House Press publishes books at the intersection of the literary arts and environmental advocacy. THP authors explore the diversity of human experiences with the environment and engage community in conversations about landscape, literature, and the future of our ever-changing planet, inspiring action toward a more just world. We believe that lively, contemporary literature is at the cutting edge of social change. We seek to inform, expand, and reshape the dialogue on environmental justice and stewardship for the human and more-than-human world by elevating literary excellence from diverse voices.

Visit www.torreyhouse.org for reading group discussion guides, author interviews, and more.

As a 501(c)(3) nonprofit publisher, our work is made possible by the generous donations from readers like you.

Torrey House Press is supported by Back of Beyond Books, the King's English Bookshop, Maria's Bookshop, the Jeffrey S. and Helen H. Cardon Foundation, The Sam and Diane Stewart Family Foundation, the Barker Foundation, Helen Bigelow, Diana Allison, Klaus Bielefeldt, Patrick de Freitas, Laurie Hilyer, Shelby Tisdale, Kirtly Parker Jones, Robert Aagard and Camille Bailey Aagard, Kif Augustine Adams and Stirling Adams, Rose Chilcoat and Mark Franklin, Jerome Cooney and Laura Storjohann, Link Cornell and Lois Cornell, Susan Cushman and Charlie Quimby, Betsy Folland and David Folland, the Utah Division of Arts & Museums, Utah Humanities, the National Endowment for the Humanities, the National Endowment for the Arts, and Salt Lake County Zoo, Arts & Parks. Our thanks to individual donors, subscribers, and the Torrey House Press board of directors for their valued support.

Join the Torrey House Press family and give today at www.torreyhouse.org/give.